The Art o.
Decisions

Chris Blake
zemlake@btinternet.
com
07973 834910

FT Prentice Hall
FINANCIAL TIMES

In an increasingly competitive world, we believe it's quality of thinking that gives an edge – an idea that opens new doors, a technique that solves a problem, or an insight that simply makes sense of it all. The more you know, the smarter and faster you can go.

That's why we work with the best minds in business and finance to bring cutting-edge thinking and best learning practice to a global market.

Under a range of leading imprints, including *Financial Times Prentice Hall*, we create world-class print publications and electronic products bringing our readers knowledge, skills and understanding, which can be applied whether studying or at work.

To find out more about Pearson Education publications, or tell us about the books you'd like to find, you can visit us at **www.pearsoned.co.uk**

The Art of Decisions

How to manage in an uncertain world

Chris Blake

Prentice Hall
FINANCIAL TIMES

An imprint of **Pearson Education**
Harlow, England • London • New York • Boston • San Francisco • Toronto • Sydney • Singapore • Hong Kong
Tokyo • Seoul • Taipei • New Delhi • Cape Town • Madrid • Mexico City • Amsterdam • Munich • Paris • Milan

PEARSON EDUCATION LIMITED

Edinburgh Gate
Harlow CM20 2JE
Tel: +44 (0)1279 623623
Fax: +44 (0)1279 431059
Website: www.pearsoned.co.uk

First published in Great Britain in 2008

ISBN: 978-0-273-71099-8

British Library Cataloguing-in-Publication Data
A catalogue record for this book is available from the British Library

Library of Congress Cataloging-in-Publication Data
Blake, Chris, 1960-
   The art of decisions : how to manage in an uncertain world / Chris Blake.
       p. cm.
   Includes bibliographical references and index.
   ISBN 978-0-273-71099-8 (alk. paper)
  1. Decision making. 2. Management. I. Title
   HD30.23.B59 2007
   658.4'03--dc22
                                    2007036909

10 9 8 7 6 5 4 3 2
11 10 09 08

Typeset in 9.5/13pt Din Regular by 30
Printed and bound by Ashford Colour Press Ltd, Gosport, Hants.

The publisher's policy is to use paper manufactured from sustainable forests.

This book is dedicated to Voley.

Contents

Acknowledgements ix
Introduction xi

1   The anatomy of decisions 1
2   Bad things sometimes happen to the good guys 11
3   In search of the perfect decision? 21
4   I *know* I am right (but I am not sure why) 39
5   Calling off the search 51
6   Investing, risk and poker 61
7   Rules of thumb: part 1 – risk and investing 81
8   Deciding close to home 89
9   Deciding far from home 105
10   Overconfidence and the entrepreneur 119
11   The trouble with winners and experts 133
12   Map making and the planning fallacy 145
13   Fear, greed and risk taking 159
14   The Dragon's Den syndrome 173
15   Rules of thumb: part 2 – fighting to win 189
16   The art of decision making 197

Glossary of poker terms used in the book 207
Bibliography 209
Index 215

Acknowledgements

Many people have played a part in the development of the ideas in this book. I must start by thanking Richard Balkwell for giving me the opportunity over the past five years to address the delegates on his courses – providing guinea pigs for the late night poker sessions and the morning lecture. Many of the ideas have developed from discussions during those sessions. In the same vein I must thank Diana Limburg and Richard Beresford for their support and allowing me to benefit from the interaction with their students at Oxford Brookes University. A special mention is needed for Professor Roger Mumby-Croft for his support and encouragement over many years and his insightful comments on an early draft.

Particular thanks are due to the many people who were prepared to give up valuable hours reading and commenting on drafts of the book, a time consuming task for which their only benefit is to be listed below. Thank you to all of you: David Apgar, Scott Button, Rod Cookson, Shelley Couper, Edward Milford, Keith Marriott, Richard McKie, Miles Ross, Jennifer Stewart and Jane Thurgood.

Lastly gratitude to my publisher Dr. Liz Gooster who had the faith to back a book which is unimaginably different from the book she (and the author) expected to emerge. I hope I can justify your intuitive judgement to back me!

Introduction

Once the ritual slaughter of the chicken was completed the entrails were examined. The bloody mess was considered in silence, the expectant hunters jostling to get a glimpse. More moments passed in silence until the destination of the hunting party was declared. Excitedly the men dispersed to prepare and say farewells. Confidence was high, the hunting would be good.

For countless thousands of years we have been turning to oracles, priests and magicians to help us make decisions. Should we go to war? Where is the best hunting to be found? British economist and statistician Ely Devons was Director of General Planning during the Second World War and in an essay (1961) likened the 'desperate search for trend signs' in economic statistics to ritual magic. He was struck not only by the futility of the science of prediction but also by the 'very large numbers of magicians and witch doctors' that the government employed. The value of forecasting, he came to believe, was not in its accuracy but in its public acceptance. The hunters could have argued for days seeking a rational justification for hunting in one direction rather than another. The magician's intervention stopped the argument. It was no longer subject to debate, they would set off united. For Devons the economists' models had the same function. There may have been very little validity in their predictions but they did provide a framework which everyone could accept. Part of the power of magic is that if the prediction is wrong and the hunting disappointing it is never the magic that is discredited. The reading may have been incorrect but the oracle is never wrong. And so with the economists' models. There is nothing wrong with the science but we promise that next time we will use better models, better data.

For most of human history we had gods to take the difficult decisions for us. They were continually directing the path of every object and the fate of every soul. We may have been ignorant of our destiny but we could be confident that the universe was unfolding as it should. But gathering momentum through the Enlightenment has been the idea that we can shape the future, that we can control our own destiny. If we could uncover the laws of society and of economics then, just as Newton's laws had given us control of nature, we could control our future. For the past 100 years management science has been trying to uncover the laws that govern how organizations operate. The aim is simple. If we can understand the rules that govern organizations and the rules of trade then we can design better and more effective organizations and management practices. We will no longer have to rely on trial and error to find out what works. A science of management will take us to a sun-lit upland of efficient organizations and fulfilled individuals.

Theories have been developed to improve nearly every aspect of management. Some of them analysing the triumphs of the great decision makers and then abstracting general principles (inductive theories). Others, borrowing the deductive logic of the physical sciences, would outline logical procedures that would inevitably improve performance. Rational models of decision making have been developed specifically to help us overcome the influence of emotion and subjective judgement. Prescriptions that call for a cool, dispassionate evaluation of the facts and promise to identify the best of all possible futures. Armed with these theories we have been able to look back into the recent past and explain both today's failures and today's successes. The management textbooks and lectures are littered with stories that illustrate good and bad decision making. Each anecdote is selected to illustrate the explanatory power of the theory. And, just like the magician's ritual magic, it is never the science that is found wanting. It is always the individual manager who didn't read the signs correctly, who didn't follow the prescribed procedure. Looking backwards in time it appears easy to explain how we arrived at today. Like walking backwards through a maze there seems to be an inevitability about every route chosen. But now, standing before the maze, choosing the right path every time it divides doesn't seem so easy. The compass that seemed so reliable for directing us backwards through the maze is spinning wildly when we turn to face the future. How are we to choose one path rather than another? Rigorous application of scientific management theory, personal judgement or just guess and hope? With the theories faltering when we need them most we have to conclude that luck must play a part.

Somewhat surprisingly the word 'luck' seldom if ever appears in the explanations of success and failure in the management literature. But I am in no doubt that luck has played an enormous part in my unusually varied career. A career that has allowed me to see the decision-making process from every angle. I have managed international companies for global publishing groups, managed the launch of a new internet venture in the late nineties, spent four years as an investment director in the private equity industry, and then more recently build up a portfolio of investments in small early stage companies. I have had to face the challenges of planning and deciding as a manager within a corporate hierarchy, as an entrepreneur and as an investor of both my own and other people's money. I have worked in the seemingly unchanging world of book publishing and the second by second world of internet retailing. I have been swept away by some of the technology changes that the past decade has wrought and stood there marvelling at how many of the old economy business models continue to thrive.

Luck was most prominent when I was establishing the on-line community www.babyworld.co.uk in 1997. It was luck that had brought me into contact with the willing business angel when the venture capitalists that would have thrown money at us a year later had all said no. Luck that saw Freeserve launch the UK's first free dial-up internet service that sparked the UK internet boom in the first month after we were funded. Luck that saw Freeserve buy us out as it became apparent that we had neither enough cash nor a sustainable business model in those early internet days. And then, most of all, luck that Freeserve (later Wanadoo) kept the business alive through the worst days of the crash, only to sell us back the assets in 2003 just as internet advertising and e-retailing were becoming sustainable business models. I am not sure that even one in a million monkeys with Excel spreadsheets could have come up with that business plan.

Why is luck never discussed? Because according to the science of management it isn't needed – we are the architects of our own destiny. After all, the promise behind each new management textbook is in essence, 'Do X and you can have Y.' Where X is a snappily packaged management practice and Y is whatever you desire – growth, profits, wealth, etc. A claim that has much in common with the snake oil salesman who knows that if you promise something people want then they will believe. These claims are based on two assumptions – both of which are false. Firstly, that management theories have the same predictive powers as scientific laws and, secondly, that in a chaotic open system such as the global economy we can necessarily make confident predictions about the future. Most management books are selling the hope of achieving certainty, a promise they can't deliver on. In this book I am going to tackle the question of how we should approach decision making once we accept that we can't control the future – how to manage with uncertainty.

Finally, giving up our dependence on the dream of certainty has a profound impact on how we look at the process of management. New metaphors are required. The dominant metaphor (starting with Taylor) is still the manager as machine operator, reading dials and manipulating levers to maximise the output from a machine – albeit a complex machine and with some of the mechanism hidden from view. In its place I offer the image of the manager as poker player – making investments decisions with the future always uncertain. Or the manager as explorer, charting unfamiliar territory and aware that the instincts acquired at home may not apply in this unfamiliar land.

One of the themes of this book is the gulf between what the management scientists have told managers how they 'ought' to behave and how they actually manage. For decades it has been assumed that the theories were right and the managers uneducated or lazy. In fact we now see that managers have been instinctively managing uncertainty and making effective judgements. Managers have been using their own judgement to make decisions quickly and effectively on minimal information – distilling past experience to help manage the future. This has proved effective in environments we know well. But what happens when we have to make decisions, as we must from time to time, in unfamiliar environments? I will look at the power and pitfalls of intuitive judgement in decision making both in familiar and unfamiliar environments. You will see how we can uncover rules of thumb from the diverse worlds of poker and from agile programming methodologies to provide a guide to the art of making decisions in an uncertain world. This book is about the art rather than the science of decision making. Learning to let go of the myth of certainty and to manage effectively in a profoundly uncertain future is the key management skill for the twenty-first century.

Chapter **1**

....

The anatomy of decisions

There is a mythology about decision making which is reinforced in the way decision makers are portrayed in film and on television. There is one pivotal moment and one all or nothing decision. His (it is nearly always a man) word setting in train a series of actions that will ripple outwards for years changing lives – destiny unfolding. But contrary to this popular image most decision making is the mundane daily task of allocating resources. Decisions that don't stand in isolation, but build on each other. Decisions made with other people's money and which therefore have to be justified. This chapter looks at the key characteristics of managerial decision making.

The $35 billion dollar gamble

It is 10 January 1995 and Robert E. Rubin has just been sworn in as President Clinton's Secretary to the Treasury. Straight after the ceremony Rubin is going to meet with the President and give him a very uncomfortable choice. The alternatives are stark: lend the Mexican government $35 billion dollars of American taxpayers' money, with no certainty that the money can ever be repaid; or sit back and watch the Mexican government default on foreign debt causing a collapse of the Mexican peso and the inevitable consequences of rampant inflation, a prolonged recession and massive unemployment. Not an easy decision for your first official day on the job.

The dilemma is not motivated by altruism towards Mexico and its people. The issue is, straightforwardly, about American interests. The consequences of a collapse of the Mexican economy for the US are well understood. The previous crisis in 1982 is still fresh in political memory. The likely immediate consequences are predicted to include a 30% increase in illegal immigration (500,000 additional economic refugees), an increase in cross-border drug movements, up to 700,000 US jobs at risk – in all between a 0.5% and 1% reduction in US GDP. The indirect consequences of a Mexican default are immense but less quantifiable. They include an increased risk that other developing economies will default on loans and initiate a global recession. But apart from putting US taxpayers' money at risk, there are other potential downsides from the decision to support the Mexican economy. Investors who took a known risk by lending money to Mexico will be 'bailed out', potentially encouraging poor private investment decisions and making a repeat of this situation more rather than less likely. By intervening Rubin would risk creating a bubble around investors, protecting them from 'moral hazard'.

The good news is that Rubin was not alone in his deliberations. He was supported by Alan Greenspan and Larry Summers. All of the outcomes were bad – it was a question of finding the least bad option. As Rubin reports in his frank and revealing memoir, *In an Uncertain World,* '[we] all came to a rough consensus... the risks of not acting were far worse than the risks of acting.' Clinton agreed and preparations were made to loan the better part of $50 billion (including funds from the IMF). As February slipped by, Mexico's foreign reserves dwindled to $2 billion, default was a matter of a few days away. Much of Congress, which a few weeks ago had fallen under Republican control, was instinctively opposed to the 'bail out'. Congressional support was uncertain and likely to take at least another couple of weeks to secure. This only raised the political stakes for both Rubin and Clinton – if the intervention was to be made it would have to be done *without* congressional approval. On the eve of the first $3 billion transfer, and with a unilateral 'right to withdraw' still available, Rubin and his colleagues tried to evaluate the chance that the financial support would succeed in stabilizing the Mexican economy and stop the capital flight. There is no science here, just an approximate weighing of probabilities. Their estimates of the chance of success, Rubin recalls, varied from '1 in 2' to '1 in 3' against. He imagines the question that he will be asked at the inevitable congressional hearing, '*So, Mr Secretary, you thought that there was only a small chance that sending billions of dollars of American taxpayers' money would help? And you sent the money anyway?*'

Rumours that the US might renege on the deal leaked into the markets and the peso was falling rapidly. What would you have done?

What do managers do?

Answering this question has filled miles of library shelves and occupied thousands of hours of lectures. Today's managers are required to play an ever-expanding number of roles: coach, controller, evaluator, visionary, monitor, resource acquirer, communicator, salesperson. A new role seems to be added with every new management book that makes it into the bookstores. But it's not that complicated. There is one role that no manager can delegate or avoid. The one role that will be used to judge our effectiveness long after the team building sessions and SMART objectives have been forgotten. Managers are paid to make decisions.

You *may* be paid to make decisions about the goals of your organisation. You *will* be paid to make decisions about how your organisation's resources are deployed to meet goals that have been set. The resources you control can be as varied as your own time, your departmental budget, a £10 million capital investment programme or a £1 billion war chest for acquisitions. Everyone from the CEO of a global corporation to the newly appointed departmental manager is making decisions about how best to deploy resources – once a decade strategy decisions, annual budget commitments, weekly target setting, minute by minute allocations of our own time.

The decisions we make as managers share some fundamental characteristics. They are usually made with someone else's money and therefore need to be justified; they build one on another and don't stand in isolation; the outcome is important to other people; and they are surprisingly forgettable – at least by us.

Decisions with other people's money

Unless we are working alone as a self-financed entrepreneur we are always making decisions about how to deploy resources that are, at least in part, owned by other people. Rubin was steering a decision on what to do with $35 billion of US taxpayers' money (not the easiest owners to please). There is nothing like running a business you have funded yourself to make you strikingly aware of the difference between spending your own money and spending it on behalf of shareholders. I admit to sometimes finding it easier to commit £1 million of shareholders' money than £10,000 of my own. It shouldn't be true, but most business managers will admit it – at least to themselves.

Decisions that need to be justified

Because we are deploying assets owned by others we have to account for our decisions. Rubin is very aware of how difficult it may be to justify his decision when he conjures up the questions at an imaginary congressional hearing. All too often the decision maker will select the route that can be justified to others. As we will see later the rational and analytically defendable decisions are not always the best. An instinctive judgement, which can't be captured in bullet points on an overhead or calculated in the cells of spreadsheet, can sometimes be correct. A lifetime's experience distilled into a hunch. But telling the shareholders you lost money on a hunch is seldom a winning strategy in the game of corporate survival. A wrong but logically plausible decision can look a lot more appealing than the intuitive judgement that others don't share.

the rational and analytically defendable decisions are not always the best

Decisions that build on each other

In business, in politics, and indeed in life more generally, no decision stands alone. Each decision builds on decisions taken the day or month before, layer after layer. This may sound obvious and unimportant, but contrast this with the stand-alone decisions that are the standard fare of textbooks on chance and decision theory. These discuss isolated decisions about which stock to pick, which horse to back, the expected gain from drawing a red rather than a black ball from the jar. Each of these discrete decisions can be judged a success or a failure in its own terms and, apart from influencing the weight of your purse, does not influence the next stock pick or your betting on the next race.

Contrast that with the manager who, over the course of a year, may decide which candidate to employ, what tasks to give him, how to monitor and support him in his new role, how to evaluate his performance, and finally whether she should terminate his employment for under performance. Each decision building on previous decisions, each decision being taken as more information becomes available. A constantly changing framework for her next decision. Navigating your way successfully through this tangled web of interlocking decisions is the mark of a good manager – the essence of good business judgement while keeping your sights on the overall goal.

Decisions that matter

Being more aware of the way we perceive and judge risk in an uncertain business world can help us make better decisions. Does this matter? It can matter for us personally of course. The better our decisions, the more likely we are to enjoy a successful career (although we can all think of exceptions to this observation). But imagine if, over the long run, every manager was able to make better decisions about the way they allocated resources. The world would be, unquestionably, a better place. Less money wasted, less time wasted, less careers blighted. Just pause for a moment and reflect on the money wasted on various dot.com dreams at the turn of the last century. This wasn't paper money earned cheaply in a rising stock market. The billions spent on PR consultants, technical research on products nobody wanted, fictional business plans and executive remuneration packages was hard won cash from pension contributions and personal savings. All spent on the promise of abnormal gains by taking (what turned out to be, in most cases) ludicrous risks. Understanding how we reach business decisions is an important undertaking. What was the opportunity cost? What could have happened if we had invested that money in another way?

Decisions that will be forgotten

Revisiting previous decisions can be a sobering experience. I spent four years at the height of the technology asset price bubble as an investment director for a venture capital company. Not a time when that profession covered itself in glory. From the vantage of half a decade it is easy to see the mistakes we made, the assets we overvalued. But we rarely look back. If the outcome is good we rewrite our own history – forgetting the doubts and uncertainty that plagued the earlier decision – constructing a confident path to glory (much of business autobiography falls into that category). When the outcome is not good we remember our doubts and reservations – we recall how we 'knew' it wasn't going to work.

Other people also twist their recollection of decisions. Once the outcome of a decision is known we tend to misremember what we thought at the time, when the outcome was still uncertain. This isn't motivated by political expediency but is a consequence of the way our memory works. Instead of recalling our previous decision we rerun the mental process that led to our original prediction. Only now, with the benefit of hindsight, we also know the outcome. This knowledge of the outcome then becomes part of the evidence we use when we recall our initial prediction. It is called the *hindsight bias* – a tendency to believe that we predicted what actually occurred, when in fact we forecast the opposite. What is even more disturbing is that experiments have shown that we are unaware that the knowledge of the outcome is affecting our judgement. We genuinely believe we were right all along. This can explain what happens when the project you championed fails. Your colleagues who originally supported the project will now claim they always had their doubts. It isn't only office politics, the hindsight bias means they are convinced they were always right.

The $35 billion dollar gamble – revisited

So what happened in the US–Mexico saga? The money was lent by the US and the IMF to the Mexican government. A tough series of economic measures were imposed which led to rising unemployment and a fall in real wages, and in the early months the peso continued to fluctuate in line with international confidence in the programme. By as early as the start of 1996 the Mexican economy was growing again. In the crisis of the early 1980s it had taken seven years for Mexico to be able to borrow again from international capital markets; in 1995 it took just seven months. The last of the loans was repaid in January 1997 including $1.4 billion of interest.

Rubin's telling of the episode (2003) illustrates many traits of the good decision maker. The money involved is beyond most people's imagination and the outcome would make a difference to millions of lives. It is difficult to imagine a more unforgiving stakeholder than the US taxpayer and with Congress divided there could be no sharing of responsibility. And yet Rubin, aware that his decision will be impossible to justify if the attempt fails, backs his instinct and his analysis. But then, blessed with a happy ending, he never forgets that it could have turned out differently – there is no rewriting of history to flatter the storyteller.

But this episode also illustrates another characteristic of decisions – outcomes are often not clear cut and our evaluation of an outcome as either good or bad can change over the course of a few years. The cloud around this particular silver lining started to emerge just two years later. Perhaps encouraged by the bail out given to the Mexican bondholders there was a surge of investment in emerging markets.

The bail out of Mexican bondholders in 1995 was followed by further packages of support for Thailand and South Korea. Finally, in July 1998, at Rubin's urging the IMF arranged a $23 billion bail out for Russia. There seemed to be no financial crisis the IMF and the G7 couldn't fix. Western banks and other investors had put billions into emerging markets – reassured by the knowledge that if things got bad the cavalry would always come riding over the hill. With this apparent safety net in place investing in emerging economies looked like a bet that couldn't lose. But only a month after the initial rescue package Russia did what nuclear powers were not supposed to do, it defaulted on its debts. But this time there was no Rubin inspired bail out. As Morris Goldstein (1998) put it, 'The fund and the G7 finally managed to say no.' This time the message finally got through to investors. No emerging market was safe. It set off a flight of capital, not just from emerging markets but from all investments perceived as high risk. The 'moral hazard bubble' (Edwards, 1999, p. 203) was finally punctured.

The challenge

For more than a century economists and management thinkers have been telling us how to manage and how we should make decisions. Again and again in the course of this book we will find examples of the gap between what the theorists tell us we ought to do and what managers actually do. The theorists tell us we should make decisions using careful logical steps; in practice many of our decisions are intuitive. The theorists tell us that emotion has no part to play in rational decision making; in practice emotional responses are essential to decision making. The theorists tell us that we should evaluate all of the possible choices and select the one that maximizes our utility; in practice we look at only one or two options and often only one aspect. The theorists tell us that the optimal decision should be independent of context; in practice we make different choices if are winning or losing, to achieve a gain or avoid a loss, if we are feeling rich or strapped for cash.

Until the last decade or so it has been assumed that because we don't do what the theorists prescribe we are bad decision makers – emotional, subjective and easily led astray. The only remedy was a more diligent application of the theory. We were being told to try harder. This view is starting to change. It turns out that in many ways humans are very sophisticated practical decision makers. Our judgements in many situations are far more subtle and complex than the rational theories we are encouraged to adopt. Many of the textbooks still advocate a purely rational decision-making model. More recently there have been a number of authors celebrating our intuition and emotional wisdom. My aim in this book is to help you understand the nature of business decision making. To look at what works and what doesn't. To understand both the power and the limits of intuitive decision making.

humans are very sophisticated practical decision makers

The science of management is in many ways a very sick patient. A patient that stands up and gets about with the help of two crutches: one is that the world is ultimately predictable; the second is that we are, or at least should be, rational decision makers that do whatever it takes to maximise our own wealth. Both crutches need to be kicked away. What we will find is that the manager can walk perfectly well unaided. In fact we can prosper if we learn to live with uncertainty and with a knowledge of how we really make decisions. The challenge is to be a better decision maker. Not by denying our instincts and following rational theories that can't work in the real world but by understanding the strengths and weaknesses of how we do make decisions and by learning to handle uncertainty.

In other words...

Every day managers are making decisions about the allocation of resources. Even the unconscious act of leaving resources deployed in the same way as yesterday is a decision. Decisions that are made, more often than not, with other people's money. And because they are made with other people's money you need to be able justify your decision. These decisions are important: to the shareholders, to the staff and other stakeholders, to you as decision maker – you have the power to create value or destroy value. But these are also decisions that get forgotten or are misremembered. We focus on our successes and forget our failures. Hindsight bias means that we also believe we chose correctly more often than was the case. We are not as good at decisions as our memory suggests.

Which means that...

> ➤ Every time you make a decision, however trivial, pause to consider how your decision is changing the deployment of scarce resources: attention, people, technology, money.

> ➤ Be aware of the extent to which you have to justify your resource allocations to people (usually other managers) who represent the interests of those who own the assets. In some organizations this can involve a disproportionate amount of time.

> ➤ It is easy to think you are a better decision maker than you really are. Selective memory and hindsight bias can make you overconfident. Keep a record of every decision you make.

> ➤ Start to become self-aware when you make decisions. What goes through your mind? Which factors get considered? Which get ignored? This isn't about criticising your mental deliberations but about increasing your awareness about what is often a barely conscious process.

Rules of thumb...

10 ◆ Record your decisions to calibrate your judgement

Chapter **2**

....

Bad things sometimes happen to the good guys

We saw in Chapter 1 that managers are paid to make decisions about the allocation of resources. Is there a scientific means of determining the best way to allocate those resources, or will there always be an element of chance about the outcome of our decisions? The scientific laws of management promise that we can make confident predictions about the future. If the world was predictable then we would be able to blame a poor outcome on a poor decision by a poor decision maker. In this chapter, I show that we manage in a world that is fundamentally unpredictable and that management theories don't have the status of scientific laws. Despite the promises of management science and our psychological need for certainty we have no alternative but to learn to manage with uncertainty. But this is exactly what poker players have been doing for over a century.

Bad beats

Poker players call it a bad beat. You are odds on to win but the cards turn against you. Des Wilson recounts his own bad beat in his vivid account of a year on the professional poker circuit, *Swimming with the Devilfish* (2006). He has made it to the final table of a tournament and by this stage is sitting behind £180,000 worth of chips – more than all his opponents between them. He is a strong favourite to win the tournament.

> 'It's the first hand and I am looking at two red aces and the guy in the first position raises £28k. I say, 'How many chips have you got left?' and he says, 'another £30k' and I say, 'Stick it in' and he does and he turns over ace-queen off suit. Another guy next to me says to him, 'I don't fancy your chances, I passed a queen.' I'm thinking I have the pot won. The flop comes 2-4-6...'

The details of how to play Texas Hold'em (the variation of poker they are playing) are not important. (This book has been written assuming no prior knowledge of poker – but if you are curious about the colourful language of the game then there is a glossary at the end that explains some of the terms that I use.) Wilson is sitting with a pair of aces. His opponent has an ace and a queen. There is around £120,000 in the pot. With one queen already passed by another player, the only way Wilson can be beaten is if the next two cards to be turned over, the 'turn' and the 'river', are both queens (to give three queens to beat Wilson's two aces).

> '...and then the turn and the river come queen – queen. I've just done about £60k in chips.'

The odds against both the last cards being queens were about 1,900 to 1. Wilson would have won in that position 99.95% of the time, only this time he didn't. Bad beats on the next two hands and he is out of the tournament.

> 'I get into my car and I drive around Russell Square and as I approach the lights I let out a scream of agony. The lights are red and in a few seconds while I wait I quickly mentally calculate the odds against me losing three hands in the fashion I did. It was 90,000 to 1.'

Business also has its bad beats. At the turn of this century both Nokia and Ericsson were world class manufacturers of mobile phones. Ericsson, as many well-managed companies had done, had adopted a single-source procurement strategy using the Philips plant in Albuquerque as their selected chip supplier. Single-source procurement can bring big advantages. By committing all of your demand to one supplier it is possible to extract considerable cost savings and develop a close and mutually beneficial relationship with that supplier. Nokia by contrast had adopted a diversified supply strategy using plants from around the world to meet its demand for chips. Two different but reasonable supply strategies had been adopted. Nokia's diversified supply chain providing flexibility and security versus Ericsson's single-source strategy that had less flexibility but could provide a crucial margin advantage in a fiercely competitive marketplace. It is perfectly possible for conscientious managers at both Ericsson and Nokia to have made well-judged decisions on behalf of their respective firms. Then, on the night of 17 March 2000 a lightning strike starts a small fire at the Philips plant in Albuquerque. The fire is out in 20 minutes and the damage appeared limited. Initially the plant's management believed the damage would only disrupt production for about a week and told Nokia and Ericsson the news. This proved to be far too optimistic. The smoke and water damage had taken out two of the four clean rooms essential for chip manufacture and supply was disrupted for weeks. Nokia's swift reaction to the crisis and its ability to work creatively with other suppliers around the globe enabled it to survive the supply disruption with little impact. For Ericsson it was, along with other product and management weaknesses, a near fatal blow. Within six months Nokia had gained 3 percentage points and now had 30% of the global handset market. During the same period Ericsson lost 3 percentage points and had fallen to 9% market share. One year later Ericsson announced a joint venture with Sony. Ericsson's solo assault on the market was over.

When management authors (see for example Apgar (2006)) recount this story the implication is clear – Ericsson's decision making was flawed. I am not in a position to evaluate whether Ericsson had or had not been cavalier with the risks associated with their single-source procurement policy. But I do think this anecdote perfectly illustrates how strongly we want to believe that chance has no place in modern management – that managers are accountable for outcomes regardless of the process. A small fire that

Is business like poker, a game of skill with a twist of luck?

didn't even make the local news and Ericsson's management is discredited. Bad management or a bad beat? When Wilson faced consecutive queens to lose a 19,000 to 1 on certainty he was unlucky. He had played well and made the right decision, except on this occasion it didn't have a good outcome.

Is business like poker, a game of skill with a twist of luck? Do we as managers always have to accommodate uncertainty that no amount of research or application can remove? Or is business a game of pure skill where, armed with the right information and the right 'laws' of management, it is possible to manage your future success? If it is then we can always   criticize the manager responsible for a poor outcome for a poor decision. But to be able to make confident predictions about the future the manager needs both to be managing in a world where causes have predictable effects, and where management theories have the status of scientific laws. As we shall see, neither is the case.

The misbehaviour of markets

For four decades Benoit Mandelbrot, the maverick mathematician and economist, has been looking at historic price data to find evidence that the market does not set prices in a way that neo-classical economics had assumed: a 'natural' price buffeted by random 'noise'. He focuses on the summer of 1998 – the very time when Rubin and the IMF were deciding whether to use taxpayers' funds to bail out the Russian economy. There was some worrying, but not catastrophic, economic news – a cash crisis in Russia, devaluation in China, recession in Japan. But the Dow Jones Industrial Average fell, on different days in August, by 3.5%, then 4.4%, and finally, on 31 August, by 6.8%. Mandelbrot recounts (2004), 'The hammer blows were shocking – and for many investors, inexplicable... . The standard theories taught in business schools around the world, would estimate the odds of the final, August 31st, collapse at one in 20 million – an event that, if you traded daily for nearly 100,000 years, you would not expect to see even once.'

Markets can be much more volatile than traditional theories would allow. Three centuries ago Newton was able to demonstrate that simple laws of motion and gravitation could act together to create a stable and predictable system. The planets would move in their orbits, in theory forever, without the need for God, or anything else, to keep them on track. If the planets are disturbed by a passing comet they will naturally come back to equilibrium – stability and order created by a few simple laws. Inspired by the success of Newtonian mechanics the challenge was on to find the laws of commerce. Adam Smith's insight in *The Wealth of Nations* was that the motivation of individuals to maximize their own wealth is sufficient to create a well-regulated market and stable prices. Random events such as wars or bad harvests may disrupt the market but it will return to equilibrium without the need for external intervention. Although the assumptions about the motivations of individuals has become more sophisticated in the past two centuries, modern economics is still based on the principle that the actions of millions of individuals can create a stable and resilient market. What Mandelbrot has shown is that, at times, markets are far more volatile than traditional economic models have predicted. Markets can be unstable, not as the result of external random events, but as an inescapable consequence of the way individuals interact.

This should come as no surprise to any student of modern physics. Newtonian mechanics, and indeed Smith's analysis of markets, has been concerned to describe systems at or close to equilibrium where forces are in balance (producing stable orbits and prices). But most of the systems that interest us are not closed systems close to equilibrium but open systems far from equilibrium and driven by an external force: living things driven by energy from food, the ecosystem driven by incoming solar radiation, or the international economy driven by the cheap energy from fossil fuels. These open, driven systems don't behave in the same, quiet, orderly manner that Newton's and Smith's laws predict. Ilya Prigogine, the Nobel Prize winning scientist, has called it 'the end of certainty' (1997). These complex, open systems exhibit behaviour that he calls 'deterministic chaos'. The behaviour of the whole system is determined but the paths of the individual components are unpredictable. Not unpredictable in the sense that we just don't have enough information to make an accurate prediction. But fundamentally unpredictable – it is not possible to predict in advance what will happen. There is no science that can predict with certainty which will prosper and which will fail. The network of interacting individuals – consumers, stockholders, manufacturers, raw material suppliers, planners, government officials – each making decisions with imperfect information and differing objectives does not create a stable system at equilibrium that traditional economic models had assumed.

The economy *is* a dynamic system of deterministic chaos. We can't make confident predictions about individual components in the system. Not because we are too lazy to properly evaluate the starting position or too stupid to correctly apply the laws of economics. Imagine two new internet companies setting up in neighbouring towns on the same day. We can evaluate their management teams, their technology, their customer proposition and make predictions about which will prosper and which will not in the first year of trading. In the long term it is impossible to predict the paths of either company with any certainty – their paths will diverge unpredictably. The conclusion for the

Our management theories fall a long way short of the necessary rigour

business manager is clear – even with comprehensive theories of management we can never be entirely certain that causes will have predictable effects. No matter how clever our theories and how exacting our analysis we can't close the door on uncertainty. But in fact our management theories fall a long way short of the necessary rigour.

The 'science' of management

The management sciences still have a resolutely Newtonian outlook. The real power of science is not in documenting theories in textbooks and libraries but in being able to say, 'I can make this happen by doing that' – being able to recreate causes to get desired effects. We throw the stone to get the pond to ripple. Thanks to science we can calculate the height and speed of the ripples. The science of management believes it can harness the same power. The ability to get predictable results from specific causes. I cut prices and my market share will increase. I implement a global human resource management programme and my profit will improve. But the physical sciences have one huge advantage over other areas of study. It is possible to set up experimental situations where everything is held the same apart from the property you are investigating. It is possible to simplify the environment to isolate cause and effect without a confusion of other factors. For the social sciences (which clearly includes management science) these experiments are rarely, if ever, possible. We can't take two identical companies that differ only in the management style of their leaders and see what happens. We can't isolate the impact of a different organizational structure on company performance. But unfortunately this hasn't stopped any of the social sciences from claiming much of the same authority for its conclusions as we give to physics and chemistry.

Management science is still presented on the basis that it has identified experimentally verified laws that have isolated cause and effect and that our actions have definitely predictable consequences. The MBA programmes and management textbooks still describe a world where the rules of organizations and markets can be used to confidently explain and predict performance. Any uncertainty is due to a lack of knowledge rather than being an essential characteristic of the economy. The business world is a lot more uncertain than the high priests of management sciences have been telling us. We operate in a system where causes may not have proportionate effects. Where the consequences of an action cannot always be predicted and where no amount of research and analysis can remove the uncertainty. Welcome to the real world.

There is one simple observation that exposes the poor state of management science. It appears much more comfortable explaining past events than it is predicting future events. It is easy to use a theory to explain something that has happened. The bursting of the technology bubble in 2000 looks inevitable with the aid of hindsight. But Irving Fisher of Yale University, the greatest economist of his time, claimed just one week before the Great Crash of October 1929 that the American economy had reached 'a permanent high plateau'. He was not alone – not one economist had anticipated the Great Crash.

Armed with these 'scientifically' proven laws it appears easy to see why one company fails and another succeeds. And every plausible story has the effect of strengthening the theory. But just like Ely Devons' observation (in the Introduction) of the enduring power of magic, counter examples don't disprove the theory. They merely indicate that there must have been other, unnoticed, factors at work in this example. Old management theories, like magic, don't get disproved by the evidence; they just go out of fashion. They are replaced by a new recipe, another 'six steps' to managerial success and more 'secrets' from top managers.

What about the lightning strike in New Mexico? Was it an unlikely random event which nobody could have foreseen, or was it just the trigger that started the inevitable unravelling of Ericsson's single-source procurement strategy? Does the lightning strike prove that single-source procurement is unwise in that specific situation, in my situation, in every situation? Bad luck or bad management?

In search of certainty

The trouble is we don't like uncertainty. We pay a lot of money to remove it. Modern cars are very reliable. The chance of mechanical failure and expensive repairs in the first year are very low (let's estimate for the sake of argument 5% require repair). And yet many of us take out insurance to protect ourselves from the financial risk of this loss – paying a premium for an extended warranty period to turn a 5% chance that we will suffer an unquantified loss into a certainty. If you think that extended warranties on cars are a good idea then you may be interested in the figures that were filed in a recent US lawsuit against Nissan. The cost of the extended warranty in this case was $795 of which just $131 went on repairs and the rest was spent on administration ($109) and the dealer's profit ($555!) (see Bazerman, 2006).

We are taught that we should know the answers. Education puts more weight on knowing about things rather than knowing how to find things out – facts rather than process. We assume that the people in senior positions are the people who know the answers. We get promoted for what we know. Knowledge about how the world works, knowledge that enables us to make better informed decisions about the future. And if we don't know the answer, the first instinct is to bluff. Admitting ignorance is a dangerous thing to do.

In organizations, having the ability to reduce uncertainty can give an individual or a department a lot of power. French sociologist Michael Crozier (1964) describes an intriguing example of how the ability to control uncertainty can influence power in his study of a state-owned cigarette factory. A stable market, a state-owned industry, and a routine production process resulted in very little uncertainty. What Crozier noticed was that the maintenance workers had power in the organization that was out of proportion with their low position in the hierarchy. Crozier discovered that with the machine operators paid on output, the maintenance of machinery was one of the key uncertainties for workers. The maintenance workers carefully guarded the knowledge of how to repair the machines. Their ability to influence this one remaining uncertainty meant that they were accorded great power, something they used to influence their own working conditions. At different points a business may face different uncertainties. During a price war with a competitor the biggest uncertainty will be the market share that can be achieved: the sales team are the people who have the power to remove the uncertainty and become very influential. If a company is facing a substantial claim from litigation, the legal team will become more powerful and will be able to influence behaviour in other departments. In normal circumstances, when little uncertainty is involved, it would be ignored.

In many organizations it is senior management's role as planners and forecasters that give it part of its power. The future uncertainties are controlled with plans and forecasts. Models are created and data are collected. The high status individuals in finance and planning weave their magic and produce forecasts that remove uncertainty. Rates of investment return are calculated to two decimal places, sales forecasts are 'verified' and everyone feels better. And if the forecast turns out to be wrong then better models are demanded, more data are collected, reporting is improved and controls are tightened.

What is needed is to manage with uncertainty

Efforts are redoubled to improve the plan and remove uncertainty. The models and the computing power have been transformed in the 50 years since Ely Devons' compared economic forecasting with ritual magic. We have tried to squeeze the uncertainty out of the future with data and processing power, only to find that the future is just as uncertain now as it was then. We have been trained to manage with certainty when what is needed is to manage with uncertainty. Accepting that we have to manage with uncertainty is going to lead to a very different management skill set than the one we use in our, ultimately futile, attempts to manage with certainty.

Poker, chance and management

I started this chapter with an anecdote about poker. I will be drawing on the experience of poker and the wisdom of poker players throughout the book. No knowledge or special interest in poker is assumed and the reader who loathes all card games can get as much from this book as the expert player. I have included insights from poker for one simple reason, poker is a game of skill where players have to make judgements about how best to deploy resources (chips) to maximize a return when not all of the information is available. Poker players have to make quick, important and skilled judgements under conditions of uncertainty. No amount of analysis or research (apart from cheating) can determine what the next card will be or what the opponents hold. The seductive appeal of certainty is not available to the poker player. The right judgement, as Des Wilson knows only too well, will often have the wrong outcome. While today's management textbooks and case studies have been criticizing managers for every poor outcome, the poker textbooks have been teaching to accept a bad beat for what it is and to look and learn and wait for another hand. I think the wisdom of poker has more to teach today's managers about handling investment decisions under uncertainty than most management textbooks.

In other words...

Bad things happen to good guys – not every winner is smart, not every loser is a fool and chance can unpick the best decisions. And – because we can never eliminate uncertainty when we plan a better future – luck is always going to be part of management. Physics, economics and management science have been built on the assumption that the world is stable and (at least in principle) predictable. Not only is this assumption wrong but management science's inability to undertake controlled experiments means that we have great difficulty identifying cause and effect. But that doesn't stop researchers and authors proclaiming the authority of science for their prescriptions for better management. But why should we believe their explanations any more than we believe their predictions? The challenge is not to try and achieve certainty but to learn to manage uncertainty.

Which means that...

> Don't judge other people, including yourself, by the outcome of decisions. The experience and wisdom that goes into the process is more important in the long run than the outcome.

> Treat with scepticism some of the assertions of management writers and researchers who claim to have identified universal prescriptions for managerial success.

> Be wary of theories that seem to be able to explain the past but can't predict the future.

> You don't need to understand either poker or chaos theory to be a better manager – you just need to acknowledge that you can't control the future. You don't manage uncertainty in the same way as you would manage certainty.

Rules of thumb

A♣   Don't judge people by the outcome of chance events

5♣   Judge a theory by its predictions not its explanations

6♣   Treat management theories as rules of thumb – not universal laws

8♠   We can't manage uncertainty in the same way we have *tried* to manage certainty

Chapter **3**

....

In search of the perfect decision?

Despite the fact that, as we have seen in the first two chapters, we can't eliminate the role chance plays in business, we are always looking for methods that can get us to the 'right' answer. We want to be 'rational' decision makers selecting the best alternative unswayed by subjective judgement – a decision that others can understand and accept. This chapter demonstrates that even the simplest recipe for selecting the best alternative always relies on human judgement. We will also find that even our goals can change as we start to decide. We have to rely on a personal judgement that will always reflect our individual experiences. The crucial question in Chapter 4 will be how do we distil personal experience into the judgement we use to make decisions? But first, why can't we follow simple rules to come up with the right answer?

Marry or not marry?

Having returned from his voyage on the *Beagle*, Charles Darwin had some important matters to attend to in his private life. Darwin was a habitual notetaker and listmaker. On a scrap of paper he wrote at the top, 'This is the question'. There were two columns.

MARRY	NOT MARRY
Children – (if it please God) – constant companion, (friend in old age) who will feel interested in one, object to be beloved and played with – better than a dog anyhow – Home, and someone to take care of the house – Charms of music and female chit-chat. These things good for one's health. Forced to visit and receive relations *but terrible loss of time. My God, it is intolerable to think of spending one's whole life, like a neuter bee, working, working, and nothing after all – No, no won't do – Imagine living all one's day solitarily in smokey dirty London House – Only to picture yourself a nice soft wife on a sofa with a good fire, and books and music perhaps – compare this vision with the dingy reality of Grt Marlboro' St.*	*No children (no second life), no one to care for one in old age...Freedom to go where one liked – Choice of Society and* little of it. *Conversation of clever men at clubs – Not forced to visit relatives, and to bend to in every trifle – to have the expense and anxiety of children – perhaps quarrelling.* Loss of time – *cannot read in the evenings – fatness and idleness – anxiety and responsibility – less money for books, etc. – if many children forced to gain one's bread (But then it is very bad for one's health to work too much).* *Perhaps my wife won't like London; then the sentence is banishment and degradation with indolent idle fool-* ...

(From Darwin, 1969)

And then, perhaps, to give us a clue to the way he may have been leaning, he wrote on the back of the sheet, 'There is many a happy slave.'

Clearly, this is a decision of great importance to Darwin. He can marry or he can remain unmarried. For each alternative he then lists some of the possible consequences. With each list complete he weighs up the costs and benefits of each course of action. Darwin, I presume, had a goal. It seems reasonable to infer that he was hoping to maximize his personal happiness over the rest of his life. I imagine him reviewing each set of expected consequences against this goal of happiness, trying to decide which course will serve him best. Darwin was following the structured search for the best outcome: having a goal, listing alternatives, identifying consequences and assessing the alternative that best meets his goal. Darwin is following a structured procedure for decision making that I expect most of us have tried at some stage in our lives.

A recipe for perfect decisions?

Management theories come in one of two styles. Firstly there are the theories that result from observing what the most successful businesses do. These are theories that are based on what is called inductive logic. I notice that all of the top performing companies have implemented management practice X (where X is any fashionable practice you care to think of). I therefore conclude that management practice X is the cause of the good performance and write a book which will be called something like *5 steps to improved performance through X*. The basic logical flaw in most of the research that leads to these theories has been powerfully exposed in Phil Rosenzweig's *The Halo Effect* (2007). Separating mere association from cause is a very challenging task. The other style of management theory uses deductive logic. These start with simple, apparently unquestionable, facts, and then use logic to deduce principles for action. The principles of decision theory described in many management textbooks is one of these deductive theories – based on seemingly irrefutable logic, but paying no regard whatsoever to what managers actually do.

The decision-making theory is in effect a recipe. A method which if followed with care would allow anyone to make the 'right' decision. An objective and general procedure that can be adapted to any context. A procedure that is neither subject to our changing moods nor dependent on our individual experiences. A method that any 'rational actor' could follow to pick the right route every time the path divides. Do the thought processes behind

The decision-making theory is in effect a recipe

Darwin's scribbled note have the elements we are looking for? Setting out the rational process more formally, the steps in our recipe to find the perfect decision become as follows:

1. Know what you want – your goal.
2. Identify all of the alternative courses of action.
3. Gather the information you need and then deduce all of the consequences of each course of action.
4. Select the course of action that best meets your goals.

The logic is clear and straightforward, the assumptions reasonable. You don't need extensive observation of managers in high-performing companies to be clear that this is the best procedure. Indeed, variations on this basic model have become part of the received wisdom of business decision making and there is an extensive literature telling you how to broaden your search for options, how to evaluate consequences and descriptions of the multi-attribute scoring systems to help balance competing goals. Simple commonsense it may appear, but it is a recipe that is very hard to follow in the heat of the kitchen. The first step in this four-step process, knowing your objective, I will examine later in the chapter. Here, I will start by looking at step 2 – identifying the alternative courses of action.

Step 2 – identifying the alternatives

Teaching a computer to play chess seemed an achievable goal – something that our rational decision-making model and modern computing should be able to achieve. Chess is a straightforward game played with just 32 pieces with prescribed moves on a board of 64 squares. All a computer has to do is select the best move in each position. There is no hidden information and no element of chance or unpredictability.

In 1996, IBM's Deep Blue first challenged the then reigning world chess champion, Gary Kasparov, to a match to be played under tournament time controls. Although Deep Blue did record one victory in the six-game series, Kasparov won three and drew two of the other games. The following year there was a rematch with the heavily upgraded computer. This time Kasparov lost, a final score of $2^1/_2$ to $3^1/_2$, the first ever defeat of a reigning world champion to a machine under tournament rules. Had Kasparov slipped up during the rematch or had Deep Blue got significantly better at making decisions? The 1996 version of Deep Blue was capable of evaluating 100 million positions a second. A year later it had doubled that capacity, making it one of the fastest and most powerful supercomputers on the planet. Was this improvement in its brute force processing power the crucial factor?

Chess playing computers take advantage of their perfect memory and very fast calculating speeds to evaluate the consequences of each legal move as far as they can into the future – far further than their human opponents can do. The doubling of processing power sounds impressive but you would need a 35x increase in processing power to see one more move into the future (based on the reasonable assumption that at any stage there are typically about 35 legal moves available to a player). So quickly do the possible moves multiply that a doubling of processing speed hardly makes a difference. No, the reason Deep Blue made so much progress is that it got better at doing what humans do. It had been programmed to start to mimic the ways in which humans play chess. We don't, because we can't, search exhaustively for the perfect move. What we do is ruthlessly reduce the number of options that we need to evaluate by learning patterns that are most likely to include strong moves. We discard very early on the majority of options so that we can train our limited memory and analytic powers on the few lines of development that look the most promising. Deep Blue had been taught how to recognize and evaluate these patterns of play by studying hundreds of thousands of grandmaster games. It captured the wisdom of 200 years of chess to identify the patterns that led to success. It could then focus its immense processing power to investigate in great depth the small number of alternatives that seemed most promising. In the end it wasn't brute force that defeated Kasparov, but a computer armed with the distilled experience of human players.

The same focus on a few options is characteristic of human decision making in many fields. The poker player will not consider or evaluate all of the probabilities for every conceivable hand that an opponent may hold. The good poker player uses judgement gained through experience to decide which of the scenarios require detailed attention. Similarly, the company looking to make an acquisition does not consider all of the potential acquisitions in enormous detail. With the benefit of experience perhaps only two or three alternative targets are considered in detail.

Step 3 – gather all of the relevant information

One of the perennial strategy questions that most management teams face at some point is whether and how to diversify the range of a company's activities. The economist has straightforward advice – all things being equal, diversify into the market where you can get a rate of return that is better than you are currently achieving. How is that to be done? You gather the information that allows you to estimate the likely return on capital from each of your alternative areas of activity. Straightforward advice that is similar to the problem faced by grazing animals – is there a rational strategy that enables an animal to know when it should move on to a new feeding ground? Just like the economist advising the board considering diversification, there is a rational 'marginal value' theorem for foraging animals. If by staying still the food available decreases, a foraging animal should move on when the rate at which food is found at the current location is equal to the highest rate that can be found elsewhere. When the grass is greener on the other side of the fence, move on. At first it seems hard to argue with this advice. Simple, rational decision making for sheep – move on when you can do better elsewhere. But from the sheep's point of view it's hard to make a practical decision based on the theorem. The sheep just doesn't know when to move on or where to move to. It has no way of knowing if the grass is greener without going there. All the time an ewe is looking she is not eating. Searching has a cost. So when does a rational sheep decide when to move on? When does the rational board decide on a diversification strategy?

When the grass is greener on the other side of the fence, move on

More practical foraging strategies have been developed from the animal's perspective. Simple strategies that can be tested in computer simulations: leave after a fixed time; leave if you find no food after a fixed time; and leave when the rate of finding food is too slow (below a pre-set level). The most effective strategy was the last one; once the current location is no longer 'good enough', it is time to move on. A simple, behavioural rule of thumb that doesn't optimise the feed rate, but enables a decision to be made with minimal information – the feeding rate at the current location and a specified minimum. It sounds too simple but in fact one species of wasp has been shown to use precisely this foraging strategy. The wasp that tried to collect data and assess the potential of every foraging site before making the optimal decision on where to go next died out a long time ago. Just as the board that was still gathering information about potential alternative diversifications has been sacked long ago.

If all the information was available then, in theory, you may be able to make an optimal decision. But in reality you never decide. There is always more information to be gathered. For sheep and businesses, decisions about when to move on to new pastures or new markets are vital to their survival. You would have expected evolutionary pressures to have weeded out the individuals with the least effective foraging strategy. What none of them do is use the rational, optimizing model that started this chapter. It seems the decision-making strategy for real situations with incomplete information are not as obvious as we first thought. In fact many poker writers propose a very similar strategy for players. They suggest that players should have a target rate of return per hour. This will vary depending on the experience of the player and the betting limits of a particular game. If, perhaps because your opponents are more experienced than usual, you are not getting that average rate of return then you should stop and try another game. Exactly the same advice, but derived from experience, not the product of rational theorizing. Once again a judgement is necessary.

Steps 2, 3 and 4 – running out of time

You are playing Texas Hold'em. You have a jack, ten in the pocket and the flop has come nine, eight, ace –two of them hearts. There is $600 in the pot and the player to your right has just placed a bet of $200 – there are two players still in to your left. What do you do?

In theory you should be able to apply the rational decision-making model to maximize your return. Unlike chess the options are few – fold (throw in the hand), call the bet (match the $200 and stay in the hand) or raise the bet (match the $200 and then increase the bet). But unlike chess some of the information is missing. You don't know what the turn and the river cards are going to be and you don't know what your opponent's cards are. But unlike the sheep that has to travel to get information on distant grazing you can use your knowledge of probabilities and the information you have gained about your opponents' playing styles to help you make a judgement. It is possible to calculate the probability that you will get a queen or a seven that you need to complete your straight (five cards in sequence). In theory you can also work out the probability that one of your opponents will make the flush (all cards of the same suit and higher rank-ing than a flush), or indeed of them holding a higher hand, or of their likelihood of reraising and bluffing you out of the hand. Because there is missing information, you can't be certain to make the right call. But if you can calculate the probabilities you should be able to uncover the bet that would give you the highest expectation – the course of action that would maximize your return in the long run. The thing that is stopping you reaching the perfect decision is time. The dealer is staring at you and restlessly fiddling with the pack. All around the table stacks of chips are being riffled, counted and restacked. The stares harden. The impatience is tangible. You have, maybe at most, another 30 seconds to make a decision – your mind full of probabilities, percentages and contingencies, fear of losing and an impulse not to walk away from the chips you have already bet. What are you going to do?

The alternatives are sufficiently few in number to make logical analysis possible. The information, although incomplete and necessarily couched in probabilities, is to hand. While the chess-playing computer was floored by the number of options, and the sheep by too little information, the inex-perienced poker player runs out of time. There simply isn't long enough during the game to do the analysis from first principles and to reach an optimized decision. In business, time-constrained decisions happen every day – negotiating face to face with a supplier, reacting to a customer's objections to close an order, dealing with personnel issues as they arise.

There are any number of situations where something needs to be done quickly. Times when you haven't got time to work through all of the consequences. Some decisions have to be made on the hoof – the manual doesn't tell you what to do in every situation. Times when you can't 'get back to you tomorrow on that one'.

Is trying your best good enough?

The recipe can't be followed in the heat of the kitchen

Our seemingly simple rational model of decision making can't be implemented. The recipe can't be followed in the heat of the kitchen. In the real world of chess-playing computers, hungry sheep and poker players the reality is too complicated. The alternatives are too many, the information too difficult to obtain or the time too constrained to allow a rational, optimized solution.

But maybe all we need to do is lower our sights a little. Maybe the rational decision-making strategy should be though of as an ideal – something we strive towards, knowing that we can never implement it perfectly. You can't gather all of the information and you can't evaluate all of the consequences, but maybe the best course is to do as much as you possibly can. Perhaps because it appears to reward the diligent decision maker over the lazy chancer this has an intuitive appeal. We may never be able to make a perfectly rational decision based on all of the information but we can try with all our might to gather as much information as we can and analyse it as thoroughly as we are able. Presumably the harder we work the closer we will get to the right answer. Without all of the ingredients we will not be able to follow our recipe for a perfect decision faithfully, but if we work hard we can get a passable result.

Many organizations appear to follow this model of decision making. Detailed analysis has its place – as we will see later – but an over-zealous attitude to information gathering for decision making has some very unwelcome consequences. But how can a tireless search for the right answer be anything other than good practice? I know of one international business services company with sales over $1 billion where the unofficial, but often repeated, mantra of the senior executives is that it is better to be 'slow and sure' than 'fast and dumb'. When a proposal for an acquisition or a new product launch is made by one of the senior managers within this company it will always go to the CEO for a decision. The response, more often than not, is a call for more research. A market report is commissioned, a few months go by, the findings are reported to the senior management team, the 'slow but sure' mantra repeated a few times to the frustrated managers. But because of the shared myth that there is a 'right' decision it is very hard to argue against another market report – how can more information, another perspective, harm the process? The organization is finding ways of avoiding a decision – hiding risk aversion behind a claim that more information is needed. In this particular company the culture also displays a profound lack of trust in the middle managers.

Tellingly, when more research is required, it is not the managers submitting the proposal that are sent away to do it. The senior executives are commissioning research for themselves from outside experts. The clear message is that they don't trust their managers to give them the full picture and they don't trust the decisions that the managers have reached. 'Slow but sure' is in fact a cover not just for risk aversion and indecisiveness but also for a profound lack of respect for the market knowledge and expertise of their staff. A situation that gives the worst of all possible worlds – paying the salaries of managers whose judgements you do not trust or accept, missing opportunities through slow decision making, all justified by the mistaken belief that, 'it can't be wrong to commission more market research, to get closer to the perfect decision'.

Reluctance to make a decision and the propensity to hide behind the need for more information has long been recognized by writers on decision making. Apgar (2006) calls them Encyclopaedists – people or organizations that avidly collect all of the information but can't commit. Etzioni (1989) calls it, 'Hypervigilance – obsessively collecting more and more information instead of making a decision'. It seems that there are real dangers in trying to aspire to the rational model of decision making. It is, after all, going to come down to judgement, to a subjective assessment of probabilities. No amount of research can make the decision safe, rational or completely objective. Personal judgement is part of decision making. Poker players know they can never collect all of the data; decisions are always matters of judgement. And because business managers are also making a decision without all of the information (with inevitable uncertainty) they will always have to make a judgement call. But personal risk taking in organizations can sometimes appear to be a suicidal strategy. The error of missing out because you said no to a risk often goes unnoticed. The error of accepting a risk and failing is often very public. The sins of omission seem less serious than the sins of commission. In most circumstances, as we shall see later, people are naturally risk averse (even gamblers) so an organizational culture of fear can be a serious barrier to innovation and change.

When more searching doesn't pay

One further modification of the simple recipe may be worth considering. What if we agreed to keep searching for options, gathering information and evaluating alternatives until the cost of doing so no longer justifies the additional searching? This seems to accord with common sense. We keep researching the market for a new product until we sense that the additional information gained from the next research report does not justify the additional cost. We keep interviewing candidates and taking up references until we conclude that the additional time and effort of seeing another candidate is not going to change our recruitment decision. This version of the rational decision-making process acknowledges that information and time have a cost and that they are both constrained. (It sometimes referred to as optimization under constraints – we do the best we can by acknowledging both limited resources and limited time.) But appealing though this may be, it is not clear that this helps us get any closer to becoming a rational decision maker.

How do you decide when you have done enough?

How do you determine that the next search effort will give results that do not justify the cost? How do you decide when you have done enough? There is no objective way of answering this question. It is going to be a judgement call. A judgement call that can't be reliably reproduced by every decision maker. Experience and psychology differ between individuals. This will lead to different managers reaching different decisions about when to stop searching. The 'right' decision is just as far out of reach.

How we actually make those judgements and the traps that lie in store for decision makers will be my focus in the rest of the book. It turns out that we are effective decision makers – it is just that we don't make decisions through an exhaustive (and theoretically never-ending) search for options, evidence and consequences. We use a whole host of psychological tools to make decisions in the real world where time and information are scarce and valuable. Psychological tools that have evolved with us to solve the problems faced by social primates: Who can I trust? Where can I find water and food? Who will make the best parent for my offspring? The good news is that in situations that are familiar to us these psychological decision-making tools are quick, clever and surprisingly effective. The bad news is that they also leave us open to well-researched and well-understood biases and, critically, they don't help us when we have to make a decision in an unfamiliar situation.

What do you *really* want?

In focusing on the search for alternatives and the gathering of information I have skipped over the first stage – deciding what we want – which is perhaps the most important and the most problematic. Darwin, I presume, wanted to maximize his personal happiness. There have been a few times in my life when, faced with a difficult decision, I have resorted, just like Darwin, to writing down the various options and listing the consequences of each choice. I can't say that it has ever worked. I always seem to start the process with a choice between two courses of action: for example, should I accept or decline a better paid but more challenging and time demanding job? I diligently list the likely consequences. But the choice between accepting the new position or staying always seems to be transformed into a decision about goals. This decision can seem just as intractable. What do I really want: the freedom to work fewer hours or more money (and the freedom, security, status and even friendship that money can bring)? What matters more: the free time next year or my financial security in retirement?

We often start by thinking that we know what we want, that our goals are simple and unconflicted. But in reality things can quickly get cloudy. Or more accurately we may know what we want – but do we know the price we are prepared to accept, in order to achieve that goal. I know my goal is to lose weight – what I don't know, but I am slowly finding out, is the extent to which I am prepared to eat less and get up early to find time to jog. My stated goal of losing weight is conflicting with other goals – eating well, sleeping in – which perhaps I had never acknowledged as goals but seem to be restricting my ability to achieve the stated goal.

These hidden conflicts come clearly to light when we search for somewhere to live. These days this process usually starts by entering our search criteria into an online property database. We enter the number of bedrooms, the price range, the postcode and other criteria that can include distances from schools and railway stations. The database is sifted against our criteria and 'matching' properties are listed. And then the difficulties start. The 'goals' that we thought were clear are suddenly in conflict. The price range doesn't allow three bedrooms close to the school. Having a garden and being close to the town centre seems to be impossible. Then you notice most of the properties are modern and a bit dull – age of construction or 'character' were not permitted search criteria. And, typically, the property that really fire the imagination is not in the returned 'hits' at all because the search algorithm couldn't 'see' that two bedrooms and the store room could be adapted to be three bedrooms.

Perhaps this is one of the reasons why, despite property databases of 500,000 and more entries and desktop 'virtual tours', there is still a role for the estate agent. A human who is instinctively able to pick his way through the conflicting goals and aspirations of the client and to narrow down the hundreds of possibilities to a manageable shortlist that reflects the complex trade offs and compromises between goals that real-life decision making requires. (At least there is a role for the agent until such time as the search interfaces to property databases start to reflect the way in which we resolve goal conflicts.)

In a business environment, I may know that my goal is to increase profits by 10% this year. But looking at the options for achieving the goal will bring out conflicts between other goals that I may not have been aware of, or at least not articulated. Is it right to reduce spending on product research to achieve the immediate goal? Should some environmental or ethical principles be compromised in order to achieve that goal? Is it acceptable to spend less on training to achieve this goal? What if this training was important to the safety of the staff or the customers? The stated goal has to be balanced against other goals: having a strong product pipeline to support future years' earnings, having a well-trained and motivated team. Goals are not straightforward. They are complex, layered and changing. Some goals, perhaps most goals, are discarded if achieving the goal looks too complicated or expensive. When we start on a decision-making process we are not always clear about what our goals are – which are sub-goals, which are the fundamental goals? This isn't poor management and fuzzy thinking – it is in the nature of goals to be slippery and ill-defined. The trouble can start when you treat goals as absolute. Then, you need to be careful what you wish for; you may make it come true.

One typical example of fixed goals causing problems is in setting objectives for performance related pay. The staff target is usually clear and uncomplicated – in fact the HR professionals will tell you that is how it should be – a simple incentive based on sales performance, on achieving a project milestone or on winning a major contract. Of course, in reality these plausibly simple objectives never capture the real complexities and contingencies. Yes, sales are the target, but at what margin? What promises can and can't be made to customers to secure the order? 100% of all customer complaints can be resolved to the customers' satisfaction within 20 days, but at what cost? Pin one goal firmly to the table and you create an incentive for managers to disregard the other goals that are layered around it. If you put enough incentive to achieve the one goal then watch out – you may just get what you wished for and a whole host of subsidiary goals may lie in tatters, including the company's standing with suppliers, its reputation with customers, its ethical standing in the community. In organizations decision making is often mired in internal politics. One of the drivers of this conflict is the fact that different individuals have different goals; goals that may not be reconcilable. If the goals are different there may be no process that can reach a consensus so the politics starts to win people over to your way of thinking – if you share my goals then you may share my solution.

In recent years the managers of Britain's National Health Service (NHS) have been incentivized to achieve targets and performance ratings. Anna Walker was recently appointed as Commissioner of the Health Commission, the body set up to assess the many health service providers. She recounted in a recent interview (*Guardian*, 11 October 2006) a conversation she had with a CEO of one of the Trusts that delivers healthcare who explained, 'you can get three stars by treating performance rating as a project; you put all your effort into achieving three stars and the rest of the organization can go hang'. The performance criteria you set will never be as complex as the layered and conflicting goals of the organization.

Objectives: a Japanese perspective

Just how much we in the West still rely on the mechanistic metaphor of organizations is beautifully illuminated in a study that William Ouchi (1981) conducted on the differences between American and Japanese managers working in the US offices of a Japanese bank. He asked the Americans what frustrated them most about working with Japanese. The reply was unanimous, 'These Japanese just don't understand objectives, and it drives us nuts!' He then asked the same question of the Japanese employees assigned to the US office. The reply was just as unambiguous, 'These Americans just don't seem to be able to understand objectives.'

Intrigued he embarked upon a second round of interviews. The Americans were encouraged to be more specific, 'We have all of the necessary reports and numbers, but we can't get specific targets from him... How can we know if we are performing well without specific targets to shoot for?' Returning to the Japanese executives, 'If only I could get these Americans to understand our philosophy of banking... If they could get that under their skin, then they could figure out for themselves what an appropriate objective would be for any situation...' Ouchi's questioning perfectly captures the difference between objectives that are by-products of a master plan and those that emerge as part of a discovery process. And although Ouchi's interviews were carried out nearly 30 years ago they still capture a truth about how most managers see their role. Indeed a recent study found that 62% of corporate executives saw their role as 'guardians' who put a strong emphasis on logistics and organization. The plan had to be nailed down and then implemented without question. But if the plan wasn't right or if something changed...?

It is not that setting objectives can't work. In my experience they work when the people setting the objectives *and* the incentivized member of staff are aware of the pay offs and compromises that haven't made it into the formal statement of the incentive plan. The goals can help set priorities – but they don't supersede the full set of objectives and values that the organization stands for. If you do pin down one goal completely – elevating it to unquestionable truth – then you lose control of the other goals.

So, for the rational decision maker, the diligent manager who wants to make the best possible decision for her firm, we have reached some uncomfortable conclusions. Getting to the best possible decision is certainly beyond us. We don't have all the information, we can't deduce all of the consequences of our actions, and we are not even sure when we start what exactly it is that we want. Even if we lower our sights, make 'good enough' our goal rather than 'the best', we still find that we are making personal judgements about when to stop searching. There seems to be no simple way in which we can train ourselves or teach our staff to be rational decision makers. We are going to have to be content with personal judgements, judgements that may differ from others because of our experiences, psychology and perception of goals.

It is still early in our journey but some initial advice is emerging from our consideration of the folly of optimal rational decision making. Focus on what experience tells you are the most promising options – don't waste time looking at every remote possibility. You will never have perfect information so you will have to make a decision with some data missing. Only experience can tell you whether what you lack is likely to be vital. When you think you have enough information – decide.

What Darwin did next

In fact Darwin made his decision and wrote 'Marry – Marry – Marry – Q.E.D.' under the first column. He didn't seem to waste much time or effort on the search for possible wives – he married his cousin the following year and they went on to have ten children together.

We have seen how Darwin thought he was deciding *whether* to marry, but how did he decide *who* to marry? Deciding on a mate is one of the most significant decisions we make (from both personal and evolutionary points of view). As you might expect, the rationalists have come up with a model that describes the best method for finding our ideal partner.

FINDING AN IDEAL MATE – THE RATIONAL WAY

Assume for a moment that in our lives we may meet 100 people who could be potential partners. Also assume, somewhat unrealistically, that the decision is one sided – that whoever we select will in fact want to become our partner. (It is possible to describe rational strategies for mutual selection but the additional complications do not alter the overall principle.) Lastly assume that we can only court one partner at a time and that once we have decided not to marry a candidate we can't go back and change our minds. Can we describe a strategy that gives us the best chance of finding and keeping our perfect partner? Using basic probability theory you can come up with a rational 'stopping rule' (the rule you follow to tell you when to stop searching). It turns out you should keep dating and moving on until you have experienced 37 of the available candidates. You should marry the first potential partner that is better than all of others so far seen. The theory captures the fact that if you stop earlier you have a high probability of missing a very good match. If you keep dating too long you increase the chance that the best match has been and gone (and can't be regained). In essence, use 37% of the field to determine the range of available candidates, then use this information to select the one that is better than all of those seen so far. Simple. Does love and romance play no role? Well, you can also argue that emotion has a powerful role to play in the decision-making process. If when we find the candidate that we think is better than the others we may fall in love. But being in love is a highly charged emotional state which has the effect of stopping the search – we lose the desire to keep looking for a better mate! So even the rationalist has a role for love.

We will never know, but I would speculate that Darwin used another strategy. I speculate that he probably had various requirements for his future wife. Social standing, education, age, health, child rearing capacity are likely to have been factors. The fact that he married his cousin makes me think he may have stopped searching as soon as he found the first candidate that met these criteria. Like the sheep that moved on when the grazing was no longer good enough, Darwin stopped searching for a wife when he met the first candidate that was good enough. This is a strategy that doesn't require knowledge of all of the other candidates to reach an optimal decision. Darwin, like the sheep, can make a decision on very limited information. But don't scoff, it's a strategy we sometimes use

We appoint the only candidate if they are 'good enough'

ourselves. We appoint the only candidate if they are 'good enough'. We select the first holiday destination that meets all of the family's competing goals. We award a cleaning contract to the first company that meets our requirements. Don't knock it. We use it frequently. Now you are aware of it as a decision-making strategy you will spot it in use.

Finally, consider the mate selection strategy of the female guppy. The female guppy will choose a mate with the brightest orange colouring on the body. Of two males on offer, the female will choose the male which has a much brighter colour. But if the two males are similar in brightness she will choose the mate that she has seen mating with others (even if it is slightly less brightly coloured). In other words, if there is no clear difference in orange appeal, choose the one that others have chosen! In this case the stopping strategy is simple and socially determined. And before we dismiss this as a simple decision-making strategy for small-brained fishes – are you sure that selecting the mate that others have chosen is not used as a 'stop search' strategy by humans? Or in the context of business, we wouldn't make a choice merely because other people have chosen it, would we? But of course we do. Doing what other people do is a very common method for making a quick decision. Corporate strategies, investment opportunities, holiday destinations. Herding is a very powerful inclination in business and in life.

In other words...

We can't follow the recipe to get the perfect answer. The alternatives are too many to evaluate (Deep Blue), the information is not available (the grazing sheep) or we don't have time (playing poker). The advice to become a rational decision maker is unusable. But just doing your best – evaluating as many alternatives; gathering as much information; and taking as long as you can – doesn't help the decision maker get any closer to an ideal decision. A subjective judgement call is always needed to tell us when to stop searching and start acting. Even our goals are not straightforward: they are layered and contingent. You don't discover what you really want until you discover what you have to give up to achieve it. Goals aren't handed down, they are uncovered.

Which means that...

> You can't make the perfect decision and it can be counter productive to try.

> There comes a point when you have to stop searching and start deciding. You have no alternative but to use your judgement.

> Don't be surprised if your goals change. They are never simple and the process of deciding will help you uncover goals that may not have been explicit.

> Setting one goal as absolute and unconditional will lead to conflict and may result in other goals being ignored.

> Sample at least a third of the field before committing to the 'best you have seen'.

Rules of thumb

K ♦ Every decision requires a personal judgement
9 ♠ Goals are discovered not handed down
7 ♥ Pass on a third of the field before choosing the best you have seen
2 ♦ You can't make the perfect decision

Chapter **4**

I *know* I am right (but I am not sure why)

We can't make the perfect decision because every choice involves a personal judgement – a judgement that depends upon our own experiences. This chapter looks at the source of our judgement – our intuitions – and how they are distilled from experience based on the emotional impact of past experiences. However effective intuitive judgements are they can cause a problem when we make decisions using other people's money. These decisions need justifying – not with intuitions but with logical analysis. I look at EMAP's stop/start internet investment strategy as an example of the influence that rational justification has on decision making.

Separating the cars from the goats

Monty Hall was the host of Let's Make a Deal – one of America's longest running TV game shows that lasted for more than two decades from the early sixties. He gave contestants a simple challenge that has become known as the 'Monty Hall problem' and generated a substantial body of academic literature. Monty showed the contestant three closed doors. The main variation has a car behind one door, selected at random, and a goat behind each of the other two doors. Monty then asks the contestant to choose one of the doors (the presumption is, of course, that they want the car and not the goat – my fondness for goats makes it necessary to point out this important detail). When they have chosen a door (which remains shut for now), Monty then opens one of the remaining doors to reveal one of the goats. He then offers the contestant a simple choice, 'Do you want to change door, or stick with your original choice?'

Imagine you are a contestant on Let's Make a Deal, you have chosen a door, and Monty has opened one of the other doors to reveal a goat. Now the crucial question, do you want to change to the other closed door or stick with your first choice? Questions of probability don't get much easier than this.

If you concluded that it doesn't make any difference if you change or stick with your original choice –'the odds of getting the car are and still are 1 in 3' – then you are in good company. Most contestants stayed with their original choice. Reproducing this problem in the laboratory typically shows about 60% will stick with their first choice and around 40% will switch. Which is a pity; you have just halved your chance of winning the car. Sticking with the original door has a 1 in 3 chance of winning the car (the original odds of selecting the correct door in the first instance). Switching to the other unopened door gives you a 2 in 3 chance of winning the car. So assuming, unlike me, you prefer cars to goats, changing is clearly the better strategy. If you are having a problem justifying this answer – I have set this problem to business leaders and students on many occasions and a proof is always required – then think about the problem in this way. Draw out three sets of three doors (left, centre and right) and put the car behind a different door in each set to represent the three different possibilities when the game begins. But remember for the contestant at this stage every door is closed and they don't know the position of the goats or the car.

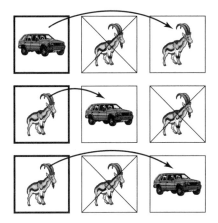

Now, imagine that you are the contestant and that you have chosen the left-hand of the three doors – with a bold outline in the diagram above. I will now pretend to be Monty and I will 'open' one of the other doors that has a goat behind it – I have put a cross through the door that I have opened. (I should add that Monty knows which door has the car behind it and he is not going to help you find the car by opening that door. Therefore he will always open a door to reveal one of the goats.) The door that you have chosen (the left-hand door) is still shut. Monty now offers you the chance to swap your selected door for the other unopened door – remembering that you are trying to find the car. You can now see that in 2 of the 3 scenarios switching to the other unopened door changes your prize from a goat to the car. In only one scenario do you switch from car to a goat. Not so hard. But, surprisingly, even when subjects had been shown the problem and given repeated trials there was only limited learning – many of the subjects were still getting it wrong. What is going on here? Why are we getting confused by such a simple problem?

Follow your instinct or follow the rules?

The Monty Hall problem is just one of many situations that show up a conflict between what people instinctively 'feel' is the right answer and the answer that can be obtained by following simple logical rules. In the Monty Hall problem a conflict arises, for most people, between the instinct that changing your choice *can't* make a difference and the simple logic that shows that changing does make a difference. Some people, even after they understand the reasoning, will struggle to accept that their initial instinct was wrong. I presented this problem in a morning session to

They just knew *they were right and I was wrong*

the senior management team of an international company and explained the logic behind the strategy of changing doors. At lunch two of the directors, both with business degrees, insisted on proving to me why I was wrong and that changing doors did not alter the probability. No amount of logical analysis could persuade two very intelligent people that their first instinct was wrong. They just *knew* they were right and I was wrong.

These conundrums have led philosophers and psychologists at various times, indeed back to Aristotle, to speculate that in fact we have two ways of reasoning. We can be guided by the associations we have built up through experience, sometimes called associative or intuitive reasoning, or we can reason by using formal rules and logic. Intuitive thinking is based on memories of our personal experiences. We learn to associate aspects of past experiences with particular outcomes – good or bad. This intuitive system of reasoning (sometimes called associative reasoning) is spontaneous and lies behind intuition, creativity and imagination; it is the hidden hand that guides our judgements and prejudices. By contrast, rule-based systems of reasoning operate with symbols, language and formal logical systems. This is the deliberate reasoning we employ when we have to provide explanations and formal analysis. The differences between intuitive reasoning and rules-based reasoning can be summarized as follows:

Intuitive reasoning is:

> Fast – it allows immediate action.

> Emotional – it is based on our emotional preferences.

> Based on experience – it captures the sum of past experiences.

> Self-evident – you are not aware of the process of deciding.

> Context specific – intuitions from one sphere may not translate to another.

Rational reasoning is:

> Slow – it takes time for analysis.

> Logical – it uses symbols and logical deductions.

> A conscious process – we are aware of the process.

> Not context specific – can be applied in any situation.

The evidence suggests that we use both systems of reasoning. If you set someone a problem, both systems of reasoning may have a go at arriving at a solution. If they come up with different answers you can get the confusion that some people experience with the Monty Hall problem – the immediate instinct that it doesn't matter if you change doors is in conflict with the logical analysis. But our confidence in our intuitive reasoning is strong. Even after the Monty Hall problem has been explained rationally some people are still convinced their intuitive answer is correct.

There aren't clear divisions between the two systems of reasoning but Steven Sloman (2002) puts forward an interesting suggestion that will sound familiar to those who are used to making decisions in organizations: 'The associative system is generally useful for achieving one's goals; the rule-based system is more adept at ensuring that one's conclusions are sanctioned.' In the corporate world this translates directly into, 'I *know* the strategy we must follow, but I will need to spend the next three months using rational arguments to get the authority to implement it.' (Which recalls one of the characteristics of business decision making that I identified in Chapter 1: when we make decisions with someone else's money we have to justify our decisions. By justification of course we mean a rationally based, logical argument, presumably with more than a passing resemblance to the idealized, rational decision-making model of Chapter 3.) Sloman also gives a neat rule of thumb to help you determine whether you have used intuitive or rule-based reasoning to get to an answer: 'When a response is produced solely by the associative system we are conscious only of the result of the computation, not the process.' These decisions go by a number of well-known names: a hunch, a gut instinct, an intuition. Something we feel is right but can't explain why.

Justification and public companies

Because we are usually making decisions with other people's money we have to spend a lot of time justifying our decisions with rational and logical reasoning. Our intuition may be very well grounded and based on years of experience in an industry. But however certain we may be we will have to create a logical argument to support our instinct. Public companies can have particular difficulties in making major long-term strategic changes. The constant need to justify the decision, especially in the face of what may be an initial deterioration in financial performance, can sometimes inhibit public companies from making important long-term investments. This following example touched on my own experience in the online community sites for pregnant women and new parents.

EMAP MISSING OUT ONLINE

EMAP are one of the UK's leading media companies and own many of the most successful consumer magazines including the market leading monthly pregnancy magazine, *Mother & Baby*. In March 2000, just one week after NASDAQ reached its all time high, EMAP announced that it would be investing £250 million over the next three years in developing its traditional print titles online. Shareholders liked the news and the share price rose on the announcement. Just eight months later, in November 2000, as the bubble was rapidly deflating, EMAP announced that it would be reducing its internet investment to just £120 million over three years and focusing on a handful of core brands. Shareholders took this promise of reduced investment as good news, and once again the shares, now sharply down from their spring highs, respond positively. Two years later, and the actual investment in internet developments was down to just £11 million a year (journalism.co.uk, 28 November 2002).

The combination of EMAP's deep pockets, a market leading brand and advertiser relationships meant that an investment in an online version of *Mother & Baby* would have been a serious problem for the still fledgling *babyworld.co.uk*. But the investment was cancelled in the cut-backs in autumn 2000. In 2006 EMAP did get round to relaunching the *Mother & Baby* website, but by then *babyworld.co.uk* and other straight to web services (either privately, or private equity, funded) had come to dominate the traffic and online advertising budgets. In fact none of the leading pregnancy and parenting magazines had established dominant positions online.

A significant factor behind EMAP missing out on this and many other online opportunities is due to its status as a public company. The board has to report to the shareholders, at least twice a year, as to how it is using the shareholders' money. In March 2000, with the internet bubble at its peak, the justification for investing in the internet was easy – market leading brands plus a quarter of a billion pounds will create significant online brands that, the evidence suggested, could be worth billions. Later the same year, with internet asset values crashing and internet advertising still dwarfed by other media, the logical justification didn't look so plausible. Cutting the promised investment was the most easily justified action – the shareholders certainly thought so and bought the stock on the back of the announcement. Like other people the management team at

> EMAP was fully aware of the internet's promise and the threat it posed to EMAP's traditional business model. But against a background of crashing asset values the long-term investment strategy could not be justified. The management team's instincts were right.

Using the NASDAQ index as a barometer of technology and internet asset values the past dozen years show a remarkable story. If you simply ignore the boom and bust from late 1998 to 2003 there is a five-fold increase in value over 12 years (from around 500 in 1994 to around 2,500 in early 2007 – a compound annual growth rate of about 15%). But now with internet advertising revenues overtaking many traditional media many of the new web-only brands are now established. The barriers to entry which were, for a few years, very low, have been raised. As with many other established media companies, having failed to migrate its own brands online, EMAP has had to pay some very high prices to acquire the newcomers. In October 2005, EMAP paid £140 million for the trade fashion site WGSN – more than 20 times the prospective profit.

Private equity and long-term planning

Many of the companies that did establish valuable brands online during the past decade had private equity backing. Surely the manager of a private equity backed venture has just as much difficulty persuading her shareholders to keep investing as her competitor in the plc media conglomerate? The answer is no. In fact it's all to do with the nature of the cash commitment. A private equity company investment is a long-term bet on a management team and an industry. The investors are, in my experience, primarily lawyers (in the US) or accountants (in the UK), and experts in deal structures and financial engineering. They typically have very little hands-on management experience. They will back a management team with a business plan for, typically, three to five years. The business plan seldom, if ever, unfolds as expected. A year in and progress is usually behind forecast. But the options available to the private equity investor are few. They have neither the time nor the experience to run the company themselves. Most of the investment in the company will be in the form of long-term loans or equity. Their only lever is usually a change of management. They may not be happy with the way things are unfolding but have little option but to wait and hope it will all turn out OK. Contrast this with the management structures in a public company. The new investment is being overseen by managers who, nearly always, have been successful operational managers in their own right. The investment budget is agreed annually. Performance is reported monthly and then passed on to head office for scrutiny. External justification for the continuing investment is continually required, either to senior management or, for the largest investments, directly to shareholders. Unlike the private equity backed venture, expenditure approvals can be rescinded at a moment's notice. Continued investment in this underperforming initiative can no longer be justified and after a difficult first year the project is abandoned. Because almost no projects go exactly to plan, at some stage most investments will be underperforming against the plan. The private equity backed initiative will have no choice but to carry on. The public company will abandon the investment. The final outcome? The plc buys the private equity backed business four years later at a very substantial premium and tells its shareholders what a great investment they have made in the future.

This, I believe, is one of the reasons that the entrepreneur can often exploit new markets more effectively than large corporations. For the self-financed entrepreneur, or for the proprietor who has secured long-term finance, intuition, whether well founded or not, can be their guide. Their intuitive reasoning doesn't need to be justified to anybody else. This gives two significant advantages. Speed of action and commitment to the long term. Less time is wasted on justifying decisions to get approval and the commitment will not be reversed if performance dips below plan. Two differences that help us understand why so many of the successful internet brands created in the past decade were established by entrepreneurs with private equity funding rather than spin offs from established franchises owned by public corporations.

The entrepreneur can often exploit new markets more effectively than large corporations

The source of our intuitions

In order to assess how we should treat intuitive reasoning it would help to understand how these associations arise. The neurologist Antonio Damasio has been able to demonstrate that our basic emotional responses play a central role in our associative learning. He believes that our powers of reasoning evolved from the automatic emotional responses in more primitive animals. As a consequence our emotional responses are deeply entwined in our decision-making processes. Damasio speculates that emotional tags, he calls them somatic markers, get associated with aspects of our experiences; effectively stamping aspects of our experiences with emotional associations. These can be either positive or negative. Faced with a decision, we search our memories for related experiences but we use the emotional tags as a short cut. We prioritize memories with particularly strong emotional associations. The use of these markers can be overt and give rise to conscious 'hunches' or can be hidden from consciousness and guide our actions without us ever being aware of the process.

Damasio's experiments and reflections on the way in which humans use emotions to tag experiences are described in his remarkable book, *Descartes' Error* (1994). One experiment he describes is particularly relevant to the risks faced by poker players and business managers. He sits the volunteer (the player) in front of four decks of cards. The player is given a loan of $2,000 (play money) with the aim of winning as much money as possible. The player can select the top card from any of the four decks and turn it over to reveal a monetary gain or loss. Two of the decks have modest gains, and occasional modest losses, but overall will lead to a steady gain. Two of the decks have bigger gains but occasional catastrophic losses. He ran these experiments both with normal members of the public and with his neurological patients that had suffered very specific brain damage that rendered them effectively without emotion. Their intelligence and capacity for logical reasoning were normal – but, like Star Trek's Mr Spock, they were unable to experience emotion.

Damasio reports that normal, undamaged patients typically played in the same way. They would cautiously test each of the decks. Initially they are drawn to the decks with the higher gains. But soon, after the first 30 or so selections, they learn to focus on the safer packs without the big losses. In contrast, brain damaged patients kept being drawn to the high-risk decks, even though they would regularly be wiped out and require further loans. Damasio's conclusion was that the brain damaged subjects were unable to lay down the emotional tags that associated two of the decks with large losses. Without this maker, and faced again and again with a decision about which deck to select, they were unable to benefit from the unpleasant emotional response resulting from previous bad outcomes. They suffered, as he puts it, 'a myopia for the future'. They were not able to learn from experience. The undamaged players were able to associate some of the decks with bad outcomes and quickly learnt to steer clear.

It appears that our basic emotional responses are essential to our learning and to our decision making. A version of this same experiment, recounted by Gladwell in his book *Blink* (2005), is even more striking. This time the experiment used undamaged gamblers but they were wired to a device that measured the activity of sweat glands on their palms. The sweat glands were more active (signifying anxiety) before they chose a card from one of the high-risk decks after selecting ten or so cards. However, it typically took 40–50 cards before they were conscious of the fact that some decks were bad news. Their subconscious brain was aware of the association long before they realized what was going on – making associations and influencing behaviour long before they were consciously aware.

Many writers portray the human brain as having several distinct functions that originate in different parts of our evolutionary past: a primitive brain that controls heart beat, breathing and other basic physiology that we share with all animals; a limbic brain of emotions that we share with mammals; and the cognitive brain that provides reason and self-reflection in primates. Perhaps influenced by Freud's conflicts between id, ego and super-ego, it is common to see human decision making as a battle between our ancient animal instincts and our human reason. We see emotions as things that are to be kept out of decision making. The ideal of pure reason, untainted by our primitive animal instincts, is seen as the pinnacle of thinking. One of Damasio's key insights is that these different systems are not in conflict. The human brain only works well when the emotional and the cognitive brains are working together. Our emotional responses play a vital role in our reasoning. It would seem that, contrary to the impression given by the scriptwriters, Spock would have been a very poor decision maker.

But I should emphasise that by using the word emotion I don't mean emotional. Damasio is using emotion to mean a feeling towards an outcome – either good or bad. Being *emotional* about a decision is a very different matter all together. Poker players, who rely very heavily on intuitive learning (as we shall see later), warn very strongly about making decisions in an emotional state. In the evocative vocabulary of poker it is called 'going on tilt'. The 'tilt' refers to the fact that your sense of balance for making sound judgements has gone. Our good judgement becomes overpowered by anger or revenge. As the poker pros would say, never make decisions when you are on tilt.

As the poker pros would say, never make decisions when you are on tilt

Just as Pavlov's dogs learnt to associate the ringing of the bell with being fed, so we learn to associate good and bad emotions with our experiences. We give the highest priority to experiences that are tagged with the strongest emotional response. Which is why, of course, the lesson of not touching the hot stove is not learnt until the child has touched it (with a strong emotional response). Telling a child not to touch the stove doesn't have sufficient emotional power to change future behaviour. There really are some lessons that we have to learn through experience and not from textbooks. There are two other important implications of Damasio's theory that we will return to later in the book. Firstly, the quality of your decision making is going to be dependent on the quality of your experiences. If your experiences are limited, if you have only experienced good outcomes and not bad, your learning will be limited. Limited learning makes for a poor decision maker. Secondly, as we start to learn that one event is associated with another, it is all too easy for us to believe that there is a causal link – that one gives rise to the other. We quickly notice that wearing the lucky suit to work is associated with the strong emotional reward of winning a large order. Before we know it we are acting as if wearing the suit causes the order to be won. A simple conjunction all too quickly becomes a causal relationship in our minds. The gambler observing he wins more often in one particular chair will come to believe that sitting in that chair is responsible for his good fortune. Even the most self-aware amongst us can be prone to this deceit. Options trader and thought-provoking author of *Fooled by Randomness* (2004), N. N. Taleb, recounts his own surprise the morning after a particularly good day's trading to be wearing the same stained tie and asking the taxi driver to drop him off at exactly the same intersection as the previous day. It doesn't take long for us to leap from spotting A followed by B to assuming A causes B – especially when A is something we have initiated. We are easily fooled into thinking we are in control.

Intuitive learning is what we distil from experience. Because it captures our most basic emotional response to events it has immense power. Enough power to overturn even the simplest and most straightforward of rational arguments. Intuitive reasoning is the power behind most of our everyday judgements. Understanding its power and its biases is essential to becoming a better decision maker and is something that we will focus on in later chapters.

In other words...

We have two ways of reasoning: intuitive (associative) and rule based. If both systems work together on the same problem and lead to different answers then we experience a tension between what we feel is right and what our logical reason tells us is right. When you are making decisions with someone else's money (which for business managers is most of the time) rule-based reasoning is usually required to justify the decision – even if your decision was based on experience and intuition. Public companies are prone to constant justification of large investment decisions to shareholders – one sequence of below-plan results and the project is abandoned. The long-term nature of private equity finance can enable quicker decision making and will see a risky venture through downturns.

The primitive emotional pathways that we share with other mammals are an essential component of our intuitive reasoning. Take the emotion out of the experience and we can't decide. Our intuitive reasoning is powerful but is based on our own experiences. The quality of your intuition is going to be directly related to the quality of your experience.

Which means that...

> Look out for conflicts between head and heart – reflect on where the conflict has come from.

> Don't try to banish emotion from decision making. Your gut feeling for or against something is there for a reason.

> Understand that sometimes you have to justify well-grounded intuitive decisions with rational arguments to the owners (or their representatives). Try to establish reasonable levels of authority for yourself (or your staff) so that you don't have to spend all of your time justifying your actions.

> Book learning and anecdotal history (case studies) can be valuable but are no substitute for personal experience – the stronger the emotion, the stronger the association, the more powerful the lesson learnt.

Rules of thumb

Q ♦ Good management is the art of good judgement – judgement based on experience

Q ♠ Don't waste time asking people for rational justification of well-grounded intuitions

Chapter **5**

....

Calling off the search

In Chapter 4 we looked at the way our brains use emotion to give significance to our experiences – making the most of our past learning to help us make choices about the future. We saw in Chapter 3 that searching can be an endless quest for alternatives and information. In this chapter I look at the way we use our intuitive judgement to stop the endless quest for information and start deciding: picking options that we like, that we recognize, or that are 'good enough'. These may seem dangerously crude decision-making strategies but in fact they can be very effective when our judgement is tuned to the environment. The problem will arise, as we will investigate later, when we try to apply the lessons learnt in one environment in a different context.

Deciding when to stop

In Chapter 4 I introduced Damasio's work with patients who had suffered very specific neural damage that left them mentally capable with the exception that they were effectively without emotion. This had rendered them unable to prioritize experience by its emotional significance and had severely limited their ability to function in the social sphere. In one poignant but amusing anecdote he recounts asking a patient to choose one of two alternative dates for a next appointment. 'For the better part of half an hour, the patient enumerated reasons for and against each of the two dates: previous engagements, proximity to other engagements, possible meteorological conditions, virtually anything that one could reasonably think about concerning a simple date. ...he was now walking us through a tiresome cost–benefit analysis, an endless outlining and fruitless comparison of options and possible consequences' (1994). Eventually Damasio could stand it no more and intervenes to stop an endless loop of speculation. Reflecting on this episode, Damasio identifies the vital role that our emotionally charged experiences play in our ability to decide: 'This behaviour is a good example of the limits of pure reason. It is also a good example of the calamitous consequences of not having an automated mechanism of decision making.'

Deciding can be seen as a search. As we saw in Chapter 3 it can sometimes be a search for goals. It is often a search for alternatives. It can also involve at times a search for evidence and a search for consequences that allow us to pick between alternatives. As we have already seen, there is no objective way of concluding the search. Just like Damasio's patient trying to evaluate two alternative dates, in theory there is no end to the searching. Looking for the perfect, optimal decision we would need to search forever. In the real world where time (i.e. money) and information are limited, decision making will always be imprecise. At some point a judgement has to be made, a personal subjective judgement to stop searching and start deciding. Sometimes the search has stopped before we are even aware that it has begun. Subconscious intuitive reasoning has the effect of stopping the search before it has even begun. At other times the decision to stop searching is a convoluted negotiation between several parties. Part of the art of decision making is knowing when to stop searching – or when to restart the search.

Stop – I like it

The stamping of past experiences with emotional tags – 'I like it' or 'I don't like it' – as we have just seen, can create a way of stopping the search. The volunteers without brain damage selecting cards from the decks in Damasio's experiment were using the memory of previous bad experiences to stop them picking cards from the deck which included big losses. In fact the decision to avoid those decks was being made subconsciously, even before the brain was conscious of the association. In this case a previous bad experience forcing the decision by avoiding the dangerous packs. Strong positive associations can have a powerful subconscious effect. If a management team presenting to a private equity firm happens to remind the investment director, even in an entirely incidental and subconscious way, of a previous team that had been very successful, then she may have a gut instinct that this is the team to back. But, of course a bad association with a previous failure can lead to an early rejection.

If you can find a similar experience in your memory that has a strong positive emotional association then the search will stop. If that association is strong enough then our conscious brains may never be aware that there were alternatives – the searching is over before we are even aware that it has begun. 'I like it' becomes one of the most powerful stopping rules. If the emotional association is powerful enough then no amount of deliberate rule-based thinking can overturn our instinct. This can be used to explain why, given that we are fundamentally risk averse (an idea we will explore in Chapter 13), we rush to buy lottery tickets especially when there are roll-over jackpots. People don't enter lotteries because they represent a rational gamble. The UK's National Lottery pays out only 50% of ticket sales as prize money. The expected value of a £1 ticket is therefore 50p – not a compelling gamble. What lottery operators the world over have found is that you need a big jackpot to get people to buy tickets – in fact the bigger the jackpot the more tickets you sell. In the UK 52% of the prize fund goes to the jackpot. Of course the odds of winning the jackpot are negligible – the lottery organiser Camelot puts the odds at about 1 chance in 14 million. But even the idea of a jackpot win has an enormously powerful emotional impact. Our

> *'I like it' becomes one of the most powerful stopping rules*

rational, rule-based selves might wish that the lottery had 100 prizes of £50,000 each, instead of one £5 million jackpot. The lottery organizers know that many of us only buy tickets when the prize has the emotional power to change lives. If the emotional impact is big enough we become insensitive to the probability of winning.

Manipulating our emotional associations with products has been one of the dark arts of marketing for as long as we have been trading with each other. Product packaging is covered in 'affective tags' – labels and images that try to create positive emotional associations with the product. New, Natural, Improved, 98% Fat Free all sound like good things and are likely to create a positive feeling with the consumer – a feeling strong enough to stop the search for an alternative product. Similarly we show a preference for a small container which is overfilled (with ice cream or popcorn, for example) over the same portion that appears to underfill a larger container. The sense that something is generously overfilled creates a positive association, the partially empty container a negative association of meanness.

Stop – I recognise it

Another frequently used method we use to stop searching and start deciding is simple recognition. If we are not sure which option to chose, we often select the one we recognize and ignore the one we don't. This sounds almost too glib to be credible, but we use recognition every day. I go to the supermarket to buy washing powder. I could undertake an exhaustive process of evaluating my goals: environmental impact, stain to be removed, washing temperature, fabric type and cost. From the back of the packets I could collect technical information and performance data. Perhaps I could balance these various criteria and make the perfect selection. Or, as I often do, I choose the first one I recognize. OK for something trivial like a detergent choice. But surely not relevant for important business decisions.

Imagine the situation where you are to appoint a new member of the team. You are down to two candidates with similar skills and experiences. Both would fit in. One of the candidates has previously been employed by a well-known public company, the other by a private firm you haven't heard of before. Most people will go for the candidate with the employment history they recognize. Recognition of one cue becomes the feature that allows us to discriminate – the reason to stop searching.

That we use simple recognition as a decision cue is the essence of brand marketing. A very striking example of this was the Benetton advertising campaign in the eighties. The adverts gave no information about the products or the company but were designed merely to be provocative and therefore memorable. Brand recognition rose quickly and Benetton was listed as one of the top five brands in the world. Brand recognition is one of the primary objectives of any marketing campaign. The logic seems inescapable – if we recognise a name then we assume that a number of other positive attributes about that organization hold true. To know is to favour.

Fast food and other branded outlets exploit the same decision-making technique. There may be two or more pizza restaurants in a town we have never visited before. There are potentially many different factors that we could take into consideration before making a selection. Perhaps we choose the one that seems to be the busiest – like the female guppy using other people's choices to guide our selection. We may, depending on how much experience we have of pizza restaurants, be able to detect subtle cues in the way the options are described, the use of authentic Italian ingredients for example. (This is an example of the way experts make decisions. Experts don't use different techniques to make decisions but they have developed a more sophisticated set of categories that can be used to decide between choices – they can see differences that appear invisible to the inexperienced pizza eater.) But the proliferation of branded chains for restaurants, coffee shops, sandwich outlets and many other outlets is testament to the fact that collectively we use simple recognition to guide our choices. Disturbingly, however, studies have also shown that we often can't recall whether we recognize a name for good or bad reasons – we just know we know them. This seems to confirm our instinct that there is no such thing as bad publicity. Being famous or infamous can both bring benefits.

Fast and effective

So far I have highlighted two simple techniques that we use to make decisions – simple emotional associations and recognition. These two triggers for deciding seem to be as far away as you can get from the ideal theoretical model that requires us to collect and then weigh the significance of each piece of data. Because of this you might assume that they are hopelessly flawed and ineffective, dangerous psychological tricks that lead to poor judgement and need to be replaced with more rational methods. But this isn't the case. Many studies have shown that fast and lean decision making (decision making that relies on assessing only one factor) can be very effective and in many environments is just as effective as attempts to systematically weigh up every factor. The reason these simple lean techniques work is because we have adapted our decision making rules to reflect the environment.

A short example may help to make this important point clear.

Imagine two worlds, each inhabited by simple creatures. In the first world the creatures' favourite food is distributed randomly and is clearly visible. The creatures in the second world don't have it quite so easy. The food is hidden from view and has to be found. Fortunately the food tends to be found close to where a particular tree grows. In the first world no clever foraging strategy is needed. Head off in any direction and you will find some food. In the second world there is an advantage in having learnt that the food is clustered near the special tree. The presence of the tree acts a cue for the presence of food. The simple strategy that says 'stop searching when you find the tree' works because the environment is structured in that way. The creatures have simply learnt a rule through experience because it works. This 'stopping rule' for finding food will almost certainly not be a conscious process. It will be an instinct – learning to associate stopping near the tree with the reward of finding food. Either creature will go hungry if transported to the other world, some creatures unaware of the significance of the tree, the others fruitlessly searching near the trees they associate with food. Learning is dependent on the environment.

Let's return to the earlier example where you had to make a choice between two candidates for a position. Both had similar skills and experiences although one candidate had previously worked for a blue chip public company, the other for a large private company that you had not heard of before. You need a reason for choosing one candidate over the other. You need a rule to tell you to stop searching for evidence and decide. By choosing the candidate with the experience from the company you recognize you are making an assumption that there is some correlation between the fact that you recognize the company and some other aspects that may help you discriminate. You are assuming, albeit subconsciously,

you use name recognition as a proxy for other cues that you don't know about

that in the environment that you inhabit, candidates from well-known firms are better than candidates from unknown firms. This decision-making strategy will be effective if that is true. Might it be true? Perhaps. The better-known company may have more rigorous recruitment procedures, or the pick of the best candidates, or better training and development programmes. In fact you don't know anything about these factors for the companies in question so you use name recognition as a proxy for other cues that you don't know about. This will be successful in discriminating between the candidates if the rule you use to make the decision fits the environment – if the larger and better known companies really do have those advantages. The stopping rule for decision making depends on the context and is learnt through experience.

The detergent I select from the supermarket shelf based on name recognition may be effective if name recognition is associated with market share. Market share may be helpful to me because other people who are more discriminating about detergent choices have chosen this brand. Or perhaps high market share indicates a more profitable company with more research that has created a better product. Or, less helpfully, market share may be merely a by-product of advertising spend. But by focusing on one factor I am able to make very quick, very lean decisions. The factor I chose isn't arbitrary, it is shaped by experience. In the world I know well it will serve me well.

Recognition is obviously not a perfect method of decision making. But it has the great advantage of requiring the minimum amount of information (it's lean or frugal) and consequently it can be fast. Using simple recognition to stop the search has a curious side effect that you may recognize when you ask experts to decide. If you recognise all of the choices then you can't use it to discriminate. Recognition as a stop rule requires some level of ignorance. This may, in part, explain the familiar stereotypes of the self-belief of the new business manager who knows very little and the indecision of the old hand. Knowing too much can get in the way of a decision.

Stop searching, 'Its good enough'

In Chapter 3, with tongue only lightly in cheek, I described the 37% rule for mate selection. Choose the first candidate that is better than any of the first 37% of the potential candidates already seen. Curiously, this gives you a 37% chance of ending up with the best mate. However you will have had to assess, on average, 74% of the candidates – not the fastest or most frugal of decision rules. What if we wanted to speed up the decision-making process? Let's assume that instead of trying to find the *best* partner we lower our sights and required only a partner in the top 10%. 'Good enough' rather than a chance of 'the best'. In this case you only need to test 14% of the sample to get an 83% chance of a top 10% per-former. The person content with a top quartile (25%) selection can get away with assessing just 7% of the sample and still have a 92% chance of meeting their goal.

This mechanism is at work whenever we have to select between alternatives which come along separately rather than all at once. This could be investment opportunities, poker hands or potential mates; you assess each one as it arises and need to make a decision to accept or wait for another opportunity. Gary Klein describes, in *The Power of Intuition* (2003), his research into the way fire-fighters and soldiers make decisions in the field when they are under stress. Expecting to find a version of the rational decision-making model being played out, he found, to his initial surprise, that they weren't consciously selecting between alternatives. His fire-fighters and soldiers came up with a single course of action and carried it out. They didn't search for alternatives; they didn't evaluate alternatives against conscious criteria. Almost without thinking they would select a course of action and carry it out. Through experience, enhanced with specific training, they had internalized patterns and sequences. They could, subconsciously, read the cues from a new situation and 'know' the best course of action. It didn't need to be the best option – it just needed to be good enough. He found that highly trained professionals that have to make critical decisions were relying on intuitive reasoning. Reasoning that had been built up through experience and reinforced with training. Klein outlines the importance of mental models – pictures built up through experience of how the world works. Fire-fighters have established through experience the way a fire will develop in certain situations. Through experience and training they learn to recognize the cues and switch immediately into acting.

But this also applies to managers. Daniel Isenberg has studied what business managers actually do to make decisions. Just like Klein's fire-fighters, he found they didn't use analytical decision-making procedures, but they did use intuition to solve problems. He identified (1984) five different ways in which managers used intuition:

1. To sense when a problem existed – 'Smell trouble'.
2. To implement well-learned procedures rapidly – 'Just get on with it'.
3. To bring together different bits of data to identify creatively patterns of significance – 'Creativity'.
4. To be a gut feel check on logical analysis – 'That's not right'.
5. To bypass rational analysis and move directly to a plausible solution – 'This will do it'.

Intuition isn't some extra-sensory new-age idea that mystically allows us to sense the solution. Intuition is simply the way in which our experience and memories are shaped to give us quick and effective guidelines on how to act in the future. It works because we adapt our decision making to reflect the particular environment we are in. It is a practical and well grounded set of experiences that allows us to make decisions when the rational model of the theorists would still have us searching and evaluating. For decades managers have been criticized as poor decision makers for their failure to meet the rational ideals of optimization (the idea that still underlies most of today's economic theory). In fact managers have been using smart, lean and effective methods to make decisions that work because they are adapted to the environment in which they have to manage (and decide).

But some new questions arise, which we will explore in the rest of the book. There is a cost to making fast, lean, intuitive decisions using the minimum of information. In certain situation intuitive judgements can lead us to make some well-documented errors – biases in our judgement which, with awareness, we can try to overcome. Secondly, and more importantly, our intuition develops within a specific environment. What is going to guide us if the environment changes or, as we need to do from time to time, we must make decisions away from the place where we acquired our experience? In Chapter 8, I will look specifically at the dangers that arise when we have to make decisions in familiar situations, 'close to home'. In Chapter 9, I look at the ways in which we make decisions when we find ourselves in unfamiliar environments, 'far from home'. But before then I want to take a deeper look at the logic of investing and the wisdom of poker.

In other words...

Deciding is a search, for alternatives, information and goals – the art of deciding is the art of judging when to stop the search. Intuition helps us stop the search – telling us to stop searching when we 'like' one of the alternatives or even when we just 'recognize' it. These fast decision-making strategies work because they have evolved to fit the environment. Change the environment and the rules don't work any more. Textbooks still want us to undergo a rational analysis of all the options but intuitive reasoning is essential to good decision making. Instead of an endless search for 'the best', we need to accept 'good enough'.

Which means that...

> Try to be aware of situations when your intuitions are closing down the search for alternatives.

> Learn to look out for positive associations and recognition strategies in marketing messages.

> Remember that accepting good enough can be a better strategy than searching for the best.

> Don't be scared of well-grounded intuition – it is an essential part of good decision making

Rules of thumb

4 ◆ Trust intuition based on well-grounded experience

J ◆ Good enough is sometimes the best decision

2 ◆ You can't make the perfect decision

Chapter **6**

Investing, risk and poker

Despite the best efforts of 'management science', luck is always going to be a part of decision making. There is no process that closes the door on uncertainty. This chapter looks more closely at the parallels between investing (allocating resources) in business and poker. Unlike managers who have been beguiled by management science's promise of certainty, poker players are experts at making investment decisions under uncertainty. Whilst both business and poker can make use of a rational economic calculation to evaluate investments (bets), it is the power of intuition based on first-hand experience that is the mark of great poker players. The wisdom of poker has much to teach the business manager

'All we have is the name'

It is early in 1998. The past three years have seen the number of commercial websites in the US rise from 2,000 to 400,000. Around the world entrepreneurs are assessing opportunities, trying to identify the part of cyberspace that they can make their own. As Ernst Malmsten (2001) recalls in his memoir, 'Build it and they will come... summed up the American attitude to the internet in 1998.' Malmsten's analysis began to focus on fashion retailing – an area where, he observed, young people spent far more money than on books or CDs. It is also a sector of strong brands with global reach and limited discounting providing good margins for retailers. The vision was huge – to develop a global, online fashion retailer from scratch. This audacious start-up plan had none of the normal competitive advantages that might attract investors. The management team were young and with no experience of the industry. Everything would have to be built from the ground up: the website and its innovative 3D product imaging, the fulfilment infrastructure and, most importantly, the brand. From a European perspective these were still early days for the internet. In Spain and Italy household internet access was below 2%. In Germany 20 hours of 56k dial-up access would cost you $75. But Malmsten and his team could see an enormous opportunity. The biggest risk was in not moving quickly enough and letting someone else establish a dominant position in the multi-billion dollar fashion industry. As Malmsten makes clear, 'The whole point was to bury the competition by cornering the market right from the start.' JP Morgan, the advisor with the challenge of raising the necessary investment, understood the nature of the risk. Malmsten recalls Samer Salty, one of JP Morgan's senior bankers seeing it as '...an all or nothing concept. If it works it'll be big.' But Malmsten tellingly recalls the raised eyebrows when they had to admit that the limited company needed to contract with JP Morgan to raise the $100 million which didn't yet exist, 'all we have is the name.'

The logic of poker

Poker players have been assessing whether the cost of meeting a bet is justified since the game was invented. Poker is a blend of skill and chance. In the short run, chance can make fools of us all, but in the long run skill will win out, the best player will prevail. Poker in many ways is the perfect metaphor for business decision making. Don't worry if you have never played poker or loathe card games – this chapter requires no knowledge of the game other than the basic principle of poker betting which I will briefly describe.

Before the cards are dealt one, two or sometimes all the players (depending on which variation is being played) must place a, usually small, bet in the pot. These bets are called the blinds or the ante – and are in effect a price that has to be paid for being part of the game before any cards are dealt. Now the cards are dealt, the players look at their cards and start to assess their prospects. A player to the left of the dealer will have the first decision. If she thinks her hand is weak she may fold (give her cards back to the dealer and pull out of that hand – losing any money she may have had to put in before the deal). But let's assume that the first player to bet likes the cards and pushes $10 into the pot. The other players to her left then have three options:

1. They can fold (chuck away their cards) put no more money in the pot and lose any money they have already bet.

2. Meet the bet (in poker called a 'call') by placing $10 into the pot. By calling they are still in the hand and have a chance of winning the pot.

3. Or they can 'raise' (literally 'raising the stakes') by meeting the initial $10 bet and then put in an additional, say, $10. Now the bet has been raised all players will either have to call the $20 bet, fold, or reraise again.

When everyone has either folded or called the last bet, cards are exchanged or revealed and a new round of betting continues. Depending on the variation of poker being played there may be between two and five rounds of betting. The last player left, when everyone else has folded will win all of the bets placed (the pot) or if there are two or more players who have called each other's bets in the final round, then the player with the best hand will win the pot (this is the showdown when players reveal their cards). The precise procedure for play, the relative importance of hands (full houses and four of a kind, etc.) and the subtleties of bluffing are of no importance here. All that matters is that each player is constantly presented with a decision, maybe up to 20 times in a single hand of poker. That decision always has the same three possibilities: should I fold (quit)?; should I call and keep playing?; should I raise the stakes? It couldn't be simpler.

should I fold (quit)?; should I call and keep playing?; should I raise the stakes?

For today's top players there are millions of dollars to be won on a never-ending circuit of international tournaments. There are thousands of professional or semi-professional players who make a decent living from the game. But of course the best players don't get dealt better cards than anybody else. The best players are dealt those frustrating low pairs and unconnected cards just as frequently as the rest of us. They will fail to complete four card flushes and straights as often as the laws of probability dictate. How, then, do the best players keep winning world championships and winning multi-million dollar tournaments?

The best poker players do two things better than the rest of us:

1. They lose less money on weak hands – they don't get tempted to fritter away small stakes on poor hands with only a small chance of success.

2. They make more money when they have good hands – they will risk more to have a chance of winning more when they have a strong hand.

Yes bluffing, psychology and being unpredictable are important – but these are just weapons in the good players' armoury to ensure that they can maximize their take from the good hands or to extract advantage when there are no players with a winning hand. But of course, this is also true of business.

The logic of business

The parallel with business decision making couldn't be more straightforward. Business decisions are decisions about the deployment of resources – people, time or money. The business manager is constantly evaluating whether the right resources are being deployed to achieve a desired outcome. As a business manager you always have the same three basic options as the poker player:

1. Quit – either decline an investment opportunity or stop an existing investment.

2. Keep playing – continue investing.

3. Raise the stakes – start a new investment or increase the rate of investment on an ongoing project.

The best entrepreneurs don't waste time and money on the smaller prospects, but they do make the most of the best prospects and do everything they can to make them successful. This suggests that, just like the best poker players, we shouldn't waste time (or money) on the mediocre.

Put everything behind the product or market where you have the biggest advantage. They don't come along very often.

So the manager's task is reduced to selecting one of three options. Simple as that. It makes management, like poker, seem a very straightforward activity. What is all the fuss about? All the manager has to do is to decide which of the three options to select. Whether you realise it or not you are making investment decisions every day. Meeting the payroll costs for a department at the end of the month may not feel like an investment decision but every month the payroll is met you are making a decision about deploying resources. In effect you are making a call, continuing with an earlier bet. Lost in a forest of management literature, best practice and the latest fads it is refreshing to get back to basics – to see the brutal logic of management decision making laid bare. The underlying logic of poker is the underlying logic of business. Of course in the heat of the battle it never seems that simple. If you have spent 18 months working to take a new product to launch it is very hard to step back and acknowledge that quitting may now be the best option in the light of new information about changing customer needs or competitor activity. In just the same way it is hard for a poker player to acknowledge that the pair of aces they have supported through three or four rounds of betting and raising are now unlikely to win the pot. The promising hand has become a probable loser and a further small bet is not justified by the $500 already put into the pot.

The simple arithmetic of betting and investing

Like all decision makers, the poker player can use either intuitive or rule-based methods for making a decision about whether to bet. I will look in more detail at intuitive decision making later in the chapter. Firstly, I will introduce the very simple rule-based reasoning that poker players can use. The arithmetic is easy.

If I asked you to say whether you would pay $10 to have a 50% chance of a $50 win, you would probably accept the wager. The expected value of the prize is $25 (the value of the prize multiplied by the chance of getting it). The cost is $10. The expected value is much larger than cost – it seems like a good wager. (In fact the psychology of these simple wagers is not as straightforward it first seems. The Nobel Prize winning economist Paul Samuelson used to give his students a simple wager on a coin toss: win $200 for heads, lose $100 for tails. Most people decline the wager even though it has a positive expectation.) But leaving these considerations for later – the arithmetic is a simple triangle of cost, probability of success and prize.

The poker player is also able to use this same rule-based logic. But there is one big difference. At the moment you have to bet nothing is known for certain. You don't know how much it is going to cost you to continue to play the hand. You may be being asked for $10 to call an existing bet. But another player may reraise. You can't be sure what the cost of seeing another card may be – the cost of accepting the wager is uncertain. Worse, there are no fixed odds (except in the rare, but delightful situations, where it is possible to *know* with 100% certainty that you have the best possible hand – in the colourful language of poker you are said to hold 'the nuts'). But every other time you have to make a judgement. What is the probability that I will end up with the best hand? I will look at the cards I hold. I will assess whatever I may have observed about the way my opponents have played. I will use my knowledge of the relative frequencies of various poker hands. A judgement based on imperfect information. Lastly, but just as importantly, you do not know the value of the final pot (the prize for having the best hand).

Judgement is everything. As in poker, so in business

Another judgement is necessary. Not just how much is in the pot now, but how much might it be when the betting is complete. And of course this matters. Being asked to call a $100 bet with a chance to win $1,000 is a very different proposition from calling $100 if the prize is only $400. But the essence of poker, and what marks it out from other forms of gambling, most of which have fixed odds, known costs of entry or known prizes, is that you must make a judgement about all three variables: the cost of betting, the probability of success and the final prize. Nothing is certain. There is no method that can eliminate doubt or secure a certain gain. Judgement is everything. As in poker, so in business.

Investments never come with exactly quantifiable price tags. With a corporate acquisition the cost of acquiring 100% of the shares of a company will be precisely agreed. And yet the actual cost of making the investment is uncertain: unbudgeted losses in the first year will have to be funded; unanticipated capital costs may become essential; the impact on the acquiring business may have been underestimated. The probability of success is always, and obviously, a judgement call. Will we be able to integrate the acquired business successfully? Can we retain the key people and their know-how? Are the cash-flow forecasts for the acquired business realistic? Looking at the historic success rates from similar transactions may not help. Knowing that the majority of acquisitions do not create long-term shareholder value may be sobering but is this acquisition one of the unsuccessful majority or the value enhancing minority? And lastly, the likely long-term gain is uncertain to a very large degree. The net gain in value will depend on many unknown factors about the market: new entrants into the market, consumer price pressures, technology changes, input cost increases – all can change and all will affect the final return.

But the business manager, like the poker player, has to make a judgement. The judgement based on the same triangle of probabilities. What is more, it isn't a one-off, out of the blue, yes or no decision. The poker player is going to be asked to make the same probabilistic judgement every time he has to call a bet or make a raise. The first decision to play the initial cards may not be expensive. Other players bet or fold, more cards are revealed. Another round of betting requires further investment decisions with new information available about each of the three probability judgements: cost, chance of winning and gain. It may have been right to bet at the start, but right to stop investing now that new information has come to light. Business decisions have the same structure. Before launching a new product some initial market research reports will not be expensive but are an essential first step. The next steps of diverting R&D resource, or taking top-performing business development managers away from profitable markets is going to start to increase the cost, but may be justified by the initial research. The final launch decision may cost millions and divert resources from across the company. At each step the business manager is evaluating the cost of the additional investment, the probability of success and the likely gain. The earlier investments were the necessary costs of being in a position to make an informed decision about the final investment decision.

Remember that one of the ways top poker players make more money is by not losing money on weaker hands. The first round of betting in a game may be cheap – perhaps just $10 to see the next cards. But there are two dangers. Firstly, if you pay $10 for every hand, even those with a very small chance of winning, then you will soon fritter away your stack. Secondly, backing a mediocre hand into the later rounds of betting can get very expensive. It is always tempting to think 'well, I have come this far'. Remember, *Every bet should be made with the idea of winning the pot*. Similarly, every expenditure should be made with the aim of making a bigger return.

One final word about overheads. Poker has small bets that must be paid just to enter the hand – called either the 'antes' or the 'blinds' (a blind bet, before the cards are seen). In poker they are the cost of entering a hand and stop people folding hand after hand and only betting when they have great cards. If you are too cautious a player these blind bets take all of your chips in the end. I see overheads as the blind bets of business. There is a certain cost we have just to be in business. It doesn't matter if we never make any product or market investments, the overheads have to be paid month after month. The more money that gets tied up in these blind bets the less we have to direct towards investments that can make a return. Overheads are a necessary cost of being in business but it is in your power to make them as low as possible – save your cash for where it can earn a return. Some overheads are just old investments that never got cancelled: the regional office that opened five years ago with a promise to grow sales that is now just seen as overhead, the client support team that was justified on the basis that it would improve client retention, and dozens of other examples. Still valid investments (worth continuing to call or raise) or just part of the overhead?

Financial models, decision making and common sense

My review of the simple arithmetic of poker may give the impression that poker players are calculating machines, their minds whirring with possibilities and probabilities. In fact most of the time poker players rely on instinct – a 'feel' for the prospects which is built up through experience. The calculating has become instinctive and only occasionally will the experienced player resort to arithmetic to assess a complex situation. Good poker players do exactly the things that management theorists have criticized managers for doing. They focus on only a couple of main variations – they don't calculate every possibility, and they use broad ideas of likelihood rather than precise mathematical probability. The experienced player will have developed a good instinctive understanding of the relationship between risk and reward. But time and time again I meet business managers, some senior people who have been running companies for years, some MBA students, who seem to have no instinctive feel for the investment proposition they are considering – be it a new product launch, an acquisition or a start up. They can answer every question about the legal documentation, they know exactly how the operational aspects will be handled. What they don't have is any 'feel' for the numbers. Ask a question about the financial implications and there will be a pause while Excel is loaded and one of the 10,000 numbers in the financial plan will be extracted in response to the question. (This is behaviour that will be familiar to some of you who watched the UK's Dragon's Den TV programme – where would be entrepreneurs try to get seed investment from angel investors. The entrepreneurial 'front man' is asked a financial question. They typically look blank and either start fumbling through the financial model or turn to the 'numbers man' to answer.) In many ways I blame the ability of spreadsheets to do very sophisticated analysis with enormous speed and flexibility. In too many companies the financial evaluation of important investments has been effectively outsourced by the commercial manager to the finance function. On the face of it this seems like a sensible move. The CFO will have the robust models, and the experience to be able to model this investment in 3 megabytes of detail. The trouble is the product manager, the CEO, the board – whoever is driving the commercial case for the investment – will often use this as an excuse not to engage with the basic risk–reward relationship.

Taking a lead from the experienced poker player I maintain that the commercial manager needs a deep understanding of three principal numbers: the overall stake being risked, a feeling for the probabilities and contingencies of success, and a feel for the likely gain. Three numbers that can be scribbled, if they need to be written down at all, on the back of the proverbial envelope. Yes, there is a place for spreadsheets, and I am not sniping at finance departments. What spreadsheets are very good at doing is adding up the easy stuff – usually the costs. These can be scheduled in enormous detail. But however sophisticated the modelling, the answer, whether it be a payback period or an IIR% to two decimal places, is no more accurate than the errors on the least certain estimate. For new ventures I judge a sales forecast a success if it's within 30% of the actual sales level. Similarly the long-term value created is likely to be plus or minus 100%. But because finance is doing the modelling the people who best understand these commercial risks pass it over as a task to be completed, just another tick box on the way to authorization. This may

> *the commercial manager needs a deep understanding of three principal numbers*

remind you of what I said earlier about the use of logical, rule-based decision-making methods when you have to justify making investments with other people's money. The financial modelling can all too easily become part of the justification of an already selected alternative. There is no substitute for an intuitive feeling for those three numbers.

The art of intuitive decision making

So far I have looked at the logic of poker (and business) and the rational rule-based approaches we can use in poker. The rule-based assessment of expected value and probabilities works particularly well for poker because, although the outcome of the hand is random (subject to the chance fall of the cards), there are known probabilities for the odds of improving from a pair to three of a kind, or the chances of your opponent holding two aces. In business, the same arithmetic of investing can be applied but none of the probabilities are known. You may be using a logical, rule-based assessment of expected value for your proposed investment, but the probabilities you are plugging into the spreadsheet are going to be based on personal judgements and subject to your personal experiences.

However, whilst the logic of expected value can be helpful in poker, it isn't how most players make most decisions. Most poker players use intuition – associative reasoning built up over many thousands of hands to make quick decisions. They don't sit there, bet after bet, carefully calculating the changing odds and the expected value of every bet. Every now and then they will pause and do a bit of mental arithmetic to make sure they are not being led astray. But the vast majority of their decisions, for beginners and experts alike will be intuitive decisions. How do poker players establish good intuitions? By practising! By playing as much as they can so that they can improve their instincts through feedback. And the internet is allowing a new generation of poker players to learn much more quickly than ever before. Des Wilson (2006) recounts a conversation with John Duthie who had recently won the televised Poker Million tournament from the Isle of Man. On the new internet generation of poker players John points out, '...they have managed to amass the poker experience in three years what has taken the majority of professionals a lifetime... I was talking yesterday to a guy who had played a million hands online, and this kid is probably 22 or 23 years old, but what he does is he plays eight tables at a time on the internet' (p.299). Playing eight hands simultaneously there is no time to assess probabilities and calculate expected values. What you get is a crash course of experience and feedback. You get a feeling for the likely outcomes of different situations. An intuition of when to fold, when to raise. After a million hands you instinctively understand the frequencies of the game. Frequencies that you have experienced, not abstract mathematical probabilities.

The Monte Carlo simulation

The same idea lies behind the Monte Carlo simulation that N.N.Taleb used to help him understand security trading strategies, described in his book, *Fooled by Randomness*, (2004). A Monte Carlo simulation is a computer program that can generate millions of the 'alternative histories' that can diverge as a result of a randomly generated sequence of outcomes. As an example, and the reason it is so called, you can simulate the random spins of a roulette wheel on the computer without any of the slight biases that a real wheel would exhibit. By running the virtual wheel again and again you can trace the possible paths that the future could take. Of course, in reality, only one path becomes history, but the Monte Carlo simulation allows you to see the different alternative paths that a random sequence of spins can generate. Each path will have different twists and turns. You don't just get the expected distribution of outcomes after 1,000 spins of the wheel, you get a sample of all of the different paths that you might take to get there. Millions of sample paths can be generated every minute. Taleb (2004, p.47–51) recounts how running one particular simulation led him into being an option trader. He built a program to examine how different security trading strategies would prosper under different market conditions over the long term. He simulated alternative histories for populations of, 'idiotic bull, impetuous bear, and cautious traders'. 'My models showed that ultimately almost nobody really survived; bears dropped like flies in the rally, bulls ended up being slaughtered... when the music stopped.' But he noticed that one type of trader survived more frequently – option traders, who 'could buy insurance against a blow-up'. So an option trader is what Taleb became.

The Monte Carlo simulation's alternative paths accelerate the learning even more quickly than playing eight simultaneous games of poker. It builds an intuitive feel for the way in which random events can act to give a distribution of different outcomes. It would take most of a lifetime, and a lot of money, sitting in front of a roulette wheel to gain an understanding of the patterns of alternative histories that can emerge from an evening's roulette. Alternatively you can run a Monte Carlo simulation for a few minutes and discover that over the long term very, very few paths lead to a gain. In fact the British roulette wheel with its one zero (American wheels have two) provides the best odds you can get from the house in a casino. The 2:1 bet for, say, any red number will pay out about 48.6% of the time (18/37, 18 red, 18 black and zero). Although play for long enough and your money will always slowly leak away.

Gain as much experience as you can

The art of intuitive decision making is to gain as much experience as you can. To get as much feedback as you can on the outcome of your decisions. By whatever means, the intuitive decision maker has a feel for the way chance will play with his decisions. Chance, as we have seen is always at work. Nothing is certain. But if you take a gamble with a 99% chance of winning and a 1% chance of a very big loss enough times you will get caught – it's just that after 50 successful gambles we start to feel invulnerable, and then, of course, the fall hurts all the more. Like Taleb's bull traders after a crash, they simply can't believe their bad luck. They go into denial. The only way to understand that the fall will inevitably come is to have played the game long enough to have seen it happen before (which is the wisdom behind the aphorism that 'all you need to make money on the stock market is a bull market and a short memory'.) Alternatively, if you haven't had 20 years' experience then you need to do all you can to understand the distribution of alternative histories. Then you won't be surprised, you may even be prepared, or, like Taleb, adopt a strategy that has the best chance of success in the long term.

adopt a strategy that has the best chance of success in the long term

Damasio's theory of somatic markers (Chapter 5) as we have already noted, means that memories that have a much bigger emotional significance are prioritized. This can have the effect of skewing a balanced assessment of our experience. The positive associations laid down by a few big wins can seem more significant than a string of small losses. (I will discuss the asymmetry of wins and losses in more detail later.) This means that gamblers often misrepresent their own rate of success. Many gamblers think they are, overall, winners (because of the significance of the few big wins) when in fact they are net losers. I had first-hand experience of this when I was working closely with a company that had developed back-end software for independent and small-chain betting shops. They could classify the punters' accounts by the rate of return they achieved over the long term. These rates were surprisingly consistent; this quarter's losers were next quarter's losers. This allowed them to segregate customers into types. One of the types they called the 'nearly men' (they were virtually all men). They had a few big wins but a string of losses resulting in a small net loss. But the 'nearly men' themselves were certain they were winners and prided themselves on their insider knowledge – the true insiders were making consistent returns, month after month.

gamblers often misrepresent their own rate of success

Record your performance

There is a way round this error that is very simple but seldom practised. Keep a record of your performance. If you rely on a judged rate of return from your memory it will be distorted. The few big gains will overshadow the many smaller losses. The many small, emotionally minor, losses add up and over time can be more than the few memorable gains. Many expert poker players recommend that a careful record is made of every session: the overall performance, the big bets that won and the big bets that lost. Only then when you review your performance objectively will you see if you are one of the 'nearly men'.

A publishing example

Book publishing has a very similar investment and risk pattern to poker – lots of small bets (relative to overall wealth) with most of the return coming from a few big winners and a lot of small losers (so, incidentally, has the private equity industry). The small publishing house I currently work with publishes about 100 new books a year. 100 small bets of approximately £5,000 each (the cost of making the stock to sell) in a global market. Just as in an evening's poker, a few of the 100 titles will do very well and make enormous returns – more than ten times the initial outlay. Many will do OK, some will lose money and not recoup the initial outlay. But it can take over a year before we know if the bet has paid off. The feed-back cycle is very long. The books that succeed grab most of the attention. It takes a conscious effort to look coldly at every bet one and two years after the event to see how good we really are at the game. Good publishers or 'nearly men'?

This diversion reminds me of an anecdote from my first job in publishing. A well-respected international firm of auditors had been in to audit the accounts at the end of the financial year. They had undertaken some simple analysis which showed, shockingly to them, that of the 70 or so books we had published that year all of the profit for the entire company was equal to the contribution from just the best performing six titles. 'Why,' they asked, 'had we wasted money publishing all of the others?' The answer, that we couldn't possibly know which six would be the big winners in advance, went straight over their heads. To an auditor (I'm entitled to be critical because I spent one year as an auditor) with Newtonian certainty that the business world is predictable, it seemed carelessness on our part. Surely, they believed, the information that would have allowed us to spot the duds was always there, if only we had known where to look. In their world prediction is as easy as explanation – we should have known.

Managers don't gamble?

If you ask managers what they think they do, you get some surprising answers. They don't see management as a gamble, although the difference between risk taking and gambling may just be down to using acceptable vocabulary, i.e. spin. As one manager put it, 'Society values risk taking but not gambling, and what is meant by gambling is risk taking that turns out badly.' But the managers that have been interviewed make an important point. They don't see themselves as accepting a fixed odds gamble and sitting back and waiting to see what happens. Management isn't the same as placing bets on a roulette wheel and hoping. A commitment is made, a risk is accepted, but then good managers do everything they can to minimize the risk. Risks, once accepted, are there to be controlled. Decisions aren't isolated, one-off, all or nothing events, but a series of related decisions that allow the future to be shaped. And although the arithmetic for calculating risk and return is available to managers they use the same generalizations as experienced poker players. Managers quickly discard low likelihood events and focus on a couple of likely scenarios. Nor do managers use probability assessments and expected outturns to reduce all alternatives to a single number (net present value, for example) to make a decision. In fact managers have more in common with poker players than they may think.

Managers quickly discard low likelihood events

Dot.com madness and the logic of investing

So is the poker players' triangle of probabilities a useful tool to for looking at business investment decisions? Let us turn our attention to one of the strangest times in my business career – the collective madness that seemed to take hold around the turn of the century in technology and, in particular, internet investments. I had an early success with an internet business, www.babyworld.com – a community and e-commerce site for new and expectant parents. I had successfully raised funding for the business from a business angel in the summer of 1998. Although the dot.com boom was well underway in the US it was in its infancy in the UK. Freeserve had not yet launched its free dial-up ISP, internet usage was low, e-commerce untrusted and a minority activity. Before embarking on the venture in late summer 1998, I can vividly recall the concerns that I had. I was about to invest most of my available capital and the next few years of my career. I tried to arrange those concerns and judgements into three categories: the likely cost, a probability of success and the likely gain. The cost was not only all of my available capital but also potentially the opportunity cost of not advancing my career within publishing's corporate hierarchy and the real possibly that, in my mid-thirities, my career may never recover from an entrepreneurial failure. The probability of the venture being successful was a very complicated and uncertain calculation. I had no doubts about the future importance of the internet as a communications and commerce medium. But I had no experience in publishing for the parenting market and no knowledge of the nursery goods industry. I was also concerned about the unfolding financial crisis in the Far East (Chapter 1) and the possibility of there being a world-wide consumer recession reducing the potential for online advertising and e-commerce. The potential gains from the venture probably got the least attention. There was a land grab starting in the UK (already well underway in the US) – you didn't need to make a profit from your internet venture – it was merely sufficient to have made a particular part of the internet frontier your own with a strong branding and loyal users – the cash would follow. The issue I kept worrying about was timing. I could see that the internet would change the world but was now the right time to be making the investment? Too early and we would run out of cash long before online advertising and e-commerce would be sufficient to pay the overheads. Too late, and there would be a host of competitors – especially the magazine publishers who published the profitable and respected titles for expectant parents. They, it seemed to me had all of the competitive advantages that could make a success of the online parenting sites: knowledge of the readership, editorial expertise, advertising relationships, free cross-promotion in the pages of the magazines.

The failure of the vast majority of the print press (newspapers, consumer and business-to-business magazines) to implement effective and consistent internet investment strategies is, to me, one of the least discussed and most blatant examples of poor investment decision making in this most curious of times. The examples where people invested and failed are well known – the lost opportunity of not investing are often harder to see. Except I would argue you can spot the missed opportunities. Every new online media brand that has achieved reasonable prominence in the past five years marks the place where a print media management team failed to exploit its competitive advantage.

'All we have is the name' revisited

I started the chapter by recounting the story of boo.com. I broke off the story in July 1998 with JP Morgan agreeing to help raise $100 million with a planned launch in May 1999 and an initial public offering (IPO) pencilled in for six months later. In fact around $100 million was raised, and subsequently spent, over the next 18 months. (It has always intrigued me as to how much management focus you must have to spend $100 million in 18 months in a industry that is not capital intensive!) There were inevitable technical problems, driven by the simultaneous launch in 18 countries and also by the, as it turned out, unnecessary requirement to have the capacity to handle 10,000 customers simultaneously. The logistical and management complexity of simultaneously launching a site to sell 4,000 different product lines in different languages across Europe and North America from dozens of suppliers was too great. In fact the site launched six months late in November 1999. The forecasts remained optimistic: $100 million sales were budgeted for in 2000/01 and $1.35 billion for 2003/04, the sales for the later period buoyed up with a budgeted $100 million marketing spend.

The early trading performance was disappointing – but despite continuing technical glitches by May 2000 gross monthly sales had climbed to $500,000. But by the end of the first quarter of 2000 the world had changed. The internet bubble had been deflating since NASDAQ hit its high on 10 March. Boo.com was losing money and despite successive waves of staff cuts and cost reductions more cash was urgently needed. The planned IPO (originally planned when the annualized rate of sales had reached $5 million, which coincidently they hit in May 2000) was no longer a possibility. The shareholders who had financed the adventure were faced with one final call to meet another round of financing – one more bet to be called or declined. Another $20 million may have given the company the time it required – on a vastly reduced overhead – but only $12 million was promised and on 18 May 2000 the site was closed and the company put into liquidation.

An unfortunate business failure that only failed because access to the capital markets closed at just the wrong moment? Or an iconic failure of the dot.com period – a tale of vaulting ambition and excess? What had made experienced investors renowned for their dispassionate logic invest tens of millions of dollars in a company with a valuation of $375 million in late 1999 before it had taken even a dollar in revenue?

The poker player's triangle of probabilities can help us here. For a while back in 1999 and 2000 internet pioneers in a number of different markets were worth billions. Amazon.com had a market valuation of $32 billion in early December 1999. Professional investors in public companies making carefully researched decisions were valuing loss-making internet businesses (in the case of Amazon.com at that time making losses at the gross margin level – not just the net margin) at incredible values. If these valuations were correct then any business that had a defendable presence in an emerging internet market had the potential to be worth billions.

The cost of setting up the site and establishing the brand was thought to be about $100 million. The prize for success could be a very big number. Let's say $1–2 billion within six to 12 months (this was the expected IPO valuation slated for early 2000) – a return of between x3 and x6 on the pre-money valuation. The one number that seemed difficult to assess is the probability of going from a bold vision to dominant market share and positive cash flows. But if the prize is big enough, even long shots appear to be worth a gamble (but see rule of thumb 5 in Chapter 7). The $375 million valuation for boo.com doesn't seem too high if you can have your share of a $1–2 billion

if the prize is big enough, even long shots appear to be worth a gamble

IPO in less than six months. Surely, a justified gamble? Nothing irrationally exuberant here. Just a cool weighing up of cost, risk and reward.

The poker player would recognize the following analogy. A quiet game of poker is taking place amongst friends for the customary bets of a few tens of dollars and occasionally a few hundred dollars. Imagine, for whatever reason, a passing world champion poker player drops $1 million into the pot saying, 'this will make it more interesting'. The logic suddenly changes. The hopeless cards you hold are suddenly a ticket for a $1 million lottery. However unlikely it is that you will be able to convert your poor cards into a pot-winning hand, it has to be worth a play. If I only have a 1% chance of winning and there is $1 million to be won, then I will happily meet the $100 bet. Of course, if moments later, the world champion reaches over, picks back up his bankroll and says, 'only joking', then we all look a little foolish.

So, what went wrong?

For the investors in boo.com it wasn't the logic that was wrong. It was the value judgements that created the error. The cost of creating a pan-European brand and the infrastructure to take on and defeat the combined might of Europe's clothes retailers was almost certainly more than £100 million. The ability of the management team to deliver on the promise was, in reality, vanishingly small. A team with no previous internet or retailing experience, no competitive advantages to be brought to bear on the new venture, no existing customer relationships, no supplier relationships, no brand recognition, no fulfilment or customer service infrastructure, and all of course before broadband and the widespread acceptance of credit card purchasing. Let's be generous and put the chance of success at 2%. Even if the prize was big enough – you would go broke waiting for the 1 in 50 bet to come off. And of course the value of the prize was vastly, and temporarily, inflated. The logic wasn't wrong but the judgements used to evaluate each side of the triangle were seriously mistaken. Bubbles are hard to spot when you are inside them. The logic of the bubble works as long as you believe you can pass on your asset at a higher value to the next buyer.

The boo.com tale also illustrates some of the pitfalls of decision making. The distorting effect of very big prizes: that with finite resources you will almost always go broke waiting for long-shot gambles to pay off (even if the expected value is positive), the persistent overconfidence in our ability to improve the odds in uncertain situations, and the confidence we gain from what everyone else is doing (themes explored in Chapter 9). Lastly, the boo.com story illustrates the differences between risks where we have some intuitive understanding of the likely outcomes and the risks where we are travelling blind with no experience to guide us. Boo's managers had no previous experience to guide them. They hadn't made similar decisions before, they hadn't got feedback. They were deciding in the dark, 'far from home'. Contrast this with the financial institutions that backed the venture. They have been making investment and lending decisions for decades (centuries in some cases). They will have built up experience (based on feedback from earlier decisions) about the success criteria for successful investments. Making equity investment and lending decisions is what they do, year after year. They were making decisions 'close to home'. The shocking part of the boo.com story is not the misplaced confidence of the entrepreneurs but the way the experienced judgement of the professionals was distorted by greed.

In other words...

The decisions that managers make about the deployment of resources are effectively investment decisions. Just like the poker player, the business manager has three options: fold, call or raise. The best managers (like poker players) do two things better than the rest: they win more when they have an advantage; they lose less when they don't. Like poker, businesses always have some expenses which are the costs of being able to compete in the market. These costs, often included as overheads, need to be kept as low as possible.

In both business and poker, rule-based decision making helps identify gambles with positive expectations – where the triangle of cost, probability of success and return is favourable. A business manager should always keep sight of three numbers: likely cost, chance of success and likely return. But the best poker players don't start with detailed probability calculations – they call on them occasionally to verify intuitive decisions based on experience. The experience that allows the experienced poker player to understand the probability of success based on a familiarity with the distribution of outcomes in many alternative futures.

When you don't have experience to guide you then use other people's experiences (captured in 'rules of thumb') but these aren't 'laws' that can be universally applied – they depend on the context. A judgement is necessary to decide whether they apply in a particular context.

Which means that...

> ➤ Management is simple – there are only ever three options: fold, call or raise.

> ➤ Make the most of any situation where you have a genuine competitive advantage and avoid investing in situations where the advantage is small or non-existent.

> ➤ Always make sure you have a 'feel' for the cost, risk and gain for an investment. These are the only numbers that really matter.

> ➤ Learn from experience by comparing your decision with the eventual outcome.

> ➤ Treat other people's stories and experiences with caution – they may not be generally applicable to every situation.

Rules of thumb

Q ♥ Invest strongly in the rare situations where you have a clear advantage

J ♥ Be cautious with investments where you only have a small advantage

A ♥ Every cost should be seen as an investment for gain

K ♥ Overheads are the blind bets we place to be allowed to play the game – keep them low

10 ♥ Focus on the three numbers that matter: probable cost, chance of success and possible return

Chapter **7**

....

Rules of thumb: part 1 – risk and investing

Business and poker have a lot in common. They both share the same challenge of making investments with uncertainty about the costs, the chance of winning and the final return. The best poker players, like the best business managers, use intuition gained through experience to guide their decision making, and both groups use the simple arithmetic of investing to validate their instincts. When we don't have, or don't trust our own experience, we can use 'rules of thumb' to guide our decisions – effectively the experience of others. Because of the similarities between poker and business it comes as no surprise that the rules of thumb in poker can be directly applied to the business environment.

Rules of thumb and other people's experience

So if you haven't had your intuition honed by playing a million hands of poker on the internet or by running a Monte Carlo simulation to understand the distribution of possible outcomes for doubling on a pair of aces, how can you improve your decision making? One way is to learn from the experience of others. This experience comes in many forms but can be captured in 'rules of thumb', quick short-hands to help you find a 'good enough' option when you face a decision. If you haven't developed the intuitions yourself and you can't or don't want to undertake a slow rule-based method, use a rule of thumb. They capture other people's associative reasoning, wisdom and experience. Consequently they don't have general applicability but are specific to a particular situation.

I have spent many years of my career in book publishing and there is a widely used rule of thumb that the cover price of a book needs to be at least five times the physical production costs. A simple rule that quickly tells you the retail price you need to make an adequate contribution to costs. I have seen this rule, or variations of it, used again and again over two decades. The rule can be very useful and allows quick decisions about whether some titles are economically viable. But, like all rules of thumb, it is very sensitive to context. This one carries a host of buried assumptions, many of which are starting to unravel with the increasing availability of print on demand and the changing distribution networks and delivery media for books. Every industry, every area of human activity, has its rules of thumb, poker amongst them. In poker, many are specific to particular variations of the game. Others capture some fundamental truths about the dynamics of risk and reward. They have distilled human experience from millions of hands of poker into a few words. Used with discretion and in the right context they can be very valuable.

In Chapter 1 I criticized the way in which management science has developed theories by observing the actions of management in top-performing companies and concluding that these actions have general applicability – laws for the better management of companies. It is clear that, despite the claims of the authors, they have none of the power or status of scientific laws. They are, in most cases, examples of association rather than proven causal relationships. But that doesn't mean that they don't have value. Perhaps they are best seen as rules of thumb. Experience distilled from one specific context but useless as general, all-purpose prescriptions. But as always we want simple answers and universal truths. These 'theories' of management will never have that power, but seen for what they are they can be valuable insights into effective strategies in specific situations. What we can't do, although we sometimes try, is switch off our brains, suspend our judgement and mindlessly implement these 'proven' theories. (Even worse, what we sometimes do is pay consulting firms millions to implement them on our behalf.) There is no substitute for good judgement in deciding which practices can be usefully applied in new contexts. For all the impressive claims they are essentially rules of thumb, not universal laws of management.

This chapter is the first of two that explores how some of the rules of thumb developed for poker can have relevance in the boardroom. In Chapter 15 I gather together some other rules of thumb that are specifically about how to mange opponents and competitors.

Rules of thumb – the logic of investing

1 Keep watching, keep thinking

At the card table: No matter how routinely the betting round seems to be unfolding never stop watching and thinking. Every bet, every pause, every gesture can carry information about your opponents' hands. You can't know what the hidden cards will be, but you can make assessments about the relative strength or weakness of your opponents' hands. Spotting patterns in your opponents' play will be one of the most effective ways of achieving an advantage. How do they bet when they have strong hands? How do they bet when they have weaker hands? Always be on the look out for the unusual: the gesture you haven't seen before, the unexpected focus. Most hands are routine for moderate gains and losses. You dismiss the very unlikely possibility that your opponent already has the flush or another strong hand. But occasionally there will be a hand with significant sums at stake. Suddenly there is a lot depending on the most subtle of judgements. If you noticed an unusual gesture five minutes ago, now it may have great significance. Perhaps it's a cue that the

The smallest trigger can alert you that the unlikely is unfolding

unlikely scenario you unthinkingly dismissed may need to be reconsidered. The smallest trigger can alert you that the unlikely is unfolding.

Round the board table: However dull and predictable your market may be you must never stop looking and thinking. It is easy to switch off and think that nothing will change. You miss the small cues that suggest that a new and aggressive competitor may be about to enter, you don't see the significance of a gradual social change. Focused on the small regular gains of routine trading you don't see the patterns that can signal a major loss. The unobservant frog never notices the rising temperature of the water. Every aspect of consumer behaviour or competitor action needs to be reviewed and tested against some of the more extreme scenarios. As Intel's Andrew Grove famously observed, only the paranoid survive.

> ➤ Keep watching and pay particular attention to the surprising and the unexpected, however trivial.

2 Position matters

At the card table: Position in poker is very important and has a very specific meaning. In poker the order in which bets are placed is always the same and starts clockwise from the dealer. The best position is to be the last person to bet. The worst position is to be first to bet. The reason is simple, betting last you have gained more information about the potential strengths of the other players' hands. Betting first you know nothing. Making a bet and risking being raised by a strong, but as yet undisclosed, opponent is a real risk for the first player to bet. Being last to make a call means that you can know for certain the cost of seeing the next card – something you can't know in an earlier position. Consequently, the textbooks suggest that to open the betting you should hold a much stronger hand than if you were in a better position, further round the table. The hand that you may be pleased to play in a good position you are advised to fold if you are betting first.

Round the board table: One of the most frequently quoted rules of thumb in business is 'first mover advantage'. The reality is often very different. Amazon.com was not the first online book store in the US, it was beaten to the punch by Charles Stack. But with Charles Stack largely forgotten we look back and are convinced that Amazon must have been first. In reality the first mover has a difficult time, and for exactly the same reasons as the player in an early position at the poker table. If you are genuinely the first into a market then there are so many things you don't know. There

the first mover has a difficult time

are no reference points for customer acceptance, no price points, no experience of which marketing messages work. The product specification is untested, there are no economies of scale or established production experience. Any one of those unknowns can trip you up. What this does is significantly increase the risk. The greater the number of unknowns the higher the risk. This can make it significantly more difficult for the first mover to either attract, or have the courage to commit, sufficient capital to a new market. A shrewd competitor can wait for early feedback from the marketplace. If that competitor has access to sufficient capital (Jeff Bezos of Amazon was able to finance a business plan which promised to be loss making for five years) a cost effective route to market or a related technological expertise, then the first mover will often struggle to compete. Later entrants have fewer unknowns, lower risk and are able to invest with more confidence.

> New markets have many more unknowns, which means much higher risks. To accept those risks you need to have a clear advantage.

> Being the first to act decisively when some risks are known can be better than being first.

3 Raising or folding can be better than calling

At the card table: If you have a good hand then you should be raising (as discussed above). Although it is worth noting that there are exceptions, such as when you have a very strong hand. Here you want to conceal your strength to draw other players in and increase the final pot – called 'slow playing' a hand. If you have a weak or moderate hand with only a small chance of winning then you shouldn't be betting. Beginners and weak players will often call a round or two of bets with a moderate hand before reluctantly ducking out when the bets increase. Doing this once or twice isn't going to hurt. Doing it hand after hand can see a chip lead leak away in small bets, none of which had any real prospect of winning. Backing a moderate hand to be second best is bad play. Remember, the best players lose less money on weak and moderate hands. So raise if you are strong, fold if you are weak – don't muddle along to see what happens. (As always there are exceptions, further rules of thumb that qualify the general principle. Sometimes you need to disguise the strength of your hand to make your play less predictable – the bluff, or the semi-bluff, which we will discuss later).

Round the board table: Real competitive advantages, like two aces in the hole, are rare things. If you have one you should back it to the full. More of a problem is continuing to back small projects with only moderate expectations. Some products or markets, which may once have seemed bright prospects, continue to receive funding long after the prospects of real returns have gone. Meeting the overheads for another year is like calling a bet. You don't feel excited enough to raise the stakes. It's not such a bad product that it should obviously be closed. So year after year overheads are paid, management time is absorbed, capital is tied up. The returns, if you looked at them properly, may well be unacceptable, but organizational inertia takes over. They can be very

organizational inertia takes over

hard projects to close. Sometimes there are good reasons for keeping them going, but as a rule of thumb, 'push it hard if the prospects are good, close it if its not'. Raising or folding can be better than calling.

> It's too easy to keep calling to see what will happen, you have to decide: is it good enough to back as a winner, or should I fold and wait for a better opportunity?

4 Avoid long shots

At the card table: In poker you want to put yourself in a position where the bets you make have a positive expectation. For example, you may only have a 1 in 5 chance of making the flush and winning the hand. However, if the cost of seeing the last card is $100 and there will be $600 to be won, then even though you will lose four times out of five, in the long run the 6 to 1 return on $100 means the bet has a positive expectation. Some bets with very long odds can have positive expectations. For example, there may be a 1 in 50 chance of winning but with a 100 to 1 return on the bet – a positive expectation. If this was a lottery ticket for $1 or a bet which was for a very small proportion of your total wealth then you should take it. But the gamble only has a positive expectation if you have enough reserves to keep taking the bet, or other bets like it, as many times as it takes to see a win. But taking a long-shot bet when it's likely you will run out of money before seeing a win is a quick way to go bankrupt. You will almost certainly run out of cash long before the bet comes in. In the language of the Monte Carlo engine, very few of the alternative histories will have a positive outcome even though the expectation is positive. This is an extreme case of a principal law of probability, captured in the drunken walk. Imagine a drunk walking along a path with a wall (which he can bounce off) on one side and the gutter on the other. The drunk shuffles forwards but, also, randomly to the left or the right at each step. The drunk will always end up in the gutter. Eventually there will be a random sequence of steps that ends up in the gutter, no matter how wide the path. For the gambler with finite resources and making a series of random bets there will eventually be a losing sequence that will take up all of your resources. Backing long shots with limited wealth just means you end up in the gutter more quickly.

Round the board table: The same logic applies. A company's capital is always limited. Backing a series of high-risk ventures, say with a 1 in 20 chance of success, will end in disaster if you can only fund a small number of these ventures, even though the one that works could make a handsome return. Many start-up ventures have this characteristic: limited capital and a high-risk proposition. Most of them don't make it, not because they were daft ideas or had appalling managers (although both limitations often apply), but, like the drunk walking along a very narrow path, one misjudgement, a slightly slower take up than expected, and the cash is gone. They are in the gutter. The expected value of the investment may have been positive but they are walking a very fine line. Frustratingly of course there is always the lucky fool, in cards as well as business, for whom the bet pays off at the first attempt. They themselves, and the business

> *One misjudgement and they are in the gutter*

journalists, will praise their foresight, their judgement, their courage. The assumption, as always, is that because they succeeded they had unique insights, that they alone were able to see through the fog to find the one certain path. Praised as business heroes they easily raise capital for a second venture based on their track record. More often than not, they don't get lucky a second time.

> ➤ You wouldn't be allowed to play the lottery with shareholders' money – so don't!

> ➤ Bad luck will put us all in the gutter eventually, the trick is to stay out for as long as you can.

5 Avoid big bets for a small advantage

At the card table: This is a different take on the previous rule of thumb. That advised against long shots because on average you will have to make a lot of bets before you can expect to see a win. This time it advises against putting a high proportion of your wealth on one bet with only a small advantage. Betting all of your chips on a 55% chance of victory is something you will want to avoid whenever you can, but in tournament play when your opponent is trying to put you out of the game, it can be unavoidable. There is no second chance. Everything is risked on the toss of a coin. Instead of the drunk shuffling along in small steps, the drunk is taking giant leaps. Unless you are very lucky, and of course there is always someone who is that lucky, you just end up in the gutter more quickly.

Round the board table: The point hardly needs elaborating. Risking a substantial proportion of the company's net worth on a single bet is something you will want to avoid. Being guided by the expected value of a gamble can be very misleading. The proportion of wealth at risk is an important consideration. But entrepreneurs take this gamble when they start a business. The failure rate for new businesses is

> *Being guided by the expected value of a gamble can be very misleading*

high, the odds of success is typically less than the 50:50 odds of a coin flip. The capital risked and the salary foregone by the entrepreneur can be very high. How entrepreneurs get themselves through this conundrum to place the bet is the subject of Chapter 10. Needless to say, it's not a proposition that suits everyone.

Years ago, I was given advice by a boss of mine who was a sophisticated gambler. His rule of thumb for business investments was simple. If you didn't have a reasonable degree of confidence that you could double your investment in three years then it probably wasn't worth it. (What does reasonable degree of confidence mean? It's a judgement call. Certainly not a 10% long shot, but neither a 95% certainty – whatever these percentages mean.) Here was someone who always had an instinctive feel for costs and returns and didn't need to wait ten days while finance completed the financial modelling. Is it just an arbitrary rule? Well, I think it's more powerful than that. Doubling your money in three years equates to about 25% return a year. That's a great return on capital but remember it's not certain, so some of the bets will fail. The return needs to match the risks in every industry, but it's a rule of thumb that I have always remembered and often applied.

> You shouldn't need to place big bets on very uncertain outcomes – where are the good bets you have overlooked?

Rules of thumb

2 ♠ Be sensitive to the surprising
3 ♣ Position matters – early movers need bigger advantages
7 ♣ Raising or folding can be better than calling
8 ♣ Avoid long shots
9 ♣ Avoid big bets for small advantage
K ♣ A narrow path (limited funds) and big steps (high stakes) just gets you in the gutter more quickly
3 ♥ A good investment will, with reasonable probability, double your money in three years

Chapter **8**

Deciding close to home

Decision making, as we have seen, is more art than science. There isn't a reliable method by which we can objectively determine the best course of action in advance. Judgements wrought from experience are always going to be our guide for making decisions. Those judgements, as we saw in Chapter 5, can serve us well when we are able to apply them in the same environment that served as our teacher. This chapter looks at decision making when we are in a familiar environment – what I term, deciding 'close to home'. The situations when these intuitive judgements can serve you well and when intuition can let you down. When, for example, we get lulled by a thousand small successes into thinking nothing can ever go wrong – which is, in a nutshell, the story of Long-Term Capital Management.

Profit without risk

By any standards Long-Term Capital Management (LTCM) had an excep-tionally intelligent management team. It boasted not one but two Nobel Prize winners for economics: Robert Merton and Byron Scholes. LTCM, in common with all hedge funds, aimed to make a profit but to minimize the risk to investors by taking one position but then 'hedging' it with another position so that the overall exposure is minimal. For the hedge fund man-ager, boasting about the reliability of profits ought to be as important as the size of those profits – sacrificing the highs for protection against the lows. LTCM's core strategy was to buy interest bearing bonds and simulta-neously sell related bonds, profiting if the 'spread', the difference in interest rates in the two bonds narrowed – so-called fixed interest arbi-trage deals. But there is a problem trying to make a lot of money by taking a bet on a well-hedged risk. The returns are very small – to make a lot of money you have to put a big stake at risk. The returns may be very reliable (the volatility low), but the spread on interest rates will only be fractions of one percentage point. To overcome this problem LTCM planned from the outset to use leverage – to multiply its stake by borrowing 20 to 30 times its own capital. This works in the same way as putting up £10,000 of your own capital to buy a house and borrowing £200,000 as a mortgage. If the value of the property goes up to £250,000, you can pay back the mortgage and keep all of the gain; a very good return on your £10,000 at risk. A 25% increase in the asset value 'leveraged' into a 500% gain in the capital at risk. But if the market goes down then you will be liable for all of the loss.

LTCM's timing was impeccable. It managed to raise an unprecedented $1 billion of investors' cash and started trading early in 1994 just as Alan Greenspan made an unexpected increase in short-term interest rates. This provoked instability in financial markets providing the conditions that a skilled team with $1 billion to invest could exploit. In its first year of trading LTCM earned a return of 28%. An amazing achievement for a year in which most bond investors lost money. Buoyed by its early success the amount of capital under management grew. The partnership had to look harder and harder for new investment opportunities. It relied upon its computer models to identify situations where the markets were tem-porarily out of step with its long-term average – exploiting temporary inefficiencies in the financial markets. LTCM wouldn't make a simple bet that a price would rise or fall, it would place a 'hedged' bet that a differen-tial between two prices that had become temporarily exaggerated would return to the usual range. It found opportunities across the globe in gov-ernment and corporate bonds, mortgage securities, S&P500 options, interest rate derivatives and other financial instruments. To maintain the returns on the ever-enlarging capital base bigger risks had to be taken, but always trying to find situations where it could make, 'a sure nickel rather than an uncertain dollar'.

Even in 1997, the year of financial turmoil in Asia, the fund made a return of 25%. $1 invested in LTCM in March 1994 was worth $4 by early 1998. But although the returns on investors' capital were high, the total return on total cash invested was modest. At the end of 1995, when the fund was leveraged 28 to 1, the return on total cash invested was just 2.45%, and if allowance is made for the fact that its derivative trades were not included on the balance sheet, almost certainly less than 1%. The overall cash returns reflected the modest risks that were being taken – the investors profiting from the high proportion of borrowing. By the start of 1998 the invested capital had grown to $4.7 billion, of which the partners had built up personal stakes of $1.9 billion. This capital was leveraged with an incredible $124 billion of borrowing. LTCM were making thousands of small bets (as a proportion of the funds total wealth), on relatively low-risk positions, in well-diversified markets. This strategy, thanks to the skills of the founders in identifying the opportunities and the power of leverage had given an exceptional return with very little volatility. It appeared that some of the finest minds in finance had finally found a way to have both high returns and low risks.

When intuition makes for good business (and good poker)

A poker player, let's call him Bob, has been playing Texas Hold'em with the same group of friends every Thursday evening for five years. He is right to trust his instincts. Bob knows, without pausing for a rule-based calculation of the probabilities, when to double and when to fold, which players can be bluffed out of the pot, which players to treat with caution. Here is the decision maker utilizing all of his experience gained in a familiar environment – deciding close to home. But into this cosy and familiar situation let us introduce a couple of changes that might give our recreational poker player pause for thought. Let us imagine that one of Bob's friends invites along his Texan cousin to join the regulars on a Thursday evening. There is new learning to be done. The familiar patterns of betting that have become second nature may no longer apply. Let us now imagine that our Texan visitor suggests that, for a change, they should play Omaha (a different variation of poker) instead of their regular game of Texas Hold'em. Omaha and Texas Hold'em, although similar, require different assessments and betting strategies. Bob's intuition developed through five years of one game could in fact be a liability under the new rules. When our guest then suggests that, to make it more interesting, the betting limits should be raised then it is probably time to for Bob to make his excuses and leave early.

Intuitive reasoning develops with experience. Experience that is not universal but shaped in one particular environment. Change the environment and not only does some of the learning no longer apply but it can be positively dangerous. If you have spent ten years of your career working in an industry then you will have acquired a great deal of experience. You will be capable of making intuitive judgements about how that industry works. Intuitions about the way customers respond at different points of the economic cycle to price changes and product quality. You will have learnt through simple observation and association the impact that fluctuations in service quality have on customer loyalty. You will have seen some investments prosper and some fail. Knowledge picked up in the heat of the battle that can't be acquired in the classroom. Some of this learning may survive being transplanted to a new environment. Almost any organizational role can teach you how to motivate staff or handle the inevitable politics. But the business development decisions, the decisions that managers have to make about the deployment of resources to generate profit,

Intuitive reasoning develops with experience

are likely to be specific to an industry. Intuition is simply what you have learnt about the environment you have been working in. Nothing more, nothing less. Eisner, Disney's former CEO, described intuition as 'the sum of millions and millions of past experiences that enable you to make reasonable decisions'. In the next chapter I will look specifically at how we overcome the challenges of making decisions in unfamiliar environments, when we are 'far from home'. But first we need to look at decision making 'close to home' in a familiar environment. When can experience be trusted to make effective decisions and when can it let you down?

Deciding close to home

So what are the circumstances that will promote good decision making 'close to home'? Put simply they will be the very situations where Bob feels at his most comfortable and is able to play his best poker. That occurs when Bob has played a lot of hands recently, honing his judgement; each hand providing fast feedback on his decision making. Bob is also happier when he is playing his familiar Texas Hold'em rather than less familiar variations.

And of course Bob is most comfortable making decisions about hands that are well within his comfort zone of betting limits. Deciding close to home will work best when the decisions are frequent, the feedback is fast, the context is familiar and the funds at risk are modest (in proportion to overall wealth). Let's look at each of these in a business context.

Frequent

These are decisions that we make with regularity. Not necessarily every day or every week, but decisions that we have made before on several occasions. For a fast-food chain the decision on where to open another branch is an example of a frequent decision that is definitely close to home. For a lending bank the decision to provide a credit facility, for the consultancy company the decision about how to staff a new assignment. Decisions that occur regularly and that will be made instinctively by the experienced manager with little or no consideration of alternatives – in many cases nothing but tick-box procedures with all decision and discretion removed from the manager altogether.

Fast feedback

Our intuitive decisions will be most effective when we get fast and unambiguous feedback. You get to see the outcome of your decision – good, bad or indifferent. Did the revised pricing strategy win the tender? Did the website relaunch increase traffic and sales enquiries? Quick, unambiguous feedback is the defining characteristic of decisions close to home. As we will explore later, experts in nearly all fields overestimate the accuracy of their judgements. Studies have intriguingly found two exceptions to this general rule – weather forecasters and card players (specifically bridge players). The reason of course is that both forecasters and bridge players get quick feedback on their decisions. They get an almost immediate opportunity to calibrate their judgement. Wait too long for the results of a decision and two things happen. Firstly, as we noted in Chapter 1, we suffer from something called hindsight bias. Knowing, much later how something turned out changes how we recall our original decision. You predicted 'heads', a year later it comes out 'tails'. A proportion of us will actually believe we always predicted 'tails'. Secondly, the longer the gap between decision and result then the more confused and uncertain will be the link between the two events. You decide to reduce prices on all products and two years later you have gained 2% of market share. Cause and effect, or were other factors involved? To support the development of good intuitive judgement we need quick feedback.

Familiar

Just as Bob prefers playing a familiar version of poker, so we like making decisions in familiar contexts. Planning how to spend next year's marketing budget is lot easier if the business context is the same as last year. Making decisions about allocating research spending is much easier if there are no disruptive technologies on the horizon.

Low proportion of wealth

We are more comfortable making familiar decisions using our experience if the proportion of our wealth (or our company's net value) at risk is relatively small. Bob was happy making $20 calls but would feel very uncomfortable evaluating a $1,000 raise. Likewise, we will trust the junior manager to use their judgement and make decisions based on their day to day experience if the value at risk is low in proportion to the company's value. The same decision with most of the company's net assets at stake will require a lot of justification and consultation with all of the stakeholders. I have commented several times on the need to use rational, rule-based logic when we need to justify decisions to others. I speculate that even when we have to make decisions that involve a high proportion of our own wealth we often hesitate to use intuition alone. Rational justification often seems to be required. It is as if the fear of regret is sufficient to make us try to justify the decision to ourselves.

Experience, rank and organizational learning

Much is made about organizational learning. The organization is learning all the time. Customer service agents, sales representatives, the people who build products or deliver services are all getting feedback about product quality, production methods and customers' per-

The organization is learning all the time

ceptions about competitors. Organizations don't stop learning but what often happens is that the people who make the strategic decisions – the decisions that involve a high proportion of the shareholders' wealth – stop learning. The people who are paid to make long-term decisions about the future of the corporation have, in many cases, lost touch with the commercial environment. Sometimes, sensing they may have lost their 'feel' for the commercial environment, they do an extraordinary thing – they employ strategy consultants. Effectively outsourcing one of the main decisions that they are paid to make to outsiders with no direct experience of the market. Why do management teams do this? Partly, I presume, to dilute any sense of personal responsibility for the decision (although the time scales over which strategy decisions are evaluated is so long this hardly seems an important concern). But more importantly because strategy consultancies are very good at providing rational justifications for important decisions. The logical justifications that are necessary to present to shareholders. The only people who are never spoken to are the people that already know – the staff on the frontline who are still open to the changing environment. What gets implemented as strategy is a rationally justifiable (for this read fashionable) strategy. The 'commonsense' strategy based on the organization's own learning is never pursued. Does this sound familiar?

Getting lost 'close to home'

But for all its strengths, intuitive reasoning can lead us astray. The good news is that many of the biases that we exhibit are very predictable. We make the same mistakes again and again. We put undue weight on a few highly significant events; we wrongly come to attribute a causal relationship between two associated events; and we quickly assume that the very rare but catastrophic occurrences will not happen to us.

The availability bias

I hate beetroot and I know why I hate it. I can remember being forced to eat it as a seven-year-old in the first week at 'big' school. I can still recall my otherwise empty plate smeared with a lurid purple stain as I aimlessly pushed the detested root vegetable with my fork. The fear and insecurity of those early weeks at a new school have left a very strong emotional tag against my memory of beetroot. One particularly powerful personal experience, whether good or bad, can overwrite any number of contrary but less significant experiences.

I imagine that most people would think that your chances of surviving a plane crash are too small to consider. We quickly recall instances of plane crashes from our memory. The catastrophic crashes that kill all on board dominate both the news reports and, because of their emotional impact, our memories. Asked to estimate our chances of surviving a crash we recall examples and conclude that our chances of survival are negligible. But if I tell you that in the 568 plane crashes in the US between 1983 and 2000, 96% of the people on board survived you would question either my sanity or my source. Professor Ed Galea's study of accidents (Galea *et al.*, 2006) found that 90% of all air crashes had survivors and only 4% of the people on board died. These misrepresentations matter. If we think we are doomed in a crash situation we pay less attention to safety procedures. The same mechanism can lead to us to misrepresenting the likely success of company acquisitions, new business start ups and new product launches. Successful examples may come more readily to mind than the failures (Chapter 10 looks specifically at the impact of this for entrepreneurs). Our intuitive estimate of success is being constructed from a very biased sample of those examples that come easily to mind. All too easily we generate an intuitive sense of confidence in the outcome of our venture that be totally unjustified by the facts.

Sometimes the availability bias is not due to overweighting rare, high-impact events but due to the fact that some of the evidence is hidden from us – it just isn't available to be considered. Once again the surprising survivability of air crashes provides an example. The more dramatic crashes, as we have just seen, are more easily recalled from memory. But many of the smaller crashes don't get reported unless we happen to live close to the incident. Very few of the less serious crashes are in our memory at all – they are not available for recall. It appears all too easy to make misjudgements about the likelihood of events, either because we tend to recall only the most significant of our experiences or because we simply are not aware of the full range of outcomes.

Presumed association

The poker player's lucky chair and N.N.Taleb's stained tie from Chapter 3 remind us of how easy it is to come to associate one event with another. Perhaps, by chance, during the regular Monday evening poker sessions I notice that when I sit in the chair facing the door I win. This starts as pure chance on a couple of occasions. But after a while I start to notice that this pattern seems to continue – perhaps not invariably, but more often than not. I am not particularly superstitious, but now I start to recall, I seem to win more frequently whenever I am in the 'lucky' chair. This is the bias of presumed association. Once the initial link has been noticed, my mind starts to believe the two events (sitting in 'the' chair and winning) occur with a greater frequency than is actually the case. There are, of course, four possibilities:

1. I sit in the lucky chair and win.
2. I sit in the lucky chair and lose.
3. I sit in another chair and win.
4. I sit in another chair and lose.

Once we have in our minds the idea of an association between the chair and winning we start to note further wins from the lucky chair but tend to skip over the contradictory occurrences of the other three possibilities. Not bothering to systematically record the real frequencies we become convinced of the association. Explaining a gambler's superstition is one thing, but presumed associations can have serious consequences. Stereotypes and received wisdom can easily lead to presumed associations. If we believe that employees trained as scientists don't have the interpersonal skills to be effective managers then our experiences will support this presumed association. For some people their prejudices will be appear to be reinforced every day. Prejudices about people, about products, about markets, and about risks.

Risk blindness

Some risks we take every day, but the danger never seems to materialise. We cross the road. We continue to live in cities threatened by earthquakes and hurricanes. Each day that passes is another day without disaster. We start to believe it will never happen. How can we learn by association if the event is never experienced? An error of induction is made. Because every day of her life the turkey has been fed and looked after she comes to believe that every day will be the same – she has no reason to think otherwise. Then, without warning, after maybe 200 days of constant feeding and being looked after, the familiar routine changes. It's nearly Christmas. Any extreme event that occurs less frequently than our typical span of experience is gong to cause a problem of risk blindness. In financial markets a price crash that may occur every decade or so can catch anybody out – especially those who did not experience the last crash and many of those that did.

The more dramatic the event, the less frequently it occurs. Imagine that San Francisco is the city that you want to live in above all others. Every day you live there and there is no earthquake you have gambled and won – the gain being the additional benefit of living in the city of your choice for another day. In fact we become blind to the risk. We are rationally aware of the danger, but because for four decades we have never experienced it we become blind to it. Then, once every few generations the gamble that was taken every day will be lost. The small gains in utility that were enjoyed every day for most of a life time are wiped out in a single event.

> *The more dramatic the event, the less frequently it occurs*

Every business has some area of risk blindness. There are the risks that we may be aware of but don't do anything about. Why don't we do anything? Because of the cost that dents short-term profitability. We can become blind to the threats to our market-leading product if over 20 years there has never been a credible competitor. Its easy to forget that tomorrow there may be one. Risk blindness can be particularly dangerous when the environment is changing slowly (I call it the boiled frog syndrome). Markets slowly evolve, customer preferences shift over time and in the absence of a galvanising crisis the company can shrink and disappear with the market.

Business models and risk

Some business models are much more susceptible to risk blindness than others. Some businesses make a profit by taking a large number of small, relatively safe risks, each with a modest return and where each individual decision only puts at risk a tiny proportion of the company's total worth. Lots of repeated small gambles, with a high probability of success and a relatively modest return based on decisions that are 'close to home' for the organization. Lending banks make thousands of lending decisions – each decision a small proportion of their total capital, and on each loan only make a modest profit (a few percentage points above base rates, plus arrangement and other fees). Professional services firms (lawyers, accountants, management consultants) charge for their services on a 'cost plus profit' basis. Each of their many clients contributing a small proportion to profit, and each assignment requiring the allocation of a small proportion of the firm's professional resources. Routine, familiar and low-risk decisions about the allocation of resources. Lots of small gains but always a small and sometimes forgotten risk of a catastrophic loss. For the lending banks the possibility of a significant global economic downturn is the risk that haunts day to day business. Normally the banks' risks are diversified across different firms, continents and sectors. A default by one particular company is unfortunate but will have no implications for the bank's outstanding loans in other parts of its portfolio. But in a global recession the separate credit risks that looked well balanced and diversified suddenly appear to be correlated. For the professional service firms there is always a risk that there will be a claim for professional malpractice that the professional indemnity insurance will not cover. The pressures to extract more profit from each client can encourage a culture of corner cutting and poor practice. For years, even decades, this can go unnoticed. Then without warning the daily gamble that was taken and won every day for a small additional profit is lost. Many other businesses have the same risk profile – small, low-risk, daily gains and the small chance of a catastrophic loss. The utility companies that cut corners on safety and food processing companies don't train staff to follow health and safety procedures are examples.

Different firms take different approaches to risk. Most ways of mitigating risk involve either additional cost or a wider spread of resources. In any particular market the rival that hasn't bothered to diversify and hasn't incurred the additional costs and protections will report higher earnings. For a decade or more they will be the stars, showing the old hands how it's done; admired by analysts, sought after by journalists. Then the unexpected (inevitably) happens. The tide changes and the single strategy runs aground. But the under-rated company that has been quietly going about its business for 100 years survives. It is all too easy in our age of instant success to overlook the achievement of survival. A decade-long blaze and bust will get the headlines but a company that can survive a century or more, half a dozen recessions, a world war and globalization? The longer time horizons of family run firms can provide a powerful alternative to quarterly reporting cycles. In any game where chance plays a part, success can only be assessed over the long term.

Getting better at deciding close to home

Despite the power of intuitive decision making we have identified a number of systematic errors that can distort our judgement: the availability bias, presumed association and risk blindness. The important question is how can we become better at decision making close to home and overcome these biases?

Keep learning

It is easy to switch off when you think you know how something works. You can quickly get out of touch if you stop listening to customers. Intuitive knowledge has to be kept up to date. It will stale – hardening into dogma – unless you keep watching and learning.

Keep a record of what actually gets decided

Write down your decisions when you make them. Jot them in the diary. They can be small everyday decisions, or bigger career changing moments. Just note down what you decided and the most significant reasons for the choice. Six months later just flick through your decision diary and reflect on how things have turned out. Learning whether you can trust your judgement – whether your judgement is well calibrated – is essential feedback. Your memory can't be trusted with an accurate assessment of your past performance; you need to write it down and review it – either for yourself as an individual, for the department or for the management team. Only by keeping a record of what has occurred can we uncover the prejudices and presumed associations that can plague judgement.

Look for the surprising

One surprise is much more powerful than a dozen routine confirmations of what you always assume. A surprise shows you that somewhere in your nested assumptions about customer needs, competitor product qualities or your own organizational strengths there is a mismatch. The surprise is a flag to the mind that the world isn't working exactly as your mental model thinks it should. Surprises can always be ignored or lamely explained away but acknowledging them and finding out why they surprise is the only way to new knowledge. Part of the act of being surprised is being sensitive to what is going on in your peripheral vision. It can be easy to focus only on the task in hand and miss the surprise unfolding at the edge of your attention.

Don't be surprised by Christmas

Your experience will not have taken in all of the rare events that can occur. But the rare events are the dangerous events, the ones that can wipe out a decade's gains in a single day. If you have never experienced these events then your intuitive judgement will not include them in your reasoning – your judgements will be made without reference to the risk. Just asking the question, 'What would the company do if this occurred?' can be enough to sensitize you to the risks. The biggest danger is when, through overconfidence, you assume it can't happen to you. One day, it will, you just don't know when.

LTCM – the downfall

Long-Term Capital Management's incredible four year run of success started to unwind in May 1998. By September it had losses that amounted to some $4.6 billion and the Federal Reserve Board had to organize a consortium of banks to provide a cash rescue to prevent further international fallout. The partners' $1.9 billion of personal equity in the fund was gone within four months. Such was their confidence in their business model that most of them had virtually all of their personal wealth invested in the partnership – they didn't think they needed to hedge against their own failure. For the LTCM turkey, Christmas had arrived. The first large monthly losses in the fund's history occurred in May and June 1998 with losses of 6% and 10% respectively. Then on 17 August Russia announced its debt moratorium (the same event that finally stopped the US government bailing foreign bond investors). Markets with no logical connection to Russia began to head

For the LTCM turkey, Christmas had arrived

south. The Russian default precipitated a global move away from risk and towards liquidity. The spreads the LTCM had bet would close started to widen dramatically. The losses soared. As investors tried to close positions and realize losses, the spreads got wider. Everyone wanted out at the same time. But not everyone can have liquidity at the same time. All of a sudden the well-diversified and separate risks that LTCM had placed around the world were all sinking together. The computer models that had brilliantly predicted how each individual derivative or bond arbitrage could be exploited for profit had assumed that the markets were not correlated. Nobody had foreseen that at a time of global financial panic all of the markets would be correlated and that their diversification strategy was now an illusion. As Lowenstein (2001) reports in his rollercoaster account of the LTCM story: '[LTCM] which had calculated with mathematical certainty that it was unlikely to lose more than $35 million on a single day, had just dropped $553 million – 15% of its capital – on that one Friday in August.' If you were losing in one market, you were losing in them all. The answer, in theory, is to sit tight, wait for the anomalous trading to pass and the positions to recover. But when the vast majority of the cash in the fund is borrowed the margin for error is slim. Some of the founders cursed their luck and blamed it on a freak 'one in a hundred year' event. Except tellingly, just 12 months later, key US price spreads were just as wide and the rescued fund was losing money once again.

In the early days of the fund LTCM was following the classic pattern of a business that is making sound business decisions 'close to home'. They understood the fixed interest arbitrage deals better than anyone else – after all two of their founders had won Noble Prizes for their analysis of how to value options. Each trade involved a relatively small proportion of the fund's wealth and they were learning (and winning) quickly making steady and seemingly risk-free returns. Two things happened. Firstly, as the returns from the trades they understood best diminished they took on new capital (and more borrowing) and had to find new contracts further from their original area of expertise. These included taking one-way bets on Japanese bonds (high-risk, unhedged betting that was a long way from their original starting point). Secondly, they either didn't see, or forgot about the risk that was always there – that the diversified bets in their various markets at a time of crisis could all become correlated. Under some scenarios there was no diversification. There is a final irony in this failure. LTCM made its money by exploiting inefficiencies in the operation of markets. If, as neo-classical economists believe, prices always incorporate all of the available information and are influenced by random events, then volatility is low and the big swings really are once a century events. But if the markets did operate in a manner predicted by neo-classical economics then there wouldn't have been market inefficiencies for LTCM to exploit. But as Mandelbrot has shown, the very inefficiencies that allowed LTCM to make money also mean that volatility is much higher than traditional models assume. LTCM took the profits from the real market and comforted themselves with the stability of the theoretical model. LTCM's was a classic 'close to home' business strategy brought down in just four years by a risk that wasn't anticipated. Victims of their own success, they had to push into riskier transactions to try to get returns on ever-increasing capital. What they either forgot or ignored was the risk of a simultaneous downturn across all of their positions. Had they not used so much borrowing they may have had the flexibility to ride out the storm. But leveraged 28 times they were like the drunk walking along a very narrow pavement, one jolt after only four years of trading and they were in the gutter.

In other words...

Your intuition embodies everything you have learnt about your environment. Your intuitions can be a good guide when you are making decisions close to home when the decisions are frequent, in familiar contexts, give fast feedback and involve only a low proportion of wealth. But even close to home judgements based on intuition can also have some predictable errors. We can be misled by the availability bias and give undue weight to very few emotionally significant events; we presume association and then reinforce our prejudice; we become risk blind. Becoming a better decision maker 'close to home' requires that you keep learning about your commercial environment, record your decisions, keep looking for the surprising and never assume that it won't happen.

Which means that...

> Intuitions (distilled experience) from one environment may mislead you in another environment.

> Never lose touch with the commercial environment – customers, suppliers and competitors.

> You can learn more about your environment by talking to front line staff than you can by talking to strategy consultants.

> Keep looking out for surprises – the events that remind you that the world doesn't work the way you think it does.

> Long-term survival (keeping out of the gutter) is the true measure of a good company.

Rules of thumb

A ♦ Intuition gained in one environment can mislead in another

Q ♣ Close to home you *do* get luckier the more you practise

10 ♠ Keep learning – stay in touch with the commercial environment

3 ♦ Pay particular attention to the surprising

Chapter 9

Deciding far from home

In the last chapter we looked at the power of intuition when we are making decisions in the environment that shaped those intuitions – making decisions 'close to home'. This chapter focuses on the more challenging problem of how we make well-grounded decisions in unfamiliar environments – when we have to decide 'far from home'. These are the rare but significant decisions that all managers face. Because these decisions are in new contexts and because the feedback is often confused and delayed we don't have well-calibrated intuition to guide us. So how do we decide? Where does the confidence we need to act, and to get others to follow us, come from? The answers are both surprising and disturbing. We are easily beguiled by previous success, either our own success or that of others. Anthony Fisher's story, retold below, is one of thousands that could have been used to illustrate the point. In fact there are sound strategies for deciding in unfamiliar territory – using a geographical metaphor, we can hire a guide or we can start making a map.

Turtle burgers

THE ANTHONY FISHER STORY

For someone of his generation and his upbringing Anthony Fisher's life started in a conventional way. Educated at Eton, an RAF pilot in the Second World War then a job in the City. The rest of his life was anything but conventional. He left his job in 1950 to try to resuscitate the fortunes of the family farm in the South of England. His first experiment was to buy 200 day-old chicks and, with the help of an electric heater designed to mimic the heat of a mother hen, started to rear them in one 12 foot square stable. A foot and mouth epidemic led to the slaughter of the farm's cattle and Fisher used some of the compensation money to fund a trip to the US. It was there that he witnessed first-hand the potential for the mass production of poultry – 15,000 birds housed in a single building. To replicate this model of intensive farming in the UK would require access to birds specially bred to reach maturity as quickly as possible. Importing either live birds or eggs was illegal so he devised a plan to smuggle 20 White Rock eggs into Britain as Easter eggs, each one wrapped in silver paper. By May 1953 he had managed to develop a 2,500-bird flock and by August the same year he had 24,000 birds on the farm and the Buxted Chicken Company was formed. Expansion was rapid and by 1964 they were producing and processing 500,000 birds a week. As the volumes grew the cost of production fell. The price of a chicken to the consumer more than halved over the decade of Buxted's operation. Anthony Fisher had achieved what many politicians had promised and put a chicken in every pot. When the company he had founded was sold in 1968 Anthony Fisher was a rich man.

His second venture into food production was less successful. In 1967 he had read an article about the plight of the green sea turtle, which through over-fishing and loss of nesting habitat was coming under increasing threat. The human global population was growing rapidly and there was considerable concern about the ability of mankind to feed itself in the coming years. Fisher devised a plan to domesticate the turtles and intensively breed them as a high-protein, low-fat food source. A base was established on Grand Cayman, a company formed and investment secured. Eggs were taken from the wild under licence and hatched at the new facility.

The ambition from the start was enormous with 10 acres of breeding pens designed to house up to 100,000 green sea turtles – a vision clearly modelled on the success he had had with chicken production in the UK. In 1973, when the first ever successful captive breeding was achieved the prospects for the company looked positive, their vision simple, 'We believe the turtle food industry can become as big as the chicken industry in years to come' (Frost, 2002). There was interest in nearly every part of the turtle: shells for lampshades, oil for cosmetics, skin for leather, the penis as a Chinese aphrodisiac, even the hatchlings that died were being freeze dried and sold for encapsulating in resin as paperweights. However, demand for the meat, the main driver of the business plan, was going to have to be stimulated. Chefs were commissioned to produce turtle-based versions of classic dishes and a turtle meat cookbook was published.

Within a year the business was being closed down – virtually all of Fisher's fortune had been lost on the venture. The blow that defeated the company and deterred investors from investing any further capital was the growing environmental movement. In late 1973 the US passed an Act preventing the trade in products from endangered species (the green sea turtle had not been on the list when Fisher had started five years earlier) and because Fisher's company could not establish that the operation was 'farming' all of the US market was closed to it. Although this regulatory change may have dealt the final blow to the company it is not clear that there was, or was ever likely to be, a profitable business from farming turtles. In 6,000 years of human farming as few as a couple of dozen wild animal species have been successfully domesticated by man. The ambition of breeding and domesticating a new species, and simultaneously developing a demand for the meat amongst notoriously conservative eaters looks, from this perspective, to be a near impossible task. Anthony Fisher didn't lack confidence: a confidence, founded on his undoubted success in producing cheap chicken meat for an existing local market, which would carry him into totally new territory.

Deciding 'far from home'

Although it has some shortcomings, our intuitive reasoning is very smart. We learn fast, we recognize patterns, we can make excellent judgements based on our experience. But how do we make decisions when we are away from the familiar comfort of our normal surroundings? How do we decide when we are 'far from home' and don't have well-founded intuition to guide us?

Occasional, rare, unique These aren't decisions that come along every day, week or month. Most of them will not occur once a year. Quite often it may be a decision that you have never had to make before. An opportunity to acquire a competitor. The prospect of increasing your geographical coverage by opening a new office in Germany. Actions that either you as manager or the company as a whole have not taken before. You can't search your memories for previous instances and make a judgement about the relative likelihood of a success.

You can't search your memories for previous instances

Unfamiliar context Not only is the decision a rare occurrence, it will also, typically, be in an unfamiliar context. Situations where the everyday experiences of 'deciding close to home' do not apply.

Slow or no feedback Crucially, many of these 'far from home' decisions can take years or decades before feedback about the course of action chosen is established. In some situations there is no feedback; or if there is it is ambivalent and subject to misinterpretation.

High proportion of wealth Whereas most operational decisions put at risk only a small proportion of wealth, the decision to make a strategic change or to buy a competitor can put at risk most or all of the company's wealth. You are making a decision that is going to have enormous impact on the organization.

But the rare and important strategic decisions need to be made – not by a cadre of strategic thinkers in glass offices and certainly not by strategy consultants. So how *do* we, and more importantly how *should* we go about making these decisions where previous experience distilled as intuition is of no use? What is the advice to the decision makers deciding 'far from home'? I have isolated four ways in which we can be guided, or misguided, to make decisions in unfamiliar environments. We can back previous winners; we can copy the success of others; we can use an expert familiar with the terrain; or, continuing the geographical metaphor, we can set about building our own map of this unfamiliar country.

1 Backing a winner

Faced with a difficult decision our first instinct is often to back a proven winner. Someone who has demonstrated they have the 'right stuff' – the good judgement to ensure a good outcome in any situation. Past performance, we imagine, is a good guide to future performance. Sometimes that 'winner' is ourselves – our confidence high from a previous success.

2 Copy the success of others

Sometimes, if we don't have a previous success to (mis-)guide us; we may latch on to the success of others. This is a form of herding behaviour. If we can't decide from our own experience what to do then we copy what other apparently successful individuals are doing (remember the guppy from Chapter 3 choosing the mate that others have chosen). If it's good enough for them then it's probably good enough for me.

3 Hire a guide

In addition to backing a winner or following the crowd, another strategy for making those difficult decisions far from home is to hire a guide. Work with someone for whom the decisions, strange and unfamiliar for you, are second nature. Employ someone who has been here before and is deciding close to home. The guide may be a hired advisor or consultant, or they may be an equity sharing business partner.

4 Make a map

Lastly, when making those 'far from home' decisions, we can accept that we are in unfamiliar territory and start exploring. Making a map of the new terrain. Working out through trial and error how this new world works, discovering the delights and dangers ourselves. Looking, learning and testing as you go in order to feel at home as quickly as you can in an unfamiliar environment.

Better decision making 'far from home'

I have briefly described four generic approaches to making decisions far from home. I will now look at each one in turn to uncover the power and pitfalls of each.

Backing winners

Backing someone with a track record of success (whether yourself or someone else) to make the difficult decisions far from home is such a commonsense approach that it hardly seems worthy of discussion. But in fact it can lead to some very poor decision making. Once, as I have already argued, we accept that chance (and therefore luck) has a role in management then reliably interpreting track records becomes impossible. The challenge of untangling the relative importance of luck and skill when all you can read is the outcome of a decision is the subject for Chapter 11. Separating the lucky fool from the wise loser is surprisingly difficult. Track records are not always what they seem.

Even if we could be sure that past success was due to skill, and that luck played no part, there is still a problem with blindly backing past winners to make new and difficult decisions. We tend to regard good judgement to be a capability of an individual. Good education and a good mind, or so it is widely assumed, are all that are needed to be able to make successful judgements in any number of situations. But as we have seen, good judgement is built on experience of one environment.

One good outcome and we label people as 'winners'. Confidence soars and we believe they can apply their proven judgement in any situation –

> *One good outcome and we label people as 'winners'*

even situations that are very different from the environments in which judgements have been developed. Would Anthony Fisher have embarked on the turtle farming venture if he had not had success from rearing chickens? Although superficially similar, the challenges facing the turtle breeding business were immense and only a fraction of the learning from Buxted was likely to be relevant. Any one of a dozen new challenges could have led to a failure in the new venture. The entire process of domestication – sourcing food, managing disease, supporting the breeding cycle – was fraught with risk and uncertainty. But success depended not only on overcoming all of these challenges but also in developing consumer demand in world markets for a novel food. As it turned out it was changing social attitudes and growing environmental awareness that was to prove critical – a risk that I doubt Fisher ever considered. One success can give rise to enormous self-confidence tempting us into ventures where the previous success has no or little relevance to the new challenge. (I will look in more detail at entrepreneurial overconfidence in the next chapter.) The strategy of backing past winners can be very misleading. A good decision maker in one environment can be a very poor decision maker in another. Better decision making far from home requires us to take a sceptical attitude of the confidence we gain from other successes.

Copying the success of others

The herding strategy of copying the success of others is another strategy we adopt when we have to make decisions far from home. Jeff Bezos's early success with Amazon in the late nineties generated an enormous amount of media coverage – articles, profiles, TV interviews. Bezos and Amazon were everywhere. The message was very clear. Here was someone who had no previous experience of either book retailing or the internet. He had the advantage of being an early mover (not the first mover, see Chapter 7), and his vision was enormous. In late 1998 I was planning for the launch of baby-world.co.uk but I had no experience of publishing for the parenting market, no internet experience, and no retail experience. All of my business knowledge had been gained under the generous safety blanket of large corporations. I did what many others did at that time, I used the Amazon story as my surrogate. I had no idea of the real chance of success (the total number of successes divided by the total number of people who tried – called the base rate) but here was a story I could understand. A plausible path from vision and commitment to enormous success. For a lot of people Amazon.com was proof that if your timing was right and your vision bold enough then you would succeed. One borrowed example, second-hand experience that I used to make life changing and very risky decisions.

Following the herd and copying what works for others is not necessarily a bad strategy but it pays to be aware of the risks that you are taking when you use other people's triumphs to encourage you to take the plunge. Your role model may have been lucky – you may not be. Your role model and her team may have a much better intuitive understanding of the market-place than your team. If that is the case then they may be able to exercise better and quicker judgements than you. You may still succeed but you will probably need luck to be on your side. The poker player can mimic the betting style of his hero having read the books and studied the online tuto-rials. But, as is likely to be the case, the pupil's judgement will be less well developed than that of the star player. To match their success will require more good fortune than can reasonably be expected.

Hiring a guide

Feel uncomfortable making decisions outside of your area of experience? Then hire someone who has been there before. Using an expert with the sound judgement that comes from experience is sound advice when we are faced with difficult decisions far from home. But it is a strategy that can be often overlooked if our confidence is buoyed up by a previous success or because we are following the herd. It isn't just entrepreneurs that overlook the vital role of using experts in far from home decision making. Investors can be just as guilty of over-reliance on track record. In the dot.com boom successful and highly regarded management consultants and investment bankers (all of whom, tellingly, kept their day jobs while they sought fund-ing) had put together immaculate business plans for new web services. That nobody in the management team had any first-hand experience of the customers they were planning to serve was of no consequence to the investors. Industry knowledge seemed a luxury not a necessity – both investors and would-be entrepreneurs making the assumption that a management team of good generalists could be relied upon to make the right decisions. More of these plans were funded than now, with hindsight, seems wise. Then, mocking the popular acronyms of the day, it was 'back to consultancy' (B2C) and 'back to banking' (B2B). But using experts to guide you is not without problems and in Chapter 11 I look in some detail at the challenges of expert overconfidence and self-serving bias.

Making a map

As we have seen, backing a winner and copying the success of others are strategies for solving the difficult problem of far from home decision making that can easily lead to inappropriate confidence. Confidence that conceals from us the true risks that we are taking. 'Map making' is my shorthand for the process of exploring new territory. But unlike the (over)confidence that can make us cavalier with risk, map making starts with the assumption that we know nothing about this new terrain. We have no special wisdom or skill that is going to guarantee success. Consequently the map maker will work slowly, taking small steps and testing the environment at every opportunity, and taking nothing for granted. Map making is a way of building expertise in a new environment step by step rather than assuming that patterns and solutions from another environment can be rolled out. Once again the Anthony Fisher story vividly illustrates the point.

ANTHONY FISHER continued

Fisher's first experiments in rearing chickens were self-financed. He took small steps, solving the problems of disease control and high-density rearing before facing the challenges of processing, and always working with an established demand from a local market. For the turtle venture the situation couldn't have been more different. Now with a track record of success Fisher was able to use both his own capital from the sale of Buxted and new capital from investors keen to back a proven winner. With Fisher's own confidence high and substantial funds available the step by step approach that characterized the first venture was ignored. The first experiment in rearing chickens was 200 chicks in a stable; the first turtle breeding facility had capacity for 100,000 turtles in specially built pens. Commercial territory that was cautiously explored in the UK was taken in one giant stride for the Cayman-based venture. But these wild creatures had never been bred in captivity let alone domesticated. The market for their products was tiny. Everything about the venture was uncertain. An opportunity in unfamiliar territory that should have been explored cautiously, one step at a time. Instead, with the confidence and cash from one previous success Fisher and his backers took enormous risks.

The art of map making in unfamiliar environments is central to the art of decision making and I will look at it in more detail in Chapter 12. But Fisher's riches to rags story (not literally because a wealthy second wife kept him from financial ruin) is a powerful testimony to the danger of overconfidence born of previous success. Good judgement is born of experience, not high IQ or a classical education.

Risk profiles and business models

In the last chapter I highlighted that some business models make predominant use of decision making that is 'close to home'. Insurance, banking, consultancy and other professional service businesses all involve a high number of very similar decisions, each involving a relatively small proportion of the total net worth, and with rapid feedback. Consequently these businesses will have all of the advantages of 'close to home decision making' but also be prone to the dangers of risk blindness and the fact that each small billing event carries with it a very unlikely, but disproportionately large, downside risk. Unsurprisingly, I will call these 'close to home' business models.

Contrast this with businesses that have to make very significant but relatively rare decisions; a film production company may only fund one project a year; Disney may fund one or two major theme parks a decade at a cost of tens of billions of dollars; a global car manufacturer that has to launch a new model; a large private equity firm making a $1 billion buyout decision. The key resource allocation decisions that are taken here are characteristic of far from home decision making. They are rare, the feedback is slow, the contexts are often different from previous decisions, and they involve a significant proportion of wealth.

The pattern of risk and return is also very different. For the business that uses 'close to home' decision making the return on each individual investment decision is small and relatively predictable. The earnings are sure and steady although there is often an associated low probability risk of a catastrophic loss. In contrast the business model that utilizes 'far from home' decision making will have a very different pattern of returns. In the film and private equity industries many investments are either loss making or make inadequate returns. But every so often one of the films or investments will do spectacularly well and more than compensate for the poor performance of the other decisions. Lots of misses but a few big wins.

These two distinct investment patterns – small and reliable but with a chance of a catastrophic loss, contrasted with big and risky with an occasional jackpot – are built into many walks of life. In soccer the defender needs to make tackle after tackle with high reliability. Lots of small constant rewards (for a successful tackle) but always the threat of a big loss (a mistake that concedes a goal). At the other end of the pitch the striker is following the opposite logic. Run after run is made for no return, maybe once a match it works and the pay-off is enormous – a goal is scored. Lots of wasted effort for no return, then one huge pay out.

These are two distinct patterns of risk and reward – two styles of investment. Organizations will have different structures and cultures depending on the predominant style of investment. The organizations that utilize lots of small, routine decisions about resource deployment will make investment decisions throughout the organization but with tight procedural controls that limit discretion. The cultural emphasis will be on procedure, training, compliance and control. These will be organizations without heroes, just good procedures and efficient management. Contrast this with organizations whose investment decisions are rare and big. Decision making is tightly held at the centre and there will be less emphasis on controls or systems. Success is whatever works. These are businesses with clearly identifiable heroes – the people associated with the few really big wins and a culture that is trying to recapture prior success with each new decision – signing the same stars for the next film project, bringing in the same CEO for the private equity turnaround. I will call these 'far from home' business models.

Which business model does your business employ? Some businesses may employ different investment styles at different stages. For example, producing a monthly magazine involves a lot of 'close to home' decision making but launching a new consumer magazine is a classic example of deciding 'far from home'. I have set out below some of the key characteristics and dangers of each type of business model.

	'Close to home' business models	'Far from home' business models
Nature of investment risk	Routine investments that: > are frequent > are in a familiar context > have reliable feedback > take a small proportion of total wealth	Lumpy investments that: > are occasional > are in new contexts > provide unreliable feedback > take a high proportion of wealth
Organizational structure	> Decentralised but with strong procedures and controls	> Centralized decision making with loose or informal controls
Management culture	> Monitoring, control and compliance > Efficiency drives and process re-engineering	> 'Flirtatious': toying with many prospects, but then... > 'whatever it takes', total commitment to one project > Heroes and villains > Gods and scapegoats
Examples	> High street banking > Professional service companies > Outsourcing service providers > Retail > Utilities	> Film and TV production > Private equity > Any large-scale consumer product launch
Business model risks	> Boiled frog syndrome (not noticing slow changes in the environment) > Risk blindness to very rare but catastrophic events > Complacency	> Backing mediocre opportunities > A series of misses that will wipe you out > Too much confidence in 'winners' in a different environment
Safeguards	> Top managers need to stay close to the front line > Be aware of the rare but ever-present risks > Constantly look for the unexpected	> See lots of opportunities before committing to the best > Back people with relevant experience – not just 'winners' > Hire an expert for each new situation

In other words...

When we decide 'close to home' we can use intuition distilled from our past experiences, but sometimes we have to make decisions 'far from home' when intuition can be a very poor guide. Decisions far from home can be characterized as: rare or unique; in unfamiliar contexts; with limited feedback; and involving a high proportion of wealth. We can still have 'hunches' about the best course of action but these may be based on some very unreliable sources: backing your own or someone else's past success in a different context or copying the successful strategy of others. It is easy for both investors and entrepreneurs to be seduced by the idea that good decision making is an innate property of the individual manager rather than the product of experience in one environment. Faced with decision making in an unfamiliar context it can be better to use a guide – someone who knows the lie of the land. But perhaps the most effective long-term strategy is to acknowledge that in unfamiliar contexts the judgements learnt in another situation may not apply. Building long-term value in an unfamiliar environment is not achieved by applying sweeping generalizations from previous experience (although don't be deceived by the few that get lucky with this strategy). It is achieved by accepting your ignorance and being willing to learn fast and fail fast.

Understand which of the two basic models your business deploys. Does it rely on a frequent and familiar investments to make a steady gain – 'close to home'; or does it rely on occasional large investments with high risk – 'far from home'. Each business model relies on a different style of decision making and each has its characteristic weaknesses and dangers. Know how your wealth-creating decisions are made so you can arm yourself against the dangers of complacency or hero worship.

Which means that...

> If you do feel confident in your judgement when faced with a decision far from home you need to reflect on where your confidence may come from – well-grounded experience or empty dreams built on other people's stories of success?

> If you are deciding in unfamiliar terrain then you should consider hiring a guide (an expert)

> Best of all, accept the novelty of the new situation and take time to build your own map of the unknown terrain. Learn to be at home in the new environment.

> As investor or entrepreneur, be aware of the false security that prior success in a different environment can bring.

> Understand the basic pattern of investment that your business uses to make money and be aware of the inevitable dangers

Rules of thumb

6 ◆ Consider hiring a guide when faced with decisions in unfamiliar terrain

7 ◆ Success can breed overconfidence

Chapter **10**

Overconfidence and the entrepreneur

In the last chapter I identified four strategies we sometimes use when faced with decisions in unfamiliar situations: backing winners, following the herd, using experts and making maps. In fact we often rely on an innate sense of confidence in our own judgement. This chapter looks at the sources of this confidence (in fact overconfidence). My focus is the overconfidence of entrepreneurs but it applies just as well to the assessment of any new venture.

A paradox – loss aversion vs. entrepreneurial optimism

Consider this opportunity. There will be a single throw of a fair die. If you throw a 1, 2, 3 or 4 you lose whatever you have been prepared to wager on the throw. If you throw a 5 or a 6 you win two and a half times your stake (plus your original stake – making a total return of three and half times the stake). Would you risk £10 on such an opportunity? Would you risk £100, £1,000 or maybe £100,000? Would you accept the wager if all your savings and possibly your home were at risk? Researchers have found that very few people would invest much money in this wager even though it has a positive expectation. (If the stake is £10 then the expected value is £11.67. The chance of winning, 1/3, multiplied by the gain of £25 plus the stake of £10 returned. Mathematically, 33% x (£25 + £10) = £11.67). They found people were willing to invest more money if they knew that they could sign up for three or more 'plays' – enabling them to spread the risk and give themselves three or more chances of the pay out (a portfolio strategy). But if it was a single throw of the die this was seen as an unattractive wager. The prize is not worth the risk. We know people are generally risk averse (this idea is explored in Chapter 13) so this is not a surprising result. The high likelihood of the loss (67%) looms larger than the unlikely gain.

What has this go to do with entrepreneurship? Exact figures for the overall failure rate of new businesses are difficult to determine. A major study by Dun and Bradstreet (1967) concluded that two-thirds of new businesses failed within the first four years. Another study of US firms (Dunne et al., 1988) recorded in a census of manufacturers between 1963 and 1982 found that 62% of new firms were gone within five years, 80% had disappeared within ten years and that business failure was the main reason for the firms' disappearance from the census. In some areas of business the failure rate can be much higher – the restaurant industry quotes failure rates for independent restauranteurs as high as 80% in the first two years. Even if the businesses survive, the entrepreneur's expectations are very often not met. A representative study of 150 new businesses in Scotland (Reid and Smith, 2000) found 19% of the businesses didn't make it to the second year and a further 42% were classified as poor performers (measured by the growth in staff, profitability and productivity). The founders' dreams of fast cars and big houses were presumably on hold.

Whatever the actual rate of new business failure the Dun and Bradstreet figure suggests that on two-thirds of occasions the entrepreneurs' investment was lost. And yet there is no shortage of new businesses being started, indeed every year the number of new enterprises grows. Would-be entrepreneurs rush in every year putting their own savings and houses on the line – accepting a wager which, in the experimental laboratory, most people dismiss. What is going on in the mind of the entrepreneur that makes this seem like a reasonable wager?

Thanks to a survey of Californian entrepreneurs on the threshold of starting a new business (Cooper *et al.*, 1988) we do have an insight into their thinking. The entrepreneurs were asked to estimate their chance of success and then to estimate the average rate of success for businesses similar to their own ventures. The self-belief was striking. A third of the entrepreneurs believed their success was certain – that is they believed there was a 100% probability of their success. Overall, more than 80% believed they had a 70% or better prospect of success. Their optimism about their own enterprise was extreme. But they are also optimistic about the prospects of their peers. They believed that similar new ventures to their own would succeed 59% of the time, a figure much higher than the actual success rate of around a third. So not only were they overconfident about their own prospects but collectively they believed that most of their peers would do better than average!

So perhaps we have an answer to the paradox that I started with – why do entrepreneurs risk failure two-thirds of the time when most people decline such a wager for small stakes? If you misread your chance of failure to be 30% rather than 67% then the wager looks very different. With these probabilities the entrepreneurial wager looks very attractive. But we now have a new question to answer. Why do entrepreneurs overestimate their chances of success? Why are we overconfident?

Everyone's a winner

One answer is the availability bias, something we first encountered in Chapter 8. When we judge the relative likelihood of an event we trawl our memories for instances and our recollections are biased towards the most recent and the most memorable events. Our perception of the frequency is skewed to those events that are most 'available' to our memory. Unfortunately for the entrepreneur, business success is a lot more visible (and therefore more 'available') than business failure. The businesses that survive are fighting for our attention every day; the successful entrepreneurs are profiled in magazines and interviewed on television. The unsuccessful businesses are almost invisible. You eat at the successful restaurant, it is hard even to remember the restaurants that have come

The unsuccessful businesses are almost invisible

and gone over the years. Asked to assess the relative frequency of successes and failures, we infer a much higher chance of success than is justified. This availability bias is also behind some spectacular misrepresentation of probabilities in many areas of life (or death). What would you expect to be the ratio of tobacco-related deaths to fatalities in motor vehicle accidents? In fact tobacco kills roughly ten times more people than traffic accidents, but because of the media reporting of a few dramatic accidents with high emotional impact we overestimate their frequency. We know about tobacco-related deaths but the deaths are unexceptional and unreported. This has serious consequences about the ways in which we perceive risks and the steps we take individually and as a society to protect ourselves. The dramatic and the over-reported dominating both the policy debate and the public purse. The moral of the story is to look at the underlying rate – what statisticians call the base rate. There may be good reasons why the base rate does not apply to your situation, perhaps you are one of the entrepreneurs that is justified in believing your prospects are better than average, but in the absence of such evidence the base rate is the best guess, whatever your experience and sense of judgement suggests. The 67% base rate of entrepreneurial failure is the reality. The burden of proof for entrepreneurs is to find the reasons why that will not apply in their case. A relevant base rate is like a rock in bog of subjective judgments. Hoard them, consider them. See how often they confound your own judgement and received wisdom.

A history of the future

But for some events we either have no memories of prior instances or so few that it is impossible to arrive at an estimate of a future probability. How do we assess the likelihood of a nearby nuclear reactor suffering a serious accident when we have no experience of such accidents? How do we make judgements when we are away from our area of experience – 'far from home'? In these situations we construct a scenario. We literally construct a story in our minds that will get us from here and now (nuclear reactor working normally) to some future state (nuclear accident). To assess the probability of the nuclear accident we may focus on a few significant issues that may 'cause' an accident: poor training, an ageing plant, an inadequate inspection regime, operating compromises caused by commercial constraints. We create a 'history of the future' – building scenarios around a few factors which seem significant. If we can easily build a scenario – a particular history of the future – then we assume it has a high probability of happening. If the scenario seems difficult to construct then we assume the outcome is very unlikely. But this kind of thinking will produce biases. In this case our focus will be on the outcome that arises from one chain of thought that follows the path of least resistance. We will ignore the outcome that may arise from a large number of different scenarios even though each scenario has a small probability and involves some 'uphill' assumptions.

This recalls the danger of deciding close to home when experience tells us to ignore the unlikely but potentially catastrophic rare events. Once again we find people not doing what the decision theorists think we should – carefully balancing the probabilities and outcomes of all the potential outcomes. We find that we decide by focusing on a few main scenarios converting 'probable' into 'certain', and 'unlikely' into 'impossible'. Contrast this thinking with the Monte Carlo engine that maps future histories of every scenario giving a reliable feel for the distribution of outcomes. In contrast, it seems, we follow just a couple of scenarios that seem plausible and assume they represent a good approximation for the likely outcome, giving no regard for the numerous future histories that give unfavourable outcomes because each of these alternatives is, by itself, improbable.

This process of mental simulation or scenario building is exactly the process that the would-be entrepreneur has to go through. They will go on a mental journey from business plan to high value exit. Step by step – from market research, to product development, to building the organization, marketing, launch and ultimate high-value sale to a competitor. If we can easily create in our minds a picture of a successful outcome, with key assumptions that appear reasonable, then we assume that the probability of success is high. If we struggle to create a plausible scenario then we tend to think of the outcome as unlikely. Building and playing with scenarios is a vital part of the creative process of building a business. We create histories of the future where we focus on the causal links that lead to success. But as we have seen one scenario worked through in exact detail can be a very poor guide to the overall prospect of success. To make the successful transition from business plan to market leader requires many steps, each one dependent on the success of the previous step. The market research needs to identify an exploitable opportunity, the product development has to be able to allow a product to be developed at reasonable cost, the right people have to be employed to plan and execute the launch, the production or service delivery has to work as planned. Success depends on a series of crucial events – none of which are certain. And yet the overall success of the business depends on a successful outcome at each step.

Even if the probability of success at each stage is 80% (i.e. we estimate that there is an 80% chance of the market research identifying the opportunity, etc.) but there are five critical stages then, mathematically, the chance of achieving the final goal is 0.8^5 ($0.8 \times 0.8 \times 0.8 \times 0.8 \times 0.8$) or about 33%. But as we have seen, we don't assess risks in this way. We do not sum all of the probabilities of each step and we don't weigh the overall gain against the cumulative risk. We focus on one main scenario and one or two main variations. We leap willingly from step to step, focusing on the most plausible scenario and oblivious of the way in which the cumulative probabilities are multiplying. So, whether by misjudging frequencies, or by being unaware of compounding risks, we underestimate our chances of failure.

Entrepreneurial optimism vs. investor scepticism

Perhaps now we can understand why, despite the unbounded optimism of entrepreneurs, that venture capitalists are so wary of start ups. Delivering a successful business and creating a return for both the investor and the entrepreneur is a risky business. Venture capitalists prefer investment opportunities where there is only one very clear and well understood risk – for example taking a successful regional business national, taking a national business across borders, adding one new product to an already established customer base. For an established business the management team, the market acceptability of the pricing strategy and the production technology are already established and will not present significant risks. In fact there is nothing the venture capitalist likes better than an investment *without* an operational risk. If financial engineering can release value with highly-leveraged bank finance without the need to take market, management, or operational risks, then so much the better. By contrast the business start up has everything to prove. Step after step along the critical path has an uncertain outcome. To the entrepreneur the scenario seems more than plausible. After all, the business plan she has spent six months refining has required her to live inside this successful scenario day after day. Confidence rises and it is possible to imag-

the business start up has everything to prove

ine why a third of the Californian entrepreneurs in the study believed they had a 100% chance of success. But the professional investor has two different perspectives. Firstly, he is much more aware of the base rate for successful start ups. Perhaps for no other reason than that he has lost money on some earlier early-stage investments and these failures will be very much 'available' to him. Secondly, looking at the business plan from the outside he will be much more aware of the individual risks that compound to give the overall chance of success. He will see each step not as part of an inevitable path to glory but as a series of mutually dependent risks – any one of which can bring down the whole.

The entrepreneur has inhabited her business scenario for so long that she will find it very difficult to step back and see the opportunity as others will see it. These different perspectives can be characterized as 'inside' and 'outside' views. The inside view is the entrepreneurs' view, focusing on the problem and the internal variables that can be controlled and altered to achieve the goal. The outside view ignores the specific details and focuses on the base rate success for projects of this type. The different views draw on different sets of information to reach probability estimates about the same situation. It is not that the inside view is wrong. Belief and confidence, even if misplaced, can be essential if you want to achieve any complex task. But as an entrepreneur you need to be aware that there is another view. You have to be prepared to look from the outside in if you want to getter a better calibration on your judgement of your probability of success. You need to be able to see your business plan as others will see it. It is far too common for entrepreneurs to blame investors' scepticism on their lack of vision rather than acknowledging the validity of their outside view and their greater awareness of the base rate.

But it is also possible for the entrepreneur to improve her 'inside' thinking – to build more realistic scenarios, with a better calibrated judgement of success. This can be achieved by taking time to look at future histories where the venture was a failure rather than a success – not something we normally like to spend much time doing. But actively spending time thinking about the reasons why a venture may fail, you not only build a more balanced view of the chances of success, but you also build an understanding of the critical issues that need to be addressed. Can you list the three most likely reasons for failure? Lack of finance, competitor response, inability to recruit necessary skills, market timing (too early or too late), poor marketing or customer apathy and a hundred other factors can lead to a business failure. However unpalatable, imagining these possible future histories builds a better understanding of the risks than an endless rerunning of the same successful scenario with a couple of minor variations. We can never give our attention to all of the millions of scenarios that a full Monte Carlo simulation can generate but we need to have worked through a range of possibilities, the good as well as the bad, in order to get a realistic appreciation of the chances of success.

The curse of overconfidence

So far I have looked at the way entrepreneurs misjudge the probability of their success based on misrepresenting frequencies or focusing on successful scenarios. But there is another trick that our minds play on us when we try to assess our prospects – we systematically overestimate our ability to influence the outcome. We are not as good as we think we are. We suffer from an illusion of control.

Experts tend to over-estimate the quality of their judgements. The same failing applies to all of us in everyday situations where we have no particular expertise. One well-documented example of this overconfidence comes from our abilities as amateur investors and stock pickers. Barber and Odean (2000) made a study of individuals' stock portfolios during a bull market when the market rose 17.9%. On average the personal portfolios performed 1.5% below the market as a whole. However, the 12,000 portfolios (20% of the sample) that were the most actively traded – where investors sought to use their expertise to adjust their selection to maximize returns – was a substantial 6.5% below the market as a whole. In a follow-up study (2001) they looked at the differing strategies of men and women and discovered that it was the men who fared less well than the women (though both underperformed the market). The men were less able than the women to sit on their hands and stick with their initial stock selections and through the course of a year changed over three-quarters of their portfolios. In contrast the women, on average, changed just over half of their portfolios. The women's better return was not because they chose better stocks but because by changing less often they experienced lower transaction costs. The men's conceit was that they could continually improve their performance by adjusting their portfolios. In fact this resulted in no improvement in stock selection but a slow leaking away of profits in commission. Both sexes, but the men to a greater extent, had the unfounded confidence that they could make stock selections that could out perform the market. They couldn't.

There is one very neat experiment (Camerer and Lovallo, 1999) that was set up to illustrate the overconfidence that plagues entrepreneurial judgement. The experiment consisted of a game with eight players (mostly business students). For each round of the game the players could decide if they wanted to enter that round or sit out and wait for the next round. Before the students decided whether to enter a round, they were told how many entrants in each round would be successful – a number that varied from two to eight. Prizes were awarded to players in each round. For example, in one round it would be announced that there would be four winners gaining prizes that varied from $20 to $5 and players who didn't win a prize had to pay $10. With this information players, with the aim of maximizing their returns, had to decide whether to enter the round or sit it out. Two versions of the game were played, one where the prizes were distributed by chance, and one where the prizes were awarded based on the ability to solve puzzles and answer trivia questions.

When the prizes were distributed by chance, the students made money from the game. They were correctly able to judge whether a round was worth entering based on the number of prizes available, the probability of winning and the cost of entry. But as soon as skill was involved more students entered the round than could win. They didn't consider themselves to be luckier than average, but they did think they were more skilful than average – even though

They overestimated their abilities relative to their competitors

they knew that the students for the study had been recruited on the basis that it would involve a test of skill or knowledge. The students were good judges of their prospects in a game of chance, poor judges in a game of skill. They overestimated their abilities relative to their competitors.

Camerer and Lovallo, the researchers who designed the game described above, used the term 'reference group neglect' to describe the phenomenon. We are aware of our own abilities, but we don't acknowledge the abilities of others and consequently overestimate our chances of winning. In support of reference group neglect they quote Joe Roth, chairman of Walt Disney explaining why so many big films are released from different studios on the same holiday weekends, 'Hubris. Hubris. If you think about your own business, you think , 'I've got a good story department, I've got a good marketing department, we're going to go out and do this.' And you don't think that everyone else is thinking the same way' (Camerer and Lorallo, 1990). Too many players enter the market. Overconfident in their ability, neglecting the competition, some are bound to lose.

Reference group neglect is not a phrase that is often heard around the poker tables. But the better players will recognize the concept. It is all too easy, having a strong hand, to keep betting and raising, paying little regard to your opponents. A good hand may not be the best hand and it takes an experienced player and an accurate reader of an opponent's hand to be able to fold a good hand when you suspect that your opponent has a better hand. But the concept is just as common around the boardroom table as it is around the poker table. Management teams, like entrepreneurs, spend a lot of time working with the 'insider's' view of the company. Focused on their own team and their own strengths they underestimate the competitors' products. They also overlook their competitors' ability to change strategy, innovate, or respond aggressively. I have repeatedly seen business plans which make no acknowledgment of how competitors may react to a new product or new sales.

Business plans: the planning fallacy and illusions of control

This reflection on the enthusiasm of the entrepreneur has brought together two of the key themes that keep recurring in this book. Managers don't do the things that the decision theorists say they should. They don't make choices between alternatives by maximizing expected utility (the product of the likely financial outcome and the probability of it occurring). Managers it seems are poor at understanding or calculating probabilities and will focus on one or two highly probable scenarios and ignore a host of low probability outcomes regardless of the consequences. But managers also believe that the future can be predicted and controlled. Intricate long-term plans can be made; risks can be managed. They have an unshakeable belief in their ability to control events. A nice example of the illusion of control comes from gamblers playing dice. They will place bigger bets before their throw than they will after a throw but before the numbers on the dice are revealed. The gambler is suffering from the illusion that she has some control over the outcome of the throw. Consequently she will gamble more when she still has the (illusory) opportunity to influence the throw.

The two managerial conceits of being able to control events and make long-term forecasts with accuracy come together in the business plan. This can be any long-term business forecast but in the context of this chapter it is the three- to five-year plan that is created to secure funding. The business plan will crystallize one scenario; one five-year prediction about costs, revenues, competitor reaction, market growth and macro-economic performance. The commentary in the business plan may have some simple scenario analysis – a few reruns of the numbers with some different market growth or market share assumptions. But in essence there will be a spreadsheet that captures in enormous and inappropriate detail a five-year chain of predictable events that is one scenario. And yet these business plans are treated, sometimes literally, as promises to investors. (I have seen investment agreements where, should the business plan not match reality three months in succession, the investor effectively acquires complete management and financial control of the company.) Seeing the business plan as a five-year promise may suit the investors by keeping the management team on the defensive but is a ludicrous misrepresentation of the reality of planning. The entrepreneur's business plan ends up as a symbol of both the mismatch of power between investor and investee (or head-office and operating company) and the fallacy that managers can plan for the long-term future. A planning fallacy established by the shared belief that the science of management can explain everything and that therefore the diligent manager can make confident predictions about the future. The comfort of inappropriately detailed plans and persistent over-confidence is a dangerous combination. Perhaps we shouldn't be surprised that two-thirds of new business ventures fail.

These days I prepare business plans for third party investment and review other managers' business plans for potential investment. The business plan has a role, but instead of seeing it as promise to investors I see it like a candidate's curriculum vitae. The business plan is an opportunity for management to demonstrate its knowledge of the market and the customer, and the relationship between cost and sales price. Management's sales forecast for the 37th month is worthless – its ability to make good decisions in the face of an unpredictable market is everything.

The glamour of entrepreneurship

Fame and fortune can be achieved for a lucky few in a number of careers. The film, music and sports industries turn their top performers into multi-millionaires and give them the status of idols. A teenager starting out at the bottom of the industry is effectively buying a lottery ticket where the jackpot is life-transforming but the prospects of success negligible and life on the bottom rung is hard and poorly remunerated. In the past few years, catalyzed by the dot.com boom entrepreneurship has become a high status activity. Our most admired business people are not the corporate leaders of previous decades but the maverick entrepreneurs who have risked all and won. So perhaps all of our care-ful evaluation of the probabilities of success is

Regardless of the odds thousands will try every year

irrelevant. The lure of the wealth and status that comes with entrepreneur-ial success is too great. Regardless of the odds thousands will try every year even though only a tiny percentage will hit the jackpot. This is in effect a lottery for career choice – a big prize with a very small chance of success. If the emotional impact of the potential prize is big enough we will buy a ticket regardless of how small our chance of winning.

Necessary confidence and biding your time

One of the arguments for overconfidence is that it is an essential compo-nent for action. If we were all realistic about our not very good prospects for achieving our goals then nothing would happen. As a society, it can be argued, and as individuals, we need an element of overconfidence. It can be argued that it is far better for the manager or entrepreneur to believe they can change the world and try (even if they are likely to fail) than to believe that nothing can be done and stay at home. But my advice is for the individual manager not society as a whole. Most entrepreneurs get only one, or if they are lucky a couple, of worthwhile opportunities in a lifetime. An honest assessment of your chances of success is not an excuse for not bothering but a reminder to make the most of the opportunities that you do get.

I have made this point to MBA students before, many of whom are planning entrepreneurial careers. They have interpreted my point here as general advice against taking the plunge. This is a point that I answer with a metaphor from poker. You have been playing most of the evening with very poor hands. You haven't had the strong hands to back and you start to get bored. Finally you are dealt a half-decent hand and become convinced that this is the hand you have been waiting for. Your frustration and boredom overcoming any doubts about the quality of the cards or your opponent's strength, you dive in with a big raise. After all, these are the best cards you have had all evening, if you don't bet now... But I have seen entrepreneurs do exactly the same thing. They have got bored with their corporate jobs and crave the glamour and excitement of being entrepreneurs. The first half-decent idea that they can hang a plausible business plan on will be the one they back. They will spend no time questioning where their gut-feeling has come from. They will not ask if their instincts are well founded. The advice to the poker player and the entrepreneur is the same. If you are going to back a hand with all of your chips make sure it is good enough. If you are not sure, pass and wait, there will be another deal; you may get a clearer opportunity. (Remember the 37% rule for mate choice – you should not commit until you have seen over a third of the likely opportunities, then chose the first one that is better than the rest.) Likewise for the entrepreneur – you may only get the one chance so make sure it the best opportunity you can. Better to pass the 'OK' opportunity and wait for a better one, than plough on because the timing feels right, or because you have got a poorly grounded sense of optimism. You will never make the commitment to starting a business without a sense of optimism and confidence. You need to be as sure as you can that that confidence is well grounded.

In other words...

Even when we don't have well-grounded intuition to guide our decision making we can still have confidence in our ability to succeed. Unfortunately, this confidence is often misplaced. When we are venturing into unfamiliar territory, which is often the case for entrepreneurs, we can be poor judges of our chance of success. We underestimate the likelihood of failure because business failures are much less visible to us than the successes. We build histories of the future that dwell on successful scenarios – we skip over the paths that lead to failure giving us an 'insider's' view and a false sense of confidence. In contrast the 'outsider' looking at the base rate is likely to be much more sceptical. This overconfidence leads to an illusion of control – a false confidence that we can plan confidently into the future.

Which means that...

> Don't rush into the first entrepreneurial opportunity – you only get to pursue a few opportunities in a lifetime, so like the poker player, wait for the best hands. (Remember the 37% rule – use the first third to assess the range, and then choose the best after that.)

> Try to find relevant base rates and incorporate them into your thinking. A low base rate doesn't mean you shouldn't proceed, it just means you are going into a risky venture with your eyes open.

> Improve your 'inside' thinking by exploring scenarios that lead to failure as well as success.

> Take time out from business planning to keep a view on what the 'outsider' sees.

> A business plan necessarily represents only one of many possible future histories – never convince yourself or allow others to believe it is literally true.

Rules of thumb

8 ♥ Take an outsider's view of your business plan
6 ♥ Don't believe your own business plan – it is just one of an infinite number of alternative futures

Chapter **11**

The trouble with winners and experts

This chapter focuses on the problems encountered with two of the strategies I outlined in Chapter 9 for making decisions far from home: backing winners and using experts. I will look in detail at track records and how separating luck from skill is much more difficult than we might imagine. I also explore some of the problems that may occur when we use an expert to guide us in unfamiliar terrain. They know the ground but there are some dangers which you need to be aware of. But I start with the story of a 13-year track record of success.

The perfect track record?

Most people are not sophisticated investors. When we are making decisions about where to invest our savings most of us are 'far from home' – we are amateurs without the experience or information of the professionals. It seems to make sense to let a professional, a fund manager, do the selection and decision making for us. And if we are going to use a professional, then it would seem to make sense to pick the one with the best track record. The assumption is that past performance is the best predictor of future performance. We back a winner.

Peter Lynch is a legend in the US's managed fund industry. He managed the Fidelity Magellan Fund from 1977 to 1990. During his tenure the performance of the fund was astounding. A $10,000 investment in the fund in 1977 would have been worth $280,000 in 1990 – an average annual rate of return of over 29%, beating the S&P500 index in 11 of his 13 years in charge. It should be remembered that this period also included the 1987 crash when markets fell by up to 23% across the world. And it didn't take long for investors to notice this star performer. The fund launched with just $20 million under management. By 1990 this had ballooned to $14 billion as shrewd investors spotted a winner and wanted some of the success for themselves. The longer the success went on – the more the investors rushed in. Peter Lynch's superior judgement shining out over more than a decade

Hot hands – streaks and runs in sport

Sport is another domain where people back winners. Players can be in form or out of form; they have runs when they are 'hot' and runs when they are not. Soccer players can score in game after game, or suffer a goal drought for half a season. Basketball players can have streaks when every shot seems to score and then another time when every shot bounces out. If you want to guess who will score next do what every sport fan knows: pick a winner – pick the player in form. Or should you?

American sport is dominated by statistics. Individual players' performances are recorded and studied in enormous detail. This provides an extraordinarily rich data source for the statistician. For basketball these data have been mined to answer the simple question: Is there a 'hot hand' in basketball? Does a player who has just succeeded in making a shot with his last two or three attempts have a better than average chance of making the next shot? In other words, do players have hot streaks where their immediate past performance influences the next shot? Or is it random – with the chance of success being independent of whether the last shot, or sequence of shots, was successful or not?

It turns out that professional basketball players make about 50% of their shots from the field (i.e. from open play and not including free throws). So the question being asked is whether the sequence of hits and misses of basketball field shots is different from a random sequence of heads and tails of a fair coin. To be honest, it seems like a fairly dumb question to ask if you talk to players, coaches and fans. When asked if they believed that there was 'streak shooting' in basketball, 91% believed there was a higher probability of a success after two or three successes. The experts who watch, play and coach the game certainly believe in streak shooting. What did the data show?

In the study of the data from the Philadelphia 76ers 1980-81 season (Gilovich *et al.*, 1985), the researchers could find no evidence that the previous success or failure influenced the next shot. The data showed no streak shooting – in fact eight of the nine players studied showed a slight negative correlation – an average success rate of 54% following a miss and an average 51% success rate following a hit. The same study also looked at the average length of runs (consecutive sequences of hits or misses) and at data from free throws. The same result. No correlation was found – each throw was independent – there was no memory of the previous throws to influence the outcome of each new shot. Why is this a surprising result? Because we think we 'know' what gives rise to the 'streaks'. We can imagine a plausible scenario that will influence the results of throws. We think we can see a causal link. Players get tired and start missing more and more shots; as shots go in players become more confident – and we believe that confidence is crucial to sporting performance. And yet whichever way you look at the data – they show a sequence that is indistinguishable from a random sequence.

Humans are very good at spotting patterns, at seeking out causes and explanations, at telling stories. It seems to be part of our nature that we will see a guiding hand in random data – attribute motives and cause. This is part of the appeal of the management theories that we use to explain past success and failure. Many of these theories are nothing more than stories, plausible tales that give us a (misplaced) sense of confidence in our ability to control events. We believe that there is a reason behind every sequence of sporting, investment or management success. If there is a reason then performance can be controlled and predicted. But when we

Backing a winner to make the next shot has no foundation

look at the data the sequence is random. It doesn't mean that some players, stock pickers and managers aren't more skilful than others – an idea we will explore later in the chapter. But in basketball, contrary to the opinions of the people who play and watch the game regularly, there is no memory from one shot to the next. The sequences we believe we see and explain are in fact random. Backing a winner to make the next shot has no foundation. But try telling that to the 84% of fans who think it is vital to get the ball to a player who is on a streak.

Backing winners on the stock market

Like American sport, the quoted prices of public companies are a statistician's dream. Not surprisingly, many studies have been done analysing the price performance of individual companies and of investment funds. Unlike sport, where refuting a received wisdom can raise an eyebrow, being able to detect patterns in share prices or fund performance is the way to a fortune. Of the hundreds of studies of price movements in stocks and funds I am going to focus on just one – the performance of mutual fund managers (Peter Lynch's peers). The study (Carhart, 1997) sought to answer the question: Does good fund performance in one year predict good performance in the next year? Just as before, when we asked whether a series of basketball throws had a memory of past performance, we are now asking whether this year's top performing fund manager helps you to predict next year's top performers. The study looked at every known mutual fund from 1962 to1993. For every year, each fund was placed into one of ten groups depending on the return it had generated, the top 10%, the next 10% and so on. The study looked at the top 10% of funds – the highest achievers – and then followed these 'winners' for subsequent years.

If the performance of the funds was random you could expect last year's winners to be evenly distributed between each of the ten groups in the following year. But that wasn't what was found. There was a tendency for last year's winners to find themselves back in the top group for the next year (roughly 20% of the time when a random distribution would have been 10%). There *was* a winner's effect – the winners did repeat (to a limited extent – although more than 10% of last year's winners also appeared in the worst performing group the next year!). However, before you rush out and put your life savings into this year's top performer – this effect only lasted one year. By the following year the performance of the funds was evenly distributed across all of the performance bands. The winner's effect in mutual fund management is small and fleeting. After the second year it is indistinguishable from a random distribution – regardless of the fortune spent analysing and dissecting the investment strategies of all of the star managers. This year's star is just as likely to be a dog (maybe not next year, but certainly the year after).

Many readers will at this point be saying, 'But I have been making a good return by picking stocks for years, this guy doesn't know what he is talking about.' In fact I wouldn't be surprised if about half of you were saying that! But surely all this talk of random events is avoiding the truth that we all know. Some business mangers, some poker players, some fund managers, know more, are more diligent, are just more skilful than others. How do we understand the relationship between chance and skill?

Shefrin's coins: a thought experiment

Hersh Shefrin, in his book *Beyond Greed and Fear* (2002), describes a neat thought experiment that helps us understand the tightly knotted relationship between luck and skill. His thought experiment models the way in which fund managers work. Imagine that each of 5,000 fund managers is given a coin – each with a head on one face and a tail on the other. One third of the coins are gold, one third are silver, one third are bronze and they are distributed at random to the 5,000 managers. Each fund manager is asked to toss the coin ten times every day and record the number of heads and tails they obtain – that is all they have to do, managers making 10 binary decisions every day. The fund managers are given $1 for every head they spin, and nothing for each tail. Every day, on average, we would expect each fund manager to have made a return of $5. At the end of each day we gather the results from all of the fund managers and publish the results so that the public can assess their coin-tossing ability. The first day's report tells us that 38% of the coin-tossing managers have beaten the benchmark return of $5 but six managers, amazingly, have earned $10 from tossing ten heads.

How are we going to select the managers that are going to beat the benchmark on the next day? If the coins are all fair (50% probability of heads or tails) then track record is of no use – statistically 38% of the managers will beat the benchmark on any day. But Shefrin then asks us to imagine that the coins are not all fair. The gold coins give heads 55% of the time, the silver coins 50% and the bronze coins only 45%. But all we can do is look at the results. We don't know which coin each manager is using. Let's suppose that the return we want is $7, seven heads, two better than the benchmark. What we want to do is identify the manager with the gold coin. If you see a manager who has historically got a return of $7 – what is the chance that they are tossing a gold coin? It turns out to be just 47% – so there is a greater than evens chance that you have chosen someone with a silver or bronze coin. Even some of the managers with the disadvantaged coins will get lucky and appear at the top of the performance tables. We never know who has the better judgement – all we have is the track record, and that track record is very difficult to read.

Of course the coins of different metal are a metaphor for the differing skills, experience and judgement of the fund managers. With a large number of managers there will always be one, or more, who have an extraordinary performance relative to the benchmark. That manager could be tossing a bronze coin. And yet based on the record we will attribute to them extraordinary powers of insight, we will assume there is a causal link – that they have a special skill – and hang on every opinion that they utter. Whenever you play this game you will identify a star – someone always gets lucky – and some people tossing gold coins will be languishing at the bottom of the performance table despite having better 'judgement'.

Luck, skill and the business manager

It is easy to see how Shefrin's thought experiment with the gold, silver and bronze coins applies to poker. Some players are more skilful. They have a better understanding of the probabilities, a better read on their opponents' play and probable hands. Some players are playing with gold coins – some with coins of a very base metal. But that doesn't stop the poker player with a gold coin being beaten, in the short term, by the poor player who bets everything on a single turn of a card, however unlikely, and wins. And we rush in to attribute greatness to the winner.

In business management we have different levels of skill and experience. We make thousands of decisions every year with imperfect information. Some are trivial. Some change lives. We can't take chance out of management decision making. Our judgements are always based on imperfect information. We sometimes get a good outcome (a head) sometimes not (a tail). Because we can't predict the future with certainty every management decision involves chance. Every manager has a coin they flip when they make a decision. In some situations those coins will give the right outcome 90% of the time. In other situations they will be less reliable. But whatever the outcomes, we attribute all of the success (and all of the failures) to the decision maker and overlook the part played by chance. Bad outcomes are the product of bad decision makers; good outcomes are made by good decision makers. We promote the manager with the successful outcome; we pass over or fire the manager who had the poor outcome. It doesn't matter if we have promoted the lucky fool and sacked the wiser loser. We don't know what coin they were tossing – all we do is judge by results. In any large organization there will be always be a few lucky fools. You can probably name them in yours.

But there are behavioural cues that help us separate the wise losers from the lucky fools. In poker one sign of a good player is that they will take a bad beat in their stride. They know they are capable of making a good decision even though the cards turn against them. When it happens they won't shout and scream and curse their luck (or the dealer). They will take the bad beat with equanimity and wait for the next hand knowing that in the long run they will win. The constant bemoaning of ill fortune is a sure signs of a weak player – someone who needs good fortune to get a good outcome.

At work there are countless cues that will reveal to the astute manager if someone understands the game, can assess risk, is sensitive to a wide range of information and its possible consequences, and is comfortable with uncertainty. The good manager can know the mettle (excuse the pun) of the decision maker, not on the outcome of a single decision, but because of the way they have handled the task and the decision-making process, because of the way they have handled dozens of decisions and dozens of different outcomes. Don't sack the manager who you think may have a gold coin – even if they are currently underperforming. In the long run they will give you a return. In the long run it can pay to back the loser – not the winner. We saw in Chapter 9 the anecdotal evidence from Anthony Fisher's rise and fall that entrepreneurial success cannot be inferred from past success. It can be hard to pick the best managers based on past performance – backing a past winner is no guarantee of success in the face of uncertainty.

Using experts

What do I mean by 'expert'? An expert is anyone with a lot of first-hand experience in a particular field. Someone who has been able to develop their instincts and judgement in one decision making environment. They are valuable when they have well-grounded judgement in an area that is new to us. But in addition to experience and the intuition that comes from direct feedback, experts also typically have an un understanding of the theoretical models that can be applied in a situation. The best experts will not just have the first-hand experience that you may lack, but also the theoretical under-standing to help them apply their knowledge in a wide range of situations. A powerful combination of experience and conceptual understanding that allows the expert to do what experts do best – recognize patterns.

Pattern recognition is the ability to look at a complex situation and identify the collection of different cues that constitute a pattern. The physician will see a pattern in a collection of symptoms that may seem unrelated to the untrained eye. The engineer can spot the warning signs that may indicate a component is about to fail, the acquisition specialist will recognize the signals that may indicate that the post-acquisition per-formance will be less than expected.

So the advice seems unambiguous. An experienced, well-trained expert can be exactly the person you need to guide you when you are making deci-sions far from home. Like an explorer in a new territory you engage the guide who knows the both the landscape and the customs in the strange land – money that should be very well spent. But there are two problems you should be aware of: experts aren't as good as they are; and it's in their inter-ests to tell you what you want to hear rather than what you ought to hear.

experts aren't as good as they think they are

The overconfidence of experts

What do we mean by overconfidence? Simply that experts think their judgements are correct more often than they are in practice. Their judge-ments are poorly calibrated. Studies have been made of physicians, clinical psychologists, lawyers, negotiators, engineers and security ana-lysts. The evidence is overwhelming. They all show the same systematic overconfidence in the accuracy of their judgements (see Griffin and Tversky, 1992, for example). One commentator even describes experts as being, 'often wrong, rarely in doubt'. We saw in Chapter 8 that only when the feedback is immediate and unambiguous do experts demonstrate well-calibrated judgements – weather forecasters and bridge players alike. In fact the good calibration of weather forecasters is restricted to regular, high-probability events like rainfall. When you calibrate weather forecasters' judgements about rare events like tornados then they suffer the same biases as other experts – they overestimate the likelihood of very rare events. In the same way doctors and psychologists overdiagnose rare conditions, lawyers overemphasise the possibility of unlikely out-comes. It is a pattern of behaviour that has been observed consistently in many different situations and has proven hard to eliminate.

It isn't just experts that are prone to overconfidence in their judgement. We are all guilty of overconfidence but the benefit of the expert is that in sit-uations where there is high predictability (e.g. will it rain tomorrow?) the expert will be less prone to overconfidence than the lay person. Where experts are consistently overconfident, more so than the lay person, is in cases of low predictability (e.g. will there be a tornado tomorrow?) where the data make predictions about the future very difficult. Similarly making a spe-cific prediction about the behaviour of a psychiatric patient or the prospects for a particular share price, for example, are very difficult (low predictability) but beguiled by their sophisticated models the experts' overconfidence will be high. Their judgement will not be as good as they think it is.

Where does this overconfidence come from? Let's imagine that you have tossed a single coin five times and obtained a sequence of five con-secutive heads. You will get a strong impression that five heads is not representative of the results we should get for a fair coin. We anchor on this one piece of evidence and then put relatively little significance on the fact that the 'weight' of evidence (from just five throws) is not (statistically) strong. We become overconfident in our judgement that the coin is biased.

Let's imagine that you are interviewing a candidate for a position with your company. If he shares characteristics with other people you know who per-form well in a similar job then we intuitively think that he will also be good – even if the characteristics he shares are not significant (e.g. personality type, interests, appearance). We put a lot of weight on the strong association between the candidate and our 'ideal' representative of what a good candi-date would be like. What we don't do very well is use the information that is genuinely predictive of performance such as relevant experience, education and training, or aptitude assessments. Or when we do use this predictive information it is only used to adjust an already formed opinion about the suitability of the candidate. We anchor on strong intuitive judgements and we make only small adjustments for genuinely predictive data.

The doctor will see the symptoms presented by the patient as being rep-resentative of the condition he has been studying for 20 years and will diagnose the condition more often than is justified, taking insufficient account of the underlying rate for the condition in the general population. The management consultant that specializes in re-engineering will recog-nise the patterns that he has spent his career identifying. He will make his diagnosis and embark on the restructuring with unshakeable confidence in his judgement. It is what experts do. All well and good, unless of course the patient didn't have the condition or the company didn't need re-engineering – which will be the case more frequently than the expert believes.

An expert's first duty is to themselves

We all know the principle that the consultant's interests and the client's interests are not always perfectly aligned. This is a risk I understand – what is good for the consultant may not be best for the client. But, we suppose, the people we engage as consultants are going to be people of good integrity. It is tempting to believe that any self-serving bias could be overcome with vigilance and professionalism. However, the research on this potential conflict of interest is not so optimistic. Max Bazerman (2006) is a researcher who has done a lot of work on this topic. He describes an experiment where he and his fellow researchers gave detailed information to students about the potential sale of a company. The students were each asked to assess the value of the company for the purpose of acquisition but each was assigned to one of four different roles: buyer, buyer's advisor, seller and seller's advisor. Predictably the sellers valued the company more highly than the buyers. The respective advisors were strongly biased towards the clients that the researchers had assigned them. The advisors were also asked for their private opinions on the value, and again there was a bias to the client. To try and eradicate this bias an impartial auditor was asked to give an impartial valuation. The sets of advisors were then given an incentive to be as close as possible to the independent valuation. Even with these safeguards in place the students taking the role of the seller's advisors were still valuing the company 30% above the buyer's advisors.

The same research team then undertook a similar experiment with 139 auditors employed by one of the US's leading firms. They were each presented with one of five ambiguous accounting scenarios, half of them taking the role of the firm's auditor and half of them an independent role. Again there was a bias in favour of the presumed client. The auditors were 30% more likely to report that the statements complied with GAAP (accepted accounting standards) when they played the role of the firm's auditor than when they were given an independent role. Even the hypothetical, implied client–auditor relationship was enough to distort the professional judgement. Bazerman (2006, p.76) goes further and concludes in the light of the Enron debacle: 'Contrary to the focus of the press and the Bush Administration on finding and punishing the few bad apples damaging the US financial system, the research evidence makes it clear that deeply ingrained institutional conflicts of interests that reward auditors for pleasing their clients were largely responsible for the crisis.'

What happened next for Magellan?

Lynch left Magellan in 1990. In the 16 years since he resigned there have been four fund managers. The fund has grown, as you would expect because investors backed this winner amongst winners, from $14 billion in 1990 to over $100 billion at its peak in 1999, and now stands at around $50 billion. The returns have lost all of their sparkle. Broadly the fund has been performing close to the index – below par for an actively managed fund with its higher costs. Measured on its ten-year return it ranked 14th of the 15 US funds with more than

The returns have lost all of their sparkle

$20 billion under investment. And yet the managers who have been put in charge of this megafund all had outstanding performances as stock pickers in their previous fund management roles. Perhaps the sheer size of the fund is part of the problem – getting high growth on $50 billion is going to be more difficult than on $20 million.

So was Lynch lucky? As Shefrin points out, given his 13-year track record Lynch was probably using a gold coin. His judgement probably was better than his peers. But chance will always throw up one winner from the 5,000 fund managers. However, predicting who they will be before they are successful – ah, that is a different matter altogether. The poker player can tell which is the lucky seat after a couple of hours' play. But she never points out the lucky seat before a card has been dealt.

In other words...

When we are forced to make decisions outside of our everyday experience – far from home – we often rely on the other people to make the decisions for us. We back past winners or we appoint experts. But previous success is not as reliable a guide to future performance as we might have thought. Luck and skill are impossible to completely disentangle from outcomes alone and we have to make judgements based on overall behaviour to find the best performers in the long run.

Experts have developed considerable experience in particular environments – experience we can use when we have to make decisions far from home. The secret of expert judgement is pattern recognition – enhanced by theories and concepts that improve the experts' ability to discriminate. But experts are overconfident – their judgements are not as good as they think they are. In particular, experts overdiagnose rare occurrences in the area of their expertise. Experts will also tend to tell you what you want to hear rather than what you ought to hear.

Which means that...

> Remember, business is a lot more random the management science has been telling us. Some things just happen.

> Since chance is always involved you can't assume the loser is a fool. You have to read the cues from their behaviour to find the managers with the gold coins.

> Use an expert when you don't have the experience necessary to make a judgement in unfamiliar territory.

> Be sceptical of experts diagnosing rare events in their area of expertise.

> Never forget that the expert will want to tell you what you want to hear.

Rules of thumb

10♣ You can't separate skill from luck by just looking at outcomes

J♣ Some winners are fools, some losers are wise

9♦ Expert judgement may be better than yours but it will not be as good as they think it is

Chapter **12**

Map making and the planning fallacy

In Chapter 9 I posed a challenge – given that good judgement is built on experience, how do we make decisions when we don't have direct experience to guide our intuitions? But this question seems not to dent the perennial optimism and overconfidence of entrepreneurs (explored in Chapter 10). Regardless of the evidence to the contrary we continue to believe we can control events – tempting us into situations in which we are much more likely to fail than we believe. Chapter 11 focused on the problems of backing winners and the difficulty of getting the most from experts. This chapter looks in more detail at the strategy of 'map making' to help us create value in unfamiliar environments. For inspiration I look to the eXtreme programming methodologies that developed in the 1990s. What emerges is an approach to decision making in rapidly changing and unfamiliar environments that places emphasis on the values and importance of trying, failing and learning quickly. A new metaphor for rapidly exploring and mapping the unfamiliar that fits closely with what managers say they do.

Lost in the woods

Kent Beck and Martin Fowlers' book, *Planning eXtreme Programming* (2001), starts with a true story. When Kent was just 10 years old he went with friends on his first fishing trip. They had looked all day for brook trout without success and decided to head for home. Before long there came the sickening realization that they were lost. The young Kent started to panic and was beset by rapid breathing, tunnel vision and a cold, clammy chill. One of the group of friends proposed a plan. They knew there was a logging road above them on the ridge. As long as they walked up hill they would hit the road and would be able to walk out. Within seconds Kent's symptoms abated. They had a plan.

eXtreme management and the planning trap

In the 1990s software projects were getting ever-more complicated and ambitious. In the middle of that decade I was running a publishing company that was part of an international group. Our billing and warehouse system ran on a mainframe computer and did everything that had been required of it when it had been planned two decades earlier. But times had changed. The new imperative was to support direct marketing and customer service, new functionality was required. A new system was commissioned and a budget of £750,000 was earmarked for the development. There then followed a six-month process during which a detailed project plan was developed by the group's in-house development team. Workshops were conducted, requirements were captured. The logic for every process was described on paper, every screen input was defined, and the architecture specified in exacting detail. At the end of this process of exhaustive deliberation we had a plan. Everything was specified, a project plan that fully acknowledged the dependencies of every part of the process was defined using the latest project planning tools. There was just one problem. The plan had cost us £500,000, two-thirds of our budget, and not a line of code had been written. All we had was a plan.

This is a story that can be retold thousands of times and with budget in orders of magnitude larger than ours. From the process-driven software project failures of the 1990s a new philosophy of software development emerged. An approach that did away with the enormous planning overhead of traditional project management. The XP (eXtreme Programming) movement was born. Perhaps the quickest way to get an understanding of the XP thinking is to consider Kent Beck's car journey analogy. When you set off on a journey by car you have a goal in mind, you probably have an idea of the route you will take. But of course both the goal and the route may change. Slow traffic on the main road may invoke a change of route, as may road closures and diversions. Even the destination may change if the meeting is cancelled or the venue shifted. But not only may your goal change but every few seconds you are adjusting your course. Avoiding cars, pedestrians and other obstacles that could not have been foreseen even a few seconds before. Project management, like the car journey, is a process that needs to be constantly directed and where even the goals can be subject to change. Contrast this with the approach that traditional project management may take to the same journey. Days might elapse while a detailed description of every change of direction is catalogued. If you set out on a journey with such a plan then bad traffic or a change of venue will leave you needing to redo the plan from scratch. Traditional project management, Beck characterizes as Aim, Ready, Fire – lots of planning and preparation and then one shot at implementing the plan and hoping you get it right first time. XP project management is Ready, Fire, Aim, Aim, Aim... the only requirement is that you get it right the last time.

Doug DeCarlo, another of the leading practitioners and writers on the XP movement, captures the difference by claiming that normal project management is about managing the known, but XP project management is about managing the unknown. You don't manage the unknown the same way as you manage the known. He puts forward a definition: 'An eXtreme project is a complex, high-speed, self-correcting venture during which people interact in search of a desirable result in conditions of high change and high stress' (DeCarlo, 2004 p.7). Which could just as easily be a description of nearly any business

You don't manage the unknown the same way as you manage the known

project in today's fast-moving and uncertain environment. In traditional project management and in Newtonian business management a plan is a prediction. An exhaustively researched plan that has been created, in part, to make everyone feel better about the future. Project managers, and indeed all business managers, are trained and socialized to believe that they should be in control. They are given positions of authority and paid more because of their knowledge and experience. Experience that, both they and their boss believe, should be able to remove the uncertainty by careful planning. In Beck's phrase, people plan in order to demonstrate that they are in control of events. But obviously we can't control events; all we can do is control our reaction to events.

Some critics believe that XP project management doesn't involve planning, but that is not the case. Planning is essential, but the planning is focused on the foreseeable horizon not the distant future. There is no point in spending days planning the detail of a future which will undoubtedly change. What you need is a clear sense of where you are going and a plan that maps the detail only as far as you can see (remember the car journey analogy). Beautifully detailed plans for the next 12 months not only waste time in preparation but, more seriously, give a false sense of security, which is probably why we spend so much time doing them. The same international publishing group that I referred to earlier in the chapter also had a business planning calendar that fell into this planning trap. Three months of the year was spent preparing and then negotiating next year's budget. Every revenue and cost line was built up in considerable detail. There was a three-month break while we were left alone to manage the business. Then the long-range planning cycle began. Another three months putting together a five-year plan. Because one of the key means of rewarding senior managers was compliance with the long-range plan this was an exercise that was subject to just as much detail as next year's budget. Three months later and the budget cycle starts over again. The planning for XP projects you can characterize as just in time (JIT) planning. Know where you want to go and keep checking. If something changes so that your plan doesn't match reality, then you have to change the plan and keep changing the plan. Contrast this with the traditional bluster of the manager faced with the reality that reality no longer matches the plan. Promises are made to deliver the plan, 'on time and on budget', and for a while everyone feels better. The XP philosophy is built on the assumption that honesty and accurate forecasting are better in the long run than bluster and promises that can't be kept.

How does traditional management keep on top of big projects, and indeed management processes of any kind? By setting and monitoring targets. The targets are a by-product of the long-term plan, the tell-tale measures that will alert management if the plan goes off track. In my experience of large organizations the monthly reporting against the same targets and key performance indicators can quickly become a dull, meaningless exercise. Excuses for missed targets lose their power on regular repetition. Not only that, but the process of data collection can often take longer and require more attention than the process being measured. Beck and Fowler, with characteristic wit, capture the folly, 'The overhead of data collection can swamp the real work. The process can become inhumane, with people – messy, smelly, distractible, inspired, unpredictable people – conveniently abstracted away to a set of numbers' (2001, p.107).

At its heart the XP process is a process of discovery. Both the goal and the route are going to evolve as part of the process. Too often, we assume that both our goals and our route for achieving those goals are unchanging; foundations on which we then set about building elaborate plans. In place of fixed goals XP places emphasis on values and vision – something that everyone can use to guide decision making when the path is unclear. The core values of XP are built around people and processes. The people-based values focus on honesty and courage. People are encouraged to be honest in their assessments – to tell it like it is, not as the plan says it should be. Courage is required because XP acknowledges that the future can't be planned with certainty and every endeavour will include a risk of failure.

Whilst the emphasis on people values is refreshing, it is the values embodied in the *processes* of XP that are central to its ability to create value in uncertain environments. The XP processes encourage fast failures and demands focus on the most difficult problems first. Prioritize on the biggest challenge: try something, fail, learn and try again. There is plenty of planning in XP management but it is focused on short-term targets – typically only two to four weeks ahead and with clearly agreed criteria for what success (or failure) looks like at the end of the planning cycle – 'ready, fire, aim' repeated again and again on a rapid cycle of careful short-term planning. Another key process value is the requirement to involve both the business sponsor and the customer continually in the process. In traditional business planning, designed for an unchanging and predictable environment, both the client's objectives and the business plan are treated as fixed. Both can be signed off in advance by the client and the senior management team respectively – providing a fixed reference point for the detailed project plan that is then implemented without further reference to the client or the bsusiness sponsor (aim, ready, fire). But XP management processes start with the assumption that both the client's objectives and the business case are going to change as the process evolves (the goals will be uncovered and are not fixed). Consequently both the client and the business sponsor need to be involved with the process – not just the traditional sign off at the start and close of the project – but throughout the process, reassessing priorities, costs and objectives. XP processes make the client and the business sponsor part of the process, responding and reassessing goals as the project progresses.

The difference between traditional project management and XP management becomes clear when you consider how each methodology reacts when a project starts to go off course. Traditional management responds by tightening controls and redoubling the planning process. XP management will go back to the guiding values and principles. Together these values provide a framework for navigating rapidly changing environments. The kind of environment where detailed long-term planning has no value (apart from its role as a security blanket). These will be the projects when the competitive environment is chaotic and unpredictable and the business goals, responding to the changing environment, can change overnight. Which, now we stop to think, is exactly the environment in which the modern business manager has to deliver value. The XP project methodology was developed specifically to create business value in a fast-moving environment where when traditional methods of planning and control were not succeeding.

XP didn't start as a theoretical abstraction but as a practical solution to the failures of planning and control in fast-moving environments. Here is a management philosophy that appears to be much closer to the way in which managers actually understand and manage risk than the probability weighted outcomes of decision theory. By rejecting the value in long-term planning the manager has to fall back on the principles of constant adjustment and review, managing each step by reference to agreed values. Values alone are the guide when goals and solutions are negotiated in the process. But it is a philosophy that works, that delivers value in the most challenging of business environments.

XP delivers value in the most challenging of business environments

Learning fast, far from home

In environments we know and understand, we can, as we saw in Chapter 8, be quick and effective decision makers – deciding close to home. The problem I posed in Chapter 9 was how do we make good decisions when we are in unfamiliar surroundings, far from home. In the last few chapters I have explored some of the techniques we use to make decisions far from home, albeit with varying degrees of success: relying on past success, copying the success of others, using an expert as a guide. One of the most effective ways of dealing with unfamiliar decision-making environments is to learn quickly. Turning the unfamiliar into the familiar. We need a process that can help us learn for ourselves, to develop intuitive judgement in a new environment without the dangers of relying on mistaken feelings of confidence or the sometimes biased testimony of experts. A way of building a map of the new terrain.

XP is a methodology that embodies the principles that characterize best practice in organizational decision making when first-hand experience can't guide us: a discovery process that doesn't jump to premature conclusions; full involvement of stakeholders; and strong values to guide the search and implementation. What can be taken from XP to help us make decisions far from home?

To help answer that question, I am going to build one of those extended metaphors that the XP teachers are so fond of – remember, by their own admission these guys are West Coast software nerds. Please bear with me. The scenario is this.

Your small company has been successfully gathering a small, green gemstone from the mountains in and around your home town, fashioning jewellery and making a decent living. Let's imagine these gemstones are abundant and easily retrieved (no difficult issues about open cast mining) but found only on the highest slopes. You have reason to believe that across the river in the neighbouring land there can be found similar but even more beautiful blue gemstones on the upper slopes of those mountains. However, you have never climbed into the mountains where the blue gemstones are found, nor even crossed the river. Whilst you know everything of importance about where to find the green gemstones close to home, you know nothing about the dangers and risks of gathering the more distant blue gemstones, far from home. But a decision is made to mount an expedition in to the hills and gather the blue gemstones. A team is assembled, but being a company conversant with XP methodology you go about the challenge in a very particular way. Firstly, your team includes one of the firm's directors with the authority to fund the project, extend the finance if necessary, but also stop the expedition if, in the light of new information once you get across the river, the project no longer seems a good idea. Another team member is the sales director. She understands both the end consumer and the needs of the shopkeepers that sell the jewellery. Her role is to represent the customer's voice, to make sure that the expedition stays focused on delivering value for the customer.

The weather is far from perfect as you set out. The mountain range that is your goal is only intermittently visible through the swirling clouds and it is far from certain what your best route will be. Guided by the XP methodology you need to quickly find a route into the mountains that avoids any significant obstacles. Assumptions based on your route to gather the green gemstones close to home

▶

almost certainly will be misleading here. There is no point in discovering later when supplies, cash and goodwill are running short that there is an uncrossable river on the path you have taken. Reconnaissance teams are sent out to test potential routes. Everything is new in this unfamiliar land. The smallest bit of information is shared with the whole team; you need to learn quickly, as you feel your way slowly through this unfamiliar terrain. At the regular planning meetings the time estimates for various routes and diversions are assessed. But decisions about costs are the domain of the director – these are business decisions – your team can provide the estimates and the assessments. At every meeting the team refocuses on the most challenging tasks ahead. The business sponsor (director) and the customer representative (sales manager) are not only aware of progress but required to remain focused on the viability of the project. Without their continued support there is no expedition.

At times the clouds clear and progress is quick. At other times the clouds are low, progress slows, and you are required to use all your skills as team leader to keep everyone focused on the goal. After several days of slow progress and some U-turns the business sponsor is getting anxious about the increasing cost estimate to find the gemstones and whether the business case is justified. New estimates are required of the number of days required to get to the highest slopes. The temptation here is to be optimistic and give an estimate that everyone wants to hear. That way the expedition can continue and hopefully things will get quicker. But no, as project leader you know that the best guide to the progress over the next few days is the progress you have achieved over the past few days. (In an unfamiliar land what else are you going to base your estimate on?) But an honest, and not overly optimistic, estimate is what the business sponsor has a right to expect. He weighs the costs, the new information and likely return, and continues to back the expedition.

Then potentially a breakthrough: earlier than you expected, and at a lower altitude than initially seemed probable, you find a few scattered blue gemstones. Excited, they are presented as a potential solution to the team. The sales director is not impressed, the quality is low; the commercial director is concerned at the thin distribution and the costs of retrieval. It is their opinion that the price that can be achieved for these stones would not justify the collection and transport costs. The easy win will not work, the path continues upwards. Then, high on the slopes, close to the retreating snow line you find the stones, thick as gravel, and of the highest quality. The team returns with samples in high spirits.

This is obviously not meant to be taken too seriously or analysed in much detail. But I wanted a story, close to the style of the Beck and Fowler or DeCarlo that could illustrate how some of the principles of XP management can be used when you are, literally, making decisions far from home.

1 Even if the problem looks similar to the last one don't assume the solution is the same. There may be superficial similarities but in unfamiliar ground the intuitions you developed in a different environment can be misleading.

2 Keep your ultimate goal in clear sight. At times this may be difficult but stay focused on the business drivers. If the project isn't going to deliver customer value you are wasting your time and the decision needs to be taken, by the business sponsor, to go home.

3 Make sure you take a business sponsor and a customer advocate with you for the journey, not just to wave you off at the barrier. They are coming along for the ride and have the power to stop the project, increase its scope or to redirect it to focus on customer value.

4 In new territory you have to learn fast (and fail fast) and you have to share your learning with everyone in the team.

5 Tackle what seems like the most difficult task first. This is the one that will require the most learning to overcome. This is the task that will need creativity and tenacity to overcome. Don't leave it until last and do the easy or the fun stuff first.

Not gambling but managing

What the story above illustrates is the way in which the fast-failing/fast-learning discovery methodology of XP tackles decision making far from home. It does it by effectively turning the unfamiliar into the familiar as quickly as possible. You tackle far from home decision making by making yourself feel 'at home' as quickly as you can. If you stay in doors and plan for months you will have learnt nothing about your new environment and your elaborate plans will be useless within days. Instead, plan only so far as you can see ahead (whilst keeping your ultimate goal in view) and learn the rules of the game as quickly as you can. This suggests that managerial decision making has more in common with small step-by-step commitments rather than the set piece all-or-nothing decisions of popular imagination.

This step-by-step commitment, with the ability to mitigate or negate risks through subsequent decisions, is not what the management textbooks recommend as a decision-making philosophy. But it is what managers do in practice – another example of the gulf between theory and practice. March and Shapira's study (1987) – which I referred to in Chapter 6 to show how managers alter preferences depending on their level of success) shows most strikingly that executives in these studies did not see risk taking as gambling. Risk isn't seen as a process of having to accept a given probability of success or failure. Risk can be avoided because the outcome was always subject to their control. Managers don't calculate a theoretical probability of success; the managers' job was to make it happen regardless of any arbitrary *a priori* probability. Risks can be managed. As one respondent explained, 'In starting my company I didn't gamble; I was confident we were going to succeed' (March and Shapira, 1987).

The reflex of course is to say that, once again, the theories are right and that these surveys just show up the poor state of management practice. Another example of managerial overconfidence (Chapter 10) and proof, if more was needed, of our (misplaced) conviction that we can influence events to our benefit. Or perhaps something else is being said here. Perhaps the executives in this study have got a better understanding of the practice of management than the theory would suggest.

In the very first chapter I set out some of the key characteristics of managerial decisions. One of them was that the decisions are not taken in isolation but they build one after another. In this respect the decisions we take as managers are very unlike the separate choices much loved by the decision theorists. A decision to accept Samuelson's coin toss wager (Chapter 13) to gain $200 but risk losing $100 is not typical of the nested and mutually dependent decisions that managers take. The executives that March and Shapira interviewed were not in need of retraining in the science of decision theory. They understood that, with the right approach and a willingness to learn and fail quickly, you can manage risks. Management isn't about one-off all-or-nothing binary decisions with binary outcomes. With an open mind and a willingness to cope with ambiguity and uncertainty (not characteristics that are usually highly sought after in senior executives) then there is a way to manage in highly-volatile environments. But to succeed in this environment requires a new kind of leadership. The plan and control management that we have been trained to implement was well suited to a Newtonian world of predictable causes and effects. In truth, however, the world was never like that. It has always been unpredictable and at times chaotic. Today, catalyzed by globalization and new technology, the volatility of markets has increased. Now, more than ever, managers are needed who can manage in a world that is profoundly uncertain. A world where the disciplines of planning and control will only sink you deeper in the mire. Not only are new approaches to managing uncertainty required but also new approaches to the management and motivation of people.

Making maps – making decisions

Every manager at some point has to make decisions that are outside of their comfort zone – far from home when intuitions built on experience can't help. Because, contrary to the textbooks, we make decisions based on our intuition rather than logical analysis – we are used to having 'a feeling' about the right route to take but not being able to explain where that feeling came from. We do use analysis and logical rules to assist in our decision making but more often than not this is to justify the decisions we have made to others

the trigger is the product of our intuitive processes

(or sometimes ourselves). But the trigger, the emotional commitment to a decision, is the product of our intuitive processes. When that intuition is based on hard-won experience then we are right to trust it, although there are some common psychological traps that we need to be aware of.

The trouble starts when we have to make decisions that are outside of our expertise. More often than not we still have an intuition, an insight that allows us to make a choice, but this insight can be very misleading and based on the flimsiest of coincidences or samples borrowed from another context. Undeterred by our lack of experience we get the confidence we need to make a decision from anything that seems plausible. We rely on a previous winner forgetting that previous successes may be due to chance rather than skill, especially if the previous winner is us, even if the context was completely different. We copy the strategies of others. We hire an expert to make the decisions for us but forget that experts are not as reliable as they think they are and that it is in their interests to tell you what you want to hear. Of course bad decision-making methodologies don't necessarily give rise to bad outcomes, but like the overconfident entrepreneurs from Chapter 10, armed with an unrealistic sense of confidence we commit resources to situations that will lose more often than not. Imagine the poker player taken in by the horoscope that foretells that today will see a big win. Infused with confidence he accepts bets that might otherwise have been declined. Then on losing he curses his luck, never suspecting that his evaluation of the opportunity was warped by the misinformation. We need to be particularly wary of our instincts in these unfamiliar situations. The intuition that suggests we should proceed is difficult to analyse – it is after all just a feeling.

What this chapter has revealed is a way to tackle decisions far from home. It isn't a theory logically deduced from first principles. This process of 'mapping' the unfamiliar terrain is based on: what managers actually say they do and a discovery process that develops specifically to create value in uncertain environments. Engage with the unfamiliar terrain, don't sit at home and make abstract plans. Focus on your ultimate goal but be prepared to change you route as the situation dictates. Take courage and act decisively, even though in the light of new information you may have to retrace your steps. Engage with the customer and focus on creating value as you go – don't postpone until the final flick of the switch. Be open and honest in you communications. Learn quickly and tackle the largest obstacles first. Be steadfast of purpose but flexible of mind.

In other words...

We can't plan with confidence when we don't know the lie of the land. What XP provides is an approach that allows us to learn quickly, keep focused on our core values and create value in unfamiliar environments. Not a detailed recipe for success, but a philosophy for navigating the unknown – you don't manage the known the same way as you manage the unknown.

The XP principles provide a compelling model for making decisions far from home: keep sight of your ultimate goal; always involve a customer representative and a customer champion; learn fast and fail fast; tackle the most difficult task first; take courage and be honest in your assessments – a change of course is not a failure.

Which means that...

> Most of the detailed planning we do is a waste of time – it makes us feel better but is constantly having to be revised.

> Plan flexibly and keep your plan in step with reality.

> Managing by targets and objectives diverts attention onto the 'plan' and away from the process that needs to be managed.

> Managers need new skills for managing in uncertainty – less emphasis on planning and control, more on relationships and values.

Rules of thumb

7 ♠ Plan flexibly – avoid detailed plans of distant futures in unfamiliar terrain

6 ♠ Use shared values and a clear vision to guide decision making when the path is uncertain

5 ♠ Build relationships rather than controls

4 ♠ Practise honesty and openness in communication – courage and determination in action

5 ♦ Far from home be prepared to fail fast and learn fast

K ♠ Changing your mind in the light of new information is a sign of strength not weakness

Chapter **13**

....

Fear, greed and risk taking

In the past few chapters my focus has been on examining ways in which we can make well-grounded decisions far from home. Now I turn my attention to the way in which our individual circumstances can change our preference when we face uncertainty. Is this a gamble for gain or to avoid a loss? Are we currently above or below target? Is it a one-off risk or part of a portfolio of similar gambles? Our choices don't conform to economic theory. Once again the poker player reminds us that the business manager is a more sophisticated decision maker than the theory would suggest. But I start with an answer to a long-standing question about our motivations to make decisions about uncertain futures – which is more powerful: fear of a loss or greed for a gain?

Why Leeson broke the bank

The story of *how* Nick Leeson broke Baring's Bank has been told in print many times, including by Leeson himself in his revealing autobiography (1996), and on film in *Rogue Trader*. Complicit in the collapse were an extraordinary catalogue of management failings:

> The staggering absence of financial controls that allowed hundreds of millions of pounds to be sent from the London head office to the Singapore trading office without any supporting documentation.

> The confused management structure, the dotted reporting lines and his managers' ignorance about the option contracts that Leeson was trading.

> And perhaps, above all, the myopic focus on the annual bonus payment (which saw 25% of the bank's profits distributed to staff) that was being inflated by the illusory profits from Leeson's misreported trading.

But my interest is not so much with the financial control and management failings that brought down the 200-year-old bank but with the state of mind that drove Leeson to continue with his unauthorized trading. Was it fear or greed that drove him on?

THE LEESON STORY

It all started on 17 July 1992 with an innocent mistake by a new employee on the busy trading desk. Twenty contracts, which should have been bought on behalf of a client, were sold in error. Leeson made a quick, instinctive decision not to crystallize the loss but to put the client right by buying 40 contracts – the 20 that should have bought in the first place and 20 to match the 20 sold in error. Leeson was only authorized to trade on behalf of clients, not to take position on his own account. The 40 contracts needed to be accounted for and were booked to the now infamous 88888 account. But however faulty Leeson's judgement had been in not accepting and reporting the loss, the bad luck that was going to haunt him over the next couple of years kicked in at once. Three days later and the market had risen strongly, and the £20,000 loss had mushroomed to £60,000. At this level he feared that reporting the loss would mean demotion to the back-office settlement role from which he had only recently escaped. But sweeping errors into the 88888 account became a habit and by the end of

1992 over 30 errors had been hidden, the losses covered by making deductions from his commission earnings.

In December 1992 a single error exposed the bank to a loss of £150,000, too big to be hidden with commission deductions. Leeson was going to need both income to hide the losses and cash to meet the margin calls from the exchange. (A margin call is a payment that a trader must make to an exchange, effectively a deposit against potential losses that might arise from the option contract.) He devised a scheme in which he could sell unauthorized options on the Nikkei and receive a premium in Yen to offset the 88888 account deficit. What he also required was cash from London to cover the margin calls. As Leeson recalls, 'I was determined to win back the losses, and as spring wore on I traded harder and harder, risking more and more.' But through the summer Leeson was lucky and the market soared. Incredibly, by doubling and then redoubling his gambles, by July he had turned a £6 million loss into a small profit. He had traded out of the hole and for one glorious weekend was free of the stress that had haunted him for a year.

However, the habits learnt during that turbulent 12 months were not easy to break, the 'five eights' account needed to be used the very next Monday to cover further trading errors. The cycle had started again and this time there would be no escape. The losses spiralled out of control. By failing to close one open position quickly a $1.7 million loss opened up in a single day. The swings became extreme. Some days would see gains of £5 million, another day a loss of £5 million. By early 1994 the losses had risen to a dizzying £50 million. He was caught needing to sell more and more unhedged positions to bring in the premium he needed to hide the shortfall. Every option he sold for the premium income meant he was taking a bigger and bigger bet that the markets would rise, 'I no longer had a clear idea where the market was heading, I only had a clear idea of where I wanted it to head.' February is the month when annual bonus payments are paid. In February 1994 Leeson was sitting on a £50 million unreported loss against group profits of £100 million. At this point Barings, had their audit procedures uncovered the losses, would have been embarrassed but relatively unscathed. In 12 months the losses would swamp the balance sheet; a banking dynasty would be over. It is often reported that the Kobe earthquake in January 1995 and the resulting fall in the Nikkei were the beginning of the end for Leeson and Barings. In fact, by taking some bold positions after the earthquake in the belief that the immediate 300-point fall was exaggerated, all of the post-Kobe losses had been recovered within two weeks. But in early February 1995 Leeson was still facing a £200 million deficit, the auditors were finally closing in, so once again he doubled up and hoped to get lucky. But in the last week of February the market dropped again. The Nikkei fell 400 points on the 23rd and every 100-point drop cost Leeson £20 million. Even in these final hours Leeson was still buying contracts to try and lift the market, a financial Canute vainly trying to hold back the tide of the global markets. Finally he accepted the inevitable, walked out of the office and headed for London; his only plan to avoid jail in Asia by being arrested in Europe. As the positions unwound the losses grew. Barings was bust.

Capturing preferences – a quick introduction to prospect theory

Economists, using the intimidatingly named *expected utility theory*, work on the assumption that we make choices that give us the biggest perceived benefit. It seems a reasonable assumption and in fact is one of the pillars of micro-economics. The trouble is, as is so often the case, the reality is a lot more complicated and confusing than the theory would have you believe. Paul Samuelson, a Nobel prize winning economist, used to offer colleagues and students a simple wager to illustrate that we don't make choices in line with expected utility theory. He would offer anyone $200 if they could predict the result of a single coin toss on condition that if they got it wrong they would have to pay him $100. The vast majority of people declined the wager even though it clearly has a positive expectation (50% × $200 − 50% × $100 = $50). The theory doesn't appear to describe the way we evaluate choices.

In the 1970s two colleagues at the University in Jerusalem, Daniel Kahneman and Amos Tversky set about trying to uncover the psychology of choice. If we don't make decisions in accordance with expected utility theory, what was guiding our choices? Their research method was unusual and, as Kahneman admits, great fun. Every afternoon they would meet and spend hours devising pairs of gambles and uncovering their instinctive preferences. They focused on constructing a model that could capture their intuitive preferences, leaving the time-consuming task of verifying that their personal choices were shared by others to later. After six months of these intense debates they felt that they had an insight into the psychology of choice. Four years of refinement and experimentation followed before they published their findings (2000) with the name prospect theory. In essence, prospect theory is nothing more than a description of the way people make choices when faced with uncertain outcomes. It doesn't offer advice on how to make the best choice; it simple describes the preferences we demonstrate. Preferences that in some situations are very far removed from the rational choices of expected utility theory.

What Kahneman and Tversky found was that in most situations we are risk averse – we don't like to gamble. We prefer the certainty of keeping what we have rather than an uncertain chance of winning more. A $100 in the pocket is worth more to us than the 50% chance of winning $200. Gambling, despite what you may have assumed, is not a fundamental part of human nature. However, this basic risk aversion was part of expected utility theory; the observation that the more money we have the less we value an increase in wealth. £10,000 is valued more by someone with no wealth than it is by someone who already has £100,000. But the insight of prospect theory, uncovered by the constant probing and creative questioning of Kahneman and Tversky, was that in some situations we do prefer to gamble. What they found was that we are *risk averse* when it comes to accepting a gamble that may give us a gain, but we are *risk seeking* when it comes to situations where we are facing a loss. Given a chance to increase our wealth with a 50% gamble that may double our money we often turn it down.

Gambling is not a fundamental part of human nature

But facing a loss we will accept the same wager if it offers a chance of getting even. Nick Leeson was gambling, admittedly with someone else's money, not for gain but to recover a loss. Leeson wasn't the one bad apple, the rogue trader out of control. He was doing what many of us would have done, taking big risks to recover a loss, risks we would not have taken for gain. Fear of losing is more important than the greed for gain.

Part of the power of prospect theory is that it is able to distil our choices into a simple graph.

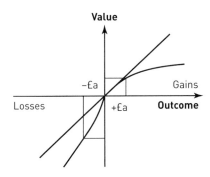

The graph maps the outcome of a gamble, the actual amount won or lost on the horizontal axis. On the vertical axis is a subjective measure of our perceived value of the outcome. The monetary change on the x-axis against the way we feel about it on the y-axis. Naively, we might expect that any gain or loss would have exactly the same perceived value to us: every £ gained or loss pleasing us or harming us to the same extent. If this were the case then the value curve would be the 45 degree line through the axis. The increase in value from £1 to £2 has just as much value to us as the increase from £999 to £1,000, or from £999,999 to £1,000,000. The curve to the right of the vertical axis is roughly the curve that you would get from expected utility theory. The more money you have (the further along the horizontal axis you start) the less value you ascribe to each gain. If you are already wealthy you get only minor increase in utility from a further gain in wealth. The main insight of prospect theory is what happens to the left of the vertical axis – in situations where you are facing losses. The curve for losses has two important features:

1 Just as for gains, the curve is at its steepest near the origin. In other words, the first loss hurts more than adding a small loss onto an existing loss.

2 The curve is steeper for losses than it is for gains. We value a gain of **£a** less than we dislike a loss of **£a**. A loss hurts us more than the same gain would please us.

But remember, this isn't a graph derived from a theoretical model. It is a graph that captures the preferences we demonstrate in hundreds of different contexts and experiments. It captures the way we actually think, not the way a theory says we ought to think. We are risk averse when seeking gains, but loss averse and therefore risk taking when facing losses.

One of the consequences of the different shape of the curves for gains and losses is that our preferences will change depending on whether we see a choice as an opportunity for gain or as a chance to recover a loss. Our choices are dependent on our frame of reference.

Imagine that you work for a pharmaceutical company and that a year ago you paid £50 million to acquire a small biotech company. Things haven't gone well in the past 12 months and there is an offer from a third party to acquire the company for just £25 million. However it is at a crucial stage in trialling a new drug. The experts tell you that there is a 50% chance of the drug getting approval, in which case the company may be worth £50 million once again. Should the drug fail to get approval then the company will be effectively worthless.

Should you accept the £25 million offer and sell the company? There is no 'right' answer here. But your answer may be influenced by your frame of reference. Do you see the reference point as the original £50 million, in which case you may be tempted to take the gamble on the drug trial, turn down the £25 million offer and hope to recover the loss? If however, you see the current £25 million as your reference point then the equal probability of doubling your money or losing everything will look like a poor wager and you may be inclined to sell and secure the value you still have. Rational economic models would point us only to the expected value. In practice our decision is driven by how we frame the question. Our choice is dependent on the context – do we see the choice as a chance to gain, or as a chance to recover a loss?

Real world examples of frame dependence

Since prospect theory describes how we make choices, it would be surprising if we couldn't find situations where our preferences changed depending on whether we were facing losses or gains. And indeed that is just what we find. I will recount two diverse examples: New York taxi drivers and on-course horse betting.

The majority of New York taxi drivers do not own the cabs they drive. They rent them in 12-hour blocks for a fixed price. They can then keep all of the fares and tips, making a good living when the demand is high, but risking losing money, by failing to cover the rental cost, when demand is low. A study (Camerer et al, 1999) has shown that on slow days, when the fare paying passengers are hard to come by, taxi drivers work longer hours than average. In contrast, when the business is brisk they work for less hours and quit early. This doesn't seem very rational, the drivers aren't maximizing their hourly earnings. You would expect the drivers to put in more hours when it is raining and business is good, but give up early on a sunny spring day when people are happy to walk. But the determination to keep putting in the hours on the slow days is exactly what you would expect from prospect theory. Every driver has a reference point – the cost of the cab and a profit that they expect or need to make every day. On a slow day, quitting early would mean accepting a loss so they keep working, taking a gamble that business will pick up so that they don't have to crystallize the loss. On good days they move

▶

into profit quickly, the reference point is passed and the lure of the additional gains from working longer hours seems less attractive. Each day is seen in isolation. Each day the driver is reluctant to accept a loss and will work long hours to avoid it. The unintended consequence is that there are less cabs on the street when the demand is high than when demand is low – now you know why you can't get a taxi when you need one most.

Another example comes from on-course horse race betting. (You can read more about this application in Camerer (2000.) This time, instead of explaining the occasionally annoying lack of taxis, it provides practical advice on how to obtain the best odds at the race track.

Most people who go for a day's racing will lose money. This of course is how the betting industry survives. Towards the end of the day the majority of people have lost more than they have won. There is one last race. Seeking to avoid a loss for the day, a high proportion of people will be drawn to one last gamble, a chance to recover their losses. Putting a bet on the favourite on the last race with its short odds and consequently low return is unlikely to earn enough to recover the accumulated losses. Consequently the high-priced long shots get heavily backed in the final race as risk seeking punters gamble to recover their loses. The favourite, seeing less money than expected, will have a more attractive price. Because of the loss aversion of the majority of punters that are trying to get back to break-even, the best odds at the race track are for the favourite on the last race. It may not win but a strategy that bets only on the favourite in the final race will have the best long-term return of any other on-course strategy. That's what the theory describes, and that is exactly what studies of results and closing prices have found.

Inevitably the psychology of buying had been understood by sellers long before prospect theory was described. By trail and error sellers have found how to get the most money from the buyer. Prospect theory predicts that the gains for the buyer should be separated and treated individually so that the buyer perceives the maximum value from each additional feature. Lots of separate gains measured against the steepest part of the curve for gains (to the right of the *y*-axis). However, the price paid (the loss to the buyer) should be bundled together into one price – taking advantage of the flatter curve in the domain of losses to the left of the *y*-axis. In industry after industry we see just that psychology at work. Different offerings are packaged together and sold for a single price: incentives to buy a subscription rather than purchase individual issues; packages of optional extras for new car buyers; a package of flight and hotel for the traveller. Experience has shown that we spend less if there is a comprehensive price list of options where every benefit (gain) has its associated cost (loss). We spend more when several products are offered at a single price.

In Chapter 4 I described Taleb's experiments with a Monte Carlo engine and how it led him to become an option trader. In fact his company, Empirica, has a very unusual business model. It buys 'out of the money options'. These are contracts which are unlikely to pay out unless something dramatic and unexpected occurs. Every day there is a high probability that the options Empirica bought will not make a profit. Day after day the business will lose the cost of the options (plus the cost of its overheads). Then occasionally, when there is turbulence in the market, the options that were cheaply acquired will be worth a great deal. This turns the psychology of investing on its head. Normally investments will see a realistic chance of a rise most days, but suffer the small, but real, risk of a crash that can put most of the value at risk. Lots of small gains followed by rare but significant losses. By contrast, Emprica's investment strategy sees an almost certain but small loss every day. There is always a small chance of a significant gain but no risk of blowing up in a crash. The constant threat of bleeding to death if the markets are steady month after month.

Prospect theory shows why this is not a business model for everyone. The value curve rewards the small regular gains of traditional investing, making the most of the steepest part of the value curve for gains and creating the illusion that we are making progress and that all is well. The occasional losses can be severe, but better, psychologically, as a single hit. Empirica's strategy needs a psychologically tough manager with almost constant small losses and the occasional heady win. But Taleb's strategy is based on a very simple observation – the market is more volatile than

the market is more volatile than most people acknowledge

most people acknowledge. If he is right, and to date his performance would suggest he is, then he will make money by buying an option on volatility that other people don't want. He just has to keep trusting the theory when, as has been the case in the past, the company can go for month after month making nothing but daily losses.

Sunk costs

Just as the urge to chase the long shot on the final race can be expensive for the punter at the race track, so the urge to continue investing in a failing project can be expensive for business. We call it the sunk cost effect, the lure of making a further, high-risk investment, with the hope that the entire project can be turned from loss to profit. This is a trap that we have already highlighted for the poker player. Good cards and strong prospects may have led to a big raise and $500 placed in the pot. When the cards disappoint it is tempting to call one more $100 bet, however unlikely the win. Once again the value curve helps us understand the error. Seen on its own, the loss of another $100 is going to hurt – on the steepest part of the value curve. If the prospects of winning are not great we will decline the bet and fold. But if we see the $100 bet as part of the already wagered $500 then the psychological impact of the loss seems less. When you are already down $500 an additional $100 loss seems less as the change in value is assessed where the value curve for losses is less steep. Integrated with the previous bet, the loss of another $100 doesn't seem so bad and we are tempted to gamble on the final card. In business the sunk cost effect is pervasive. Lending managers for banks will advance further loans to struggling companies when another manager who was not involved in the first lending decision will decline the request for more lending. Private equity companies are tempted to make a follow-on investment rather than accept the write-off. But as every good poker player knows, every bet must be made on its own terms. The money already in the pot has gone. If the final bet doesn't have a positive expectation, walk away. But it can be very hard advice to follow.

Combining bets to win

Remember Samuelson's gamble on a single flip of the coin. Despite expected value being positve, most people decline. But if instead of being restricted to a single flip you are offered three successive attempts, each on the same terms, then the gamble has instant appeal. The only way you can lose money with the three attempts is if you call incorrectly three times in a row. You would lose $300 but this is only going to happen 1 time in 8. Putting together a portfolio of risks can turn unpalatable gambles, although with a positive expectation, into a very safe proposition. And this is, of course, what the poker player does. Accepting a bet that will win if the last card is a heart may only pay off once in five attempts. A prospect that, since even gamblers are basically risk averse, we may turn down as a standalone opportunity. But in a game of poker there will be dozens of such opportunities in the course of an evening. Taken together the portfolio of different risks, in the hands of a player who understands the probabilities well, can have a very high return.

The importance of this principle was nicely captured by economist Richard Thaler (1999) when he was talking to a group of senior managers. He offered each of them in turn an opportunity to invest in a project that had a 50% prospect of making $2 million but a 50% prospect of losing $1 million (the mathematical equivalent of Samuelson's coin toss scaled up for the corporate environment). As students of prospect theory we will not be surprised to learn that 22 of the 25 managers turned down the offer. In corporate situations the perception of the loss may be complicated by more than just the financial loss. The anticipated damage to career prospects may be significant. The fear of being associated with a $1 million loss can be enough to reinforce the natural tendency to be risk averse. But Thaler then turned to the CEO of the company who was also attending the session. He offered the CEO a portfolio of 25 bets on the terms described. Without pause for thought the CEO accepted the offer. By seeing each bet as a separate gamble, and allowing each manager to make an isolated decision, the inherent risk aversion of each manager turned down a portfolio of bets with an expected value of $12.5 million and an almost negligible risk of losing money.

The thin line between extinction and success

We have seen that not only do the choices we make depend on whether we are seeking a gain or seeking to recover losses, but they also depend on whether we see the gamble as being a one off or as one of a series. However there is another factor that can alter how we evaluate a risk – something that the poker player knows only too well but that the decision theories ignore. We can change our perception of a risk depending on how much money we have.

As you will have noticed throughout this book, so many of the studies that underpin decision theory have been done in the laboratory. For understandable reasons the typical lab rat is the MBA student, available, willing and free. A number of surveys have sought to find out how we perceive and handle risks. The results have been a surprise for the theorists

– but not for the poker player. March and Shapira reviewed the major surveys to date and came to some striking conclusions (1987). Managers, they concluded, don't convert all of the alternatives into a single number (e.g. expected value) in order to make choices. They don't multiply financial outcome by the probability of its occurrence. It seems that managers don't have an intuitive understanding of probability distributions – what exactly does a 40% chance of rain tomorrow mean? High probabilities we treat as effective certainties. Low probabilities we ignore. But, most surprisingly, managers don't see risk as something that has to be accepted, like the odds on a horse race or the odds of hitting an ace on the River. Risk is seen as something that can be managed. Managers assume that once the decision has been made they can control the world to manage away the risk. The day-to-day management of emerging situations being seen as more typical of the managers' burden than the cool evaluation of alternative courses of action.

What March and Shapira also found was that how we view risks is dependent on how we are performing. Our choices are influenced by how we perceive ourselves relative to two benchmarks of performance. Two lines in the sand that mark survival and our aspiration level. These two lines define three zones of achievement.

> Performance below survival level is extinction.
> Performance above survival but below target is failure.
> Performance above target is success.

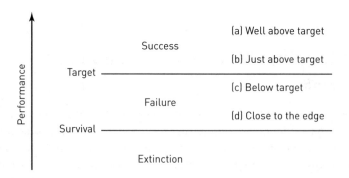

What the interviews with managers showed was what any poker player could have told you; how we evaluate risks depends on your current standing. Below target, for example at (c) in the diagram, just as prospect theory predicts, we will take risks to recover below-target performance. Above the target level, say at (b), we will be more risk averse, fearing that a loss can turn our current success into failure. If we are way above the target level we can feel liberated to take additional risks since even unsuccessful gambles are unlikely to threaten our success. And most pertinently, close to the survival threshold we become necessarily risk averse. One error, one bad call, one bit of bad luck and our very survival is threatened. The drunk walking along a very narrow pathway between wall and gutter will shorten his step and take deep breaths to summon the control he needs to stay on the path, always a short step from falling into the gutter.

For poker players this is commonsense and doesn't need theoretical exposition. When you only have a few chips left you have to pick your fights very carefully. The high-risk opportunity to win a big pot that you would happily accept, assuming it had a positive expectation, now has to be declined. Every decision becomes a matter of life or death. Risk aversion becomes extreme. In tournament poker the players' chance of success is directly related to their share of wealth. If you start on the final table as the underdog with less chips you will either have to get lucky or make some very good calls – or probably both.

Risk aversion becomes extreme

In business the stunting effect of imminent extinction is a paralysing fear. The medium-term investments that can secure greater market share and security have to be turned down. Management becomes a series of small, almost no-risk opportunities which inevitably never give the returns that can allow more freedom. Once you are close to the edge it is a very difficult road to safety.

In other words...

Despite the popular image of the manager or entrepreneur as a risk taker we are basically risk averse. We prefer the dollar we have to the uncertain prospect of more (or no) dollars. But fear of losing is more powerful than our greed for gain and consequently we will take much larger risks to recover a loss. Expected utility is a poor guide to managerial decision making and we change our preferences depending on the context.

Prospect theory describes our preferences when we evaluate gambles for gain and to recover a loss. Our attitude to gambles will depend on our frame of reference – a fact much exploited in the way products and services are packaged and promoted. We don't let go of costs we have already committed (sunk costs), tempting us to keep gambling to recover what we have already spent. Risk aversion can make us turn down one-off gambles (even when they have a positive expectation). We change our preferences depending on how much money we have got and how we think we are doing. Below target and we will gamble, close to extinction and we will become very risk averse.

Which means that...

> Experiment by changing your frame of reference when thinking about an uncertain choice. Try to see it both from the perspective of a gain and as chance to recover a loss.

> Make a conscious effort not to include sunk costs in your evaluation of further investments – see each investment on its own terms.

> Are you making full use of prospect theory in your pricing and product options?

> It is easy to become risk averse when gambles are seen in isolation: when taken together they offer a good return at low risk. Subordinates may be turning down gambles which, collectively, you should be accepting.

> Be aware of how the size of your purse and your relative performance to target will affect your attitude to risk. Being very close to extinction leaves you almost no options and it can be very hard to escape.

Rules of thumb

8 ♦ Test a judgement by changing the frame of reference
9 ♥ Look for a portfolio of similar investments rather than looking at each opportunity in isolation
2 ♣ On limited resources even good bets with positive expectations have to be turned down
2 ♥ Ignore sunk costs – each new investment must be evaluated on its own terms

Chapter **14**

....

The Dragon's Den syndrome

This chapter centres on an intriguing question: why do so many entrepreneurs turn down offers of finance? This enables me to bring together many of the ideas that have occurred in the book:

- the power imbalance between investors and entre- preneurs as they make decisions close to home and far from home respectively;
- the futility of detailed business plans as predictions of the future;
- inside thinking and overconfidence in entrepreneurs;
- the clash between intuition and logic;
- the need to justify decisions to other people with rule-based justifications;
- the impact of sunk costs;
- the endowment effect as an extension of prospect theory – the fear of losing what we own.

Taken together, the factors that contribute to the art of decision making.

The Dragon's Den

For the past couple of years there has been a TV programme in the UK called the Dragons' Den that has generated a number of clones around the world. The programme allows entrepreneurs to pitch their business proposition to 'Dragons' – self-made millionaires with cash to invest in the best ideas. The programme has been an extraordinary success and put the vocabulary of business plan, burn rate and equity dilution on prime-time television. The programme makers understand the fundamental power inequality between the entrepreneur and the investors. The entrepreneurs have to climb the narrow staircase and stand on the bare stage before the comfortably seated Dragons. Time is limited, a few minutes to explain the idea and establish credibility. There are no second chances.

Having watched a number of episodes, there are two patterns that seem to repeat again and again. Firstly, and most obviously, the majority of the ideas presented each week appear to have no prospect of commercial success. They are testament to overconfidence and the power of 'inside' thinking (Chapter 10). The entrepreneurs have lived with their ideas for so long that they seem blinded to the realities of consumers and their needs. With the Dragons exchanging looks of incredulity the entrepreneurs shuffle away without offers of investment. The second pattern occurs less frequently but is just as marked. After four or five no-hope presentations a business idea of some merit is pitched to the Dragons. They sit up and pay attention. Their questions are focused; they are attentive to the answers. The Dragons have no opportunity to investigate the markets being described. They are required to make intuitive judgements about the product, the market and above all the management capability of the entrepreneur. If they like what they see, one or more of the Dragons can make an offer to invest. Cash is offered and a price, an equity stake in the company, is proposed.

Great television can distil and frame one moment of human drama. This is one of those moments. The camera has the entrepreneur in close up. A brief hesitation betrays the indecision. An exchange of equity for cash is being evaluated. Gain the long-sought investment and lose some equity in the business, or walk away and maintain the status quo. Time after time the offer is rejected. The price too high, the equity too precious. The entrepreneur departs, frustrated that the value of their idea has not been appreciated and angry with the Dragons' demand for a pound of flesh. Indeed in one series 16 offers of investment were made to entrepreneurs but only a quarter of those offers were accepted, the rest rejected. At this point I am usually screaming at the screen – demanding that they accept the offer. I know first hand how difficult it is to get investment in early stage companies. Why is it so difficult for entrepreneurs to part with equity and accept investment?

100% of nothing

Over the past few years I have worked with several small or early stage companies and assisted them in raising funding from business angels or private equity investors. Without exception the entrepreneurs have been intelligent, well-educated and experienced in business. The issue of valuation and the equity that has to be given up in return for funding always arises at an early stage – usually in the form of an ultimatum, a minimum valuation for the business that is non-negotiable. Almost without exception I find myself having to bring down the owners' expectations of valuation. Trying to align their expectations with the reality of early stage funding. At this point I usually have to resort to leading them through the simplest of calculations (which they either already understand or are more than capable of completing for themselves). The purpose of the calculation is to show that after accepting funding their equity stake is worth exactly what it was before the investment. The example I work through goes something like this.

Imagine that you own 100% of the equity in an early stage business. You need funding to realize the opportunity and after a lot of meetings and presentations you have secured an offer from one prospective investor of £100,000. She requires 33% of the equity in return for her investment. This effectively values your early stage business at £200,000. (If 33% is equivalent to £100,000 then the entire company with the cash investment will be worth £300,000 – £100,000 in cash and therefore a pre-money valuation of £200,000 is implied for the company.) Before investment you own 100% of an asset that has just been valued at £200,000. After the investment you own 67% of an asset that is, in total, worth £300,000 (the £200,000 for the business assets or value of the opportunity and £100,000 in cash). In other words after investment you still own an asset worth £200,000. But instead of owning 100% of an asset that without investment will probably be worthless (100% of nothing) you now have an asset of equal value that has the ability to create lasting value. No value is lost and the opportunity for creating value much enhanced.

The logic is so simple and self-evident that I feel reluctant even to waste time leading you through the workings. But the logic isn't the full story.

the rule-based logic doesn't have a chance against our intuitions

There is an instinctive reluctance to let the equity go, a reluctance that the mathematical logic doesn't dispel. (A clash of instinct and logic that recalls the disbelief when I explain the Monty Hall problem – see Chapter 4.) Intuitive and rule-based reasoning solving the same problem and reaching different answers. And as is so often the case, the rule-based logic doesn't have a chance against our intuitions.

Inevitably these discussions turn on what is a fair valuation for the early stage business. Entrepreneurs have various ways of convincing themselves that their business can objectively be given a high valuation. Sometimes this is done by adding up the money invested to date, including, typically, the opportunity cost of the salary foregone. Needless to say, for the potential investor, the cost of reaching the current position has no bearing on the business's current or future valuation. Another favourite valuation justification is comparing a very early stage company with another business, usually far more advanced with significant revenues and established customers, that has recently been acquired for a large sum. The entrepreneurs will chorus, 'Well, with our better technology we must be worth at least what they were worth.' Of course the market for equity investment is a very sticky market with very few transactions and no real notion of a market value. The value of a company is, and can only ever be, judged by the offers for investment that you receive. There are hopes and dreams, and then there are the deals that can actually be done.

The endowment effect – sticking with what we've got

This apparent overvaluation of what we own has been termed the endowment effect. Since prospect theory (Chapter 13) is a description of how we make decisions when faced with uncertain outcomes, the value curve can explain this obsession with holding on to what we own. The certain loss of something we currently own (the entrepreneur's equity, for example) is going appear more significant than an uncertain but potentially larger future gain (the exit value for the company). There is a natural bias to keep what we have and maintain the status quo. In fact you can see this bias in many walks of life. The psychology of the value curve and the endowment effect is behind the typical voter's abhorrence to paying tax, especially income tax which seen as a deduction from earnings – something we already see as ours. The politicians have the gradient of the value curve working against them. We perceive that exchanging a certain and unavoidable loss of income (through tax) with the gain of public service provision is for most of our lives of uncertain or negligible value (until of course we desperately need those services). Prospect theory suggests we may be happier with consumption taxes such as sales tax and value added tax. These increase our costs but don't take away something that we already see as ours.

This tendency to over-value what we own is called the endowment effect. A deceptively simple and effective experiment (reported in Kahneman *et al.*, 1990) was devised to illustrate the endowment effect.

A MUG'S GAME

The researchers gave new mugs at random to a group of students. They then asked the students to complete a form asking them to indicate the prices at which they would be prepared to sell the mugs they had recently acquired. These were the prospective sellers. They then asked another group of students, prospective buyers, to complete a form indicating the range of prices at which they would be prepared to buy the mugs. The sellers and buyers were then matched and the mugs exchanged for cash whenever the specified buying and selling prices allowed. Now it seems reasonable to assume that all of the students could be divided into those that are relatively mug loving and those that are relatively mug hating. Since the mugs were distributed at random you might also imagine that, on average, half of the students being given mugs are mug haters and keen to sell. Likewise, half of the students not receiving a mug may be mug lovers and keen to acquire. On this logic you would expect roughly half of the mugs to be exchanged as students express their preferences for buying and selling through the values they set. In fact, typically, only 25% of the mugs are exchanged. The reason soon becomes apparent. The sellers, on average, set a selling price of $7.12 but the buyers set an average price of $2.87. The endowment effect is at work. Those randomly assigned a mug value them more highly than those who are not assigned mugs.

The market for mugs is what economists describe as 'sticky'. There are less trades and a bigger price differential than you might expect if there was a rational exchange of goods to match the desire to own a mug. This stickiness in the market is exactly what you get in the very imperfect market for investing in businesses – the private equity market. Despite the need for young businesses to acquire capital and despite the appetite of investors to find investment opportunities, transactions are hard to achieve. There may be several factors behind this. The entrepreneurs' extreme reluctance to give up equity may be a significant contribution. But the endowment effect goes both ways. The investor has cash and there will be the same endowment effect at work. The investor will tend to value the cash in hand more highly than the uncertain future gain from a share-holding. The business angel may be investing as a hobby, a side interest. The consequence is that if they don't find any companies worthy of investment then there is no great loss. For the professional private equity investor they have to find investments. They are paid to find high-return investments and holding the money on deposit for five years is not what they are rewarded for doing. Perhaps for that reason it can be easier to deal with a professional investor than a part-time business angel who has no drive to overcome the inevitable endowment effect that keeps their cash under lock and key.

Courtship and the entrepreneur

I have had the opportunity of seeing the endowment effect in action from both sides of the table having been an investment director for a private equity firm and a private investor. I have also raised money for small and new ventures from professionals and business angels. There is a knowledge asymmetry between the investor and the entrepreneur which it helps to be aware of. In Chapter 8 I introduced the distinction between deciding close to home and deciding far from home. When it comes to issues relating to the structure of the investment, the various controls and protections to be negotiated into the investment agreement, the private equity investor is making decisions 'close to home'. Their intuitive judgements are well calibrated. They will have made dozens of investments and be experienced at assessing market opportunities and management capabilities. In contrast the entrepreneur has probably never raised finance before and has almost certainly never seen an investment agreement. What strategy should entrepreneurs use to support them through the unfamiliar challenge of raising external finance? This isn't a situation where taking time to explore this unfamiliar domain is going to be possible so hiring an expert guide is the best strategy.

hiring an expert guide is the best strategy

But the information advantage is not all with the investor. Investors are, in nearly every case, generalists. They don't make a dozen investments in the one same market sector, they spread their risks. Consequently, they can't be specialists in any one market. Even a specialist new technology investor may have made some investments in mobile technologies, some in web businesses, some in infrastructure. They will have a basic knowledge, and may be deceptively fluent in the technical vocabulary, but they will not be able to match the detailed knowledge that the entrepreneur and her management team have of their marketplace. When it comes to detailed knowledge of the market the positions are reversed – now the investor is far from home. Investors gets round this knowledge gap by employing an expert. They commission a due diligence report from a trusted industry insider. But this is usually part of the final process of investment approval. Professional investors are making decisions with other people's money. They need to be able to justify their decisions and the commissioned report will be part of a final package of due diligence checks. The intuitive decision to back a management team (subject to satisfactory due diligence) will have been taken long ago based on the investors' previous experience of assessing management teams and investment opportunities. An early commitment and then the slow process of justification. The rational, rule-base analysis is part of the decision support process, the external justification. At the heart of the investment decision is an intuitive decision based on trust and all of the cues that we use to make intuitive judgements: for example, the similarity of the next investment opportunity to previous successful investments, or the extent to which the management team are typical of 'good' managers seen before. (And of course subject to any of the usual 'close to home' decision traps from Chapter 8 – for example, the presumed association that a management team with MBAs and smart suits will be more successful.)

With my tongue only slightly in my cheek, you can characterize the process of building trust between the investor and the entrepreneur as a courtship. A courtship that may lead to marriage (albeit with an 80-page pre-nuptial agreement). A process in which the investor will behave in accordance with some simple rules, rules that every entrepreneur should know.

The rules of courtship and marriage for private equity

If you ever find yourself seeking funding from an investor the following 'rules' might help you understand the relationship. Don't get the impression that I am not in favour of external investment. Private investment can be a transforming experience and the long-term nature of the relationship can make it a far better prospect in uncertain environments than bank finance. But it is important for the entrepreneur or shareholders in the company considering investment to be able to understand the nature of the relationship and the rules that govern the actions of the investor.

1. **The courtship will take a long time, it can't be rushed.** It's all about trust. The investor may be about to give you £1 million. Money that will be in your bank account under your day-to-day control (there are some exceptions, see rule 5(b) below). So of course it's about trust. But trust doesn't build quickly. It is established slowly through a courtship process. One step at a time, finding out more and more about each other, the investor assessing you as a prospective marriage partner. A first meeting at the investor's home ground. If they like you then they will come round to your place. There will be lots of enthusiasm from the investor, they want your undivided attention and playing it cool at this stage would only encourage you to look elsewhere (see Rule 2). Expect emails and phone calls, and lots of positive encouragement. More questions, more meetings maybe a lunch or even a dinner. They may introduce you to some of their friends (industry experts and advisors) but you are always on show, you are always being assessed: How well do you understand the customer? How will you react in a crisis? Do you have good judgement? The same questions being subtly asked in different contexts. There is nothing you can say in the courtship that will fast forward you to a marriage proposal but you can say something that makes them walk away. Because it is an emotional process of building trust rather than a rational evaluation of a business plan and market opportunity it will take months rather than weeks.

2. **Keep playing the field, even though the investor doesn't want you to.** There are two reasons why the investor (your suitor) doesn't want you talking to other potential partners. Firstly, they are going to put a lot of effort into the courtship. The time of their investment managers is a scarce resource so they don't want to waste that time on a courtship that you may call off. Secondly, if they are going to proceed to make an offer of investment then they don't want to be in competition with anyone else. The last thing the investor wants is a tall dark stranger whispering alternative terms in your ear. But playing the field is not as easy as it sounds. Rule 1 says that the courtship takes time. Courting two prospective partners at the same time may be a good idea in principle but it can take all of your time to keep both relationships moving forwards. While you are rushing around being courted who is running the business?

   One alternative to trying to juggle several prospective investors is to appoint a financial advisor or broker to handle the approaches from outside parties. If you are going to use a professional advisor then I would recommend one where the cost is paid as a fee and or a few percentage points of equity on a 'no deal, no fee' basis. Then, if they take you on as a client, you know they believe they have a fair chance of securing funding and not just taking your cash and wasting your time. It may seem expensive (endowment effect kicking in?) but a good advisor can get you more offers than you may otherwise be able to manage yourself and the competitive pressure can lead to improved terms that can justify the intermediaries' fees.

There is no right answer but going nearly all the way with just one investor is going to leave you vulnerable for a late rejection. It also leaves you in a very poor negotiating position over the terms of the investment agreement. After six months or more of effort invested you will be very reluctant to walk away (sunk cost effect). The investor's barrage of enthusiasm was partly an attempt to keep you loyal and is no guarantee that a final offer will emerge. And if you don't get the proposal after a long courtship then there is no option but to update your profile on the website, dress up and start dating again.

3. **The business plan can't be part of your vows.** The business plan is not a promise. Although some investors will try to hold you to the implied promise, it only maps one of the many possible futures. It is just one of the means by which the investor will assess your judgement and your knowledge of the market. The investors know, but will seldom admit, that in six months' time the business plan is likely to be completely out of date (especially for young and early stage companies). See it as an opportunity to show your understanding of the market, the customer and the costs of service delivery. Making the assumption that the business plan is 'true' is to fall into the error of believing we can predict the future over the medium- and long-term. The trouble is, as we have seen in so many contexts, we don't like uncertainty. Both the writer and the reader of the plan will want to believe it is true. If you can, find an investor with a more enlightened view of planning and decision making. They should be backing your judgement and your experience not a spreadsheet model.

4. **There is no marriage until the ceremony is over.** The longed for investment offer (marriage proposal) finally arrives. Typically a letter that outlines the principal terms of the investment, establishes a number of conditions and requests a formal period of exclusivity. Once this letter is signed and the terms accepted the investor will start spending money on lawyers and advisors to complete due diligence so it is not unreasonable at this point to agree to a period of exclusivity. But be under no illusions, the investor will retain the right to withdraw at any point for any reason and for no reason. The offer letter will always be subject to 'investment committee approval'

so if they get worried, or just see a better opportunity elsewhere, there is no obligation to invest.

The first offer letter is negotiable and now is the time to get professional advice and test how much the investor wants to invest. This period of negotiation can take several weeks but also serves as a useful period to chase along any other potential suitors in case better terms may be forthcoming. Once the terms are agreed and the letter signed your days of playing the field will be over. However the period of exclusivity should not be for longer than is reasonably necessary to complete the final checks and negotiate the investment agreement. The courtship will have taken from a few to many months, don't expect this last part of the process to take less than a couple of months. If you manage to get the cash in the bank within six months of first contact with an investor then you will have done well, even though many investors will suggest the whole thing can be completed in two months when you first meet (see Rule 1).

But there is still a lot that can go wrong. Some fundamental trust has been established but the investor can pull out at any moment for any reason (remember they suffer from the endowment effect as much as you do – it's no easier for them to part with cash than it is for you to part with equity). Paid experts will be brought in to assess your customer proposition and the market potential (remember investors are not typically experts in your sector). Professional investors (but not business angels) have to make investments so they are usually on your side by this stage. They don't want to back down now with so much effort already put into the relationship (sunk cost effect is working in your favour). The investor is now in the process of gathering the information they need to justify, by rational rule-based logic, their investment decision to others (the investment committee). You may suddenly feel that after months of being on trial they are suddenly on your side and working with you to get the decision through the necessary hoops. But however comforting and encouraging this may be it can take only one serious doubt to stop an investment. Ninety-nine out of 100 boxes may all have been ticked but it can take only one black mark to block the investment. Be particularly wary of the industry experts that are brought in at the last minute to do 'due diligence' on your market assumptions and forecasts. Treat them with caution. One word from them and the deal may be off. You need to earn their trust; don't just assume it.

5. **There will always be a fight negotiating the pre-nuptial agreement.** The letter that contained investment offer will only have covered the most basic terms. The offer letter may look good but the first site of the full investment agreement can be a shock. You must have experienced commercial and legal advice at this stage. Remember you are out of your comfort zone, deciding far from home, the

investor is doing what they do every week, so you need an experienced guide to help you through this unfamiliar terrain. Some investors have some unusual ideas about how the marriage should work, or more particularly how the divorce will be handled once the relationship is over.

(a) **The investor will want to leave the relationship with as much of their fortune intact as possible.** How will they do that? Several ways. They can make the investment in separate stages with the release of each investment dependent on meeting milestones or performance targets. I don't like this. The future is uncertain, the business plan a reasonable guess at the time it was created, possibly up to 12 months ago. The advantage of an equity investment is having the funds in the business for the long-term so that the money can't be withdrawn if you have a bad quarter. You should insist that all of the funds are invested in one go, without condition.

Another device that enables the investor to keep one hand on the cash is for a portion of the funds to be invested as a loan rather than as ordinary shares (a similar effect can be achieved with preference shares, which can earn dividends and get paid before ordinary shares). The investor will get the equity entitlement for the full investment but part (sometimes nearly all) of the funds are then advanced as a loan. What is the advantage to the investor? If the business doesn't prosper and there is a trade sale at a low price or a liquidation of assets then the investor's loan notes will be paid out before shareholders get any of the proceeds. For the investor this is 'downside protection'. It also has the effect of increasing the investor's take on exit, a so-called 'double dip'. Imagine an investor acquired 50% of a company for a £1 million investment but putting all of the money in as a loan. If there was a sale of the company for £4 million the first £1 million would go to redeem the loans. The residual £3 million would be divided in proportion to the shareholdings. The original shareholders getting just £1.5 million and the investor £2.5 million. If the sale proceeds are only £1 million then the original shareholders will get nothing. These loans are pretty much standard practice in the UK private equity industry so resisting them may not be possible. Minimizing the proportion of loan may be the best you can achieve.

(b) **They reserve the right to bring their mother to live with you if they don't like the way you run the house.** In the early days when trust is high you will be left to run the business as you see fit. There will be all sorts of provisions in the investment agreement about investors having the final say on senior appointments, capital expenditure and budget approval. But these, in general, are there to stop you putting your cat on the payroll and paying him £100,000 a year. If the trust is high then you will be left to run the company without interference. It is when the trust breaks down that the trouble will start. Instead of the non-executive director who comes to board meetings and hardly speaks, a consultant or advisor may turn up and start participating in every decision. In the best tradition of mother-in-law jokes, they will start telling you how to run the business, suggestions that it may be difficult to ignore.

(c) **They reserve the right to evict you completely and move in their lover.** The investor in reality has very few levers to pull when things are not going well. One of them is to change the management. The investment agreement may give them rights, under certain circumstances, to force you off the board and to appoint new managers to run the business. This can be devastating but be very wary of the provisions in the draft agreement which could mean that if you are forced to step down as a director you are forced to sell your shares, often at par or below market value. Losing management control is one thing, losing your economic interest in the business is another.

(d) **They will want to charge you rent on the family home.** Under Rule 5(a) you may end up with some of the incoming investment in the form of loan notes or preference shares. The investor will often attach an interest rate to the loan or a dividend to the preference shares so that the first take of any profit goes to the investor. Failure to make the interest payments or the dividend can often be used as a trigger to invoke more draconian controls: taking control of the board (and therefore the ability to sack other directors) and sometimes allowing the issue of new shares, which would allow the investor to take full control of the company and its worth.

(e) **You will be paying for the wedding and covering the costs of all of their guests.** Make no mistake, you will be paying for the cost of the deal and all of the investor's incidental costs. You will be paying for this out of the incoming investment but it can be a big proportion of the money in some cases. The company, subject to investment being completed, will be picking up the investor's legal fees, due diligence costs and sometimes a non-specific 'arrangement' fee. I have seen a term sheet where for an incoming investment of £1 million, £250,000 was going straight out in fees! OK, it is the investor's money that is paying the bills but you will not need reminding that you have sold equity in order to provide the income to pay the fees. Do your calculations on the equity exchanged for investment based on the funds that will be available after all the costs have been covered.

I offer these rules, not to deter you from seeking investment, but so that you have a better idea of what to expect. Overall the combination of capital and your management can create value. However, the division of risk and the division of benefits between management and investors is a zero sum game. A game the investors have played before. A game most management teams have not. The investor has all the advantages of decision making 'close to home', the entrepreneur all of the disadvantages of decision making 'far from home'. More often than not, in my experience, investors and managers can have a very good relationship that is beneficial to both sides. The investor gets a good return; the managers and business owners get the ability to develop a business and create long-term value. But it helps to be aware of the rules that investors follow and to understand how the endowment effect and the sunk cost effect play a part in the decision-making process.

The endowment effect and global warming

One final but important aside on the endowment effect reinforces my pessimism about our collective ability to tackle global warming and other environmental crises. The certain and immediate loss of the perceived benefits of our modern life – cheap flights, cheap meat and a reckless use of cheap fossil fuels – weighs very heavily on our minds. The promised payback – a vague notion of environmental stability to future generations – is easily ignored by most people. Giving up what we currently enjoy to achieve the uncertain payback seems an unattractive exchange. We stick with the 'endowment' of our current way of life, regardless of the longer-term consequences. And of course generating rational, economic justifications as to why we should make the exchange in terms of net present value calculations which, for example, was the approach taken in the Stern Report, will have little impact on our intuitive assessment of the choice. Our long-term future depends upon our ability to change our instinctive preference on this vital exchange. An understanding of the psychology of choice is vital to the future of the planet.

In other words...

This chapter weaves together many of the main themes in the book by looking at the decisions that are made by entrepreneurs and investors.

Entrepreneurs negotiating an investment agreement are making decisions far from home – use an expert to guide you. But the investor is, relative to the entrepreneur, far from home when assessing the business opportunity and will engage an industry expert to help them verify their investment decision.

Investors will make an initial decision to back a management team based on intuitive reasoning and then use rule-based logic to justify the decision to others. This initial judgement can be prone to biases such as presumed association and may be skewed by previous experiences (either good or bad).

Investment relationships are built on trust, not a cold analysis of facts. Trust takes time to develop. That is why, even thought the information could be exchanged in a few days, investment agreements take months to conclude. Don't treat business plans as detailed plans about the future. And certainly don't promise that they are true. A business plan is part of the entrepreneur's CV and a chance to demonstrate knowledge about a market – not a detailed financial plan for the next three years.

Be aware of how loss aversion leads to the endowment effect, which can hinder growth.

Which means that...

For the entrepreneur...

➤ Don't be too precious about equity in early stage companies. 100% of nothing is nothing. Better to do the deal and create value than don't do the deal and wonder what if...

➤ If you are looking for investment keep as many channels as you can handle open at once. You may need the negotiating strength that comes from having an alternative.

➤ Most entrepreneurs are in new territory negotiating investment agreements. Get an experienced advisor on your side.

➤ Understand the rules that govern investor behaviour, it will improve your negotiating power.

➤ Do seek investment for your business ideas. Without it most of them will only ever be dreams.

For the investor...

> Don't pretend that business plans are true.

> The initial decision to back a management team will often be intuitive – then supported and justified with rule-based logic. Therefore be aware of the dangers of 'close to home' decision making – especially the influence of a few prior investments that had either very good or bad outcomes. Also beware of presumed association influencing your judgements.

> When considering follow-on investments into failing companies be aware that the sunk cost effect may be influencing your judgement. What you have already invested – time or money – is gone and shouldn't interfere with the assessment of risk for new investments.

Rules of thumb

5 ♥ Know the 'rules' of private equity
4 ♥ You don't lose value selling shares to investors

Chapter **15**

....

Rules of thumb: part 2 – fighting to win

In Chapter 7 I looked at some of the rules of thumb from poker and how they apply to the logic of investing in business. This time my rules of thumb relate specifically to competing against an opponent, the art of misinformation and strategies for fighting strong and weak opponents.

Rules of thumb – competing, misinformation and strategies

1 Know yourself / know your enemy

At the card table: Self-knowledge is one of the most important aspects of the game. At the most basic level you need to know accurately, and without the bias of optimism, the various hands you may achieve and their relative probabilities. If you misjudge your own strength you will err again and again. Likewise, it is just as important to make an honest assessment of your opponent's potential. In poker knowing your own hand and potential is a simple matter of fact. Knowing your opponent's hand is a matter of great uncertainty and considerable judgement, which fundamentally comes from observing how they play and handle themselves in different situations (observation, experience, feedback). The fact that you know everything you can about your prospects, and have to make difficult judgements about your opponent's prospects, gives rise to one of the most expensive mistakes that beginners can make. After waiting all evening you finally get dealt a pair of aces. You know you have a good hand and you correctly assess the odds of making three aces or a full house. Excited by your own hand (for which you have full information) you take less notice of the strong betting of your opponent which may also indicate a strong hand. Eventually, when a lot of bets have been made, raised and called, you finally have to decide to make a final call or raise. You will find yourself balancing the fact that you definitely have a strong hand against a possibility (just a judgement based on a few cues) that your opponent potentially has a stronger hand.

It is all too easy to be overconfident in your own known strength relative to an opponent's unknown potential. One of the hardest things to do in

> *One of the hardest things to do in poker is to fold a strong hand*

poker is to fold a strong hand. Beyond estimating the relative strengths of the cards you also need to understand about both your own and your opponent's playing style. How often do they bluff? Do they play an aggressive, loose game? Last time they had a strong hand how did they play? What did they say? Are there patterns or flags from their past behaviour that can help you identify the best course of action now?

Round the board table: Business, in this regard, is more difficult than poker for the simple reason that understanding your own company's strengths and weaknesses is not a matter of fact (or probability) as it is in poker, but is a matter of judgement. A judgement that can be prone to bias. Too many companies get to believe their own hype. If the company has been told often enough and for long enough that they are the best then everyone gets to believe it (there may be real advantages in this kind of talking up). However, when difficult strategic choices have got to be made then an honest assessment of capabilities, strengths and past performance is vital. It is also easy to fall in to the same trap as the poker player and underestimate the strength of a competitor. Testimony about the strength of your own company's products is available every day. The same information about your competitor's products is more difficult to obtain, is usually second or third hand and may be out of date. You may overestimate your own relative strength based on the quantity and the quality of the information you have. Paranoia is a useful trait when it helps to negate our natu-

don't let healthy paranoia get in the way of action

ral tendency to ignore or underutilise vital but patchy and uncertain assessments of your competitors' capabilities. But don't let healthy paranoia get in the way of action – make an honest assessment then have the courage to act.

> Be honest when assessing relative strengths and weaknesses

> Don't ignore your opponent because the information is not to hand

> Always be paranoid, but don't be fearful – have courage

2 Don't give your opponent free or cheap cards

At the card table: There is nothing your opponents like more than a chance to stay in the hand at no cost. It means that even if they have a poor hand but can stay to see the next card for free, they will. One day they will get lucky and win. In most circumstances, if you think you have the best hand at the table early in a hand of poker you need to make it expensive for your opponents to stay in the hand. The logic is simple – with the best hand you have the best chance of winning the pot once all the cards are seen. Not every time, but you will win the pot more often than any of your opponents. The odds are in your favour. Making a big bet when you are winning achieves two things. Firstly, if the other players call your bet then the size of the pot has gone up, which increases your winnings if you do end up with the best hand at the showdown. (Remember the best poker players do well because they win more when they have good hands.) Secondly, if some of them fold then you have increased your chances of winning – any player, even with bad cards, may get lucky and beat you. The less of them in the later rounds the greater your chance of scooping the pot. So the worst thing you can do if you have a strong hand, is to bet weakly and let other players stay in the hand for a few dollars, or sometimes for nothing (a so called 'free card'). If enough players stay in then there is a good chance that one of them will get lucky and beat you.

Round the board table: Competitive advantage comes in many guises. Your market reputation and the habits and attitudes of your customers, your organizational knowledge and expertise, perhaps a defendable patent or other intellectual property right, an exclusive distribution partnership or other route to market. There will always be competitors aiming to grow their market share at your expense. If competitors are allowed to compete in your market without a significant cost or organizational commitment then more competitors will be tempted to try. If enough companies are competing with you then you increase the chances that one or more will

Don't give a competitor a free card

get lucky. They may find a compelling marketing strategy or customer proposition, recruit a transforming sales director, raise equity finance to fund an expansion or an acquisition. If you don't compete aggressively when you have an advantage then you increase the chance that you will lose your market dominance or it will get very expensive to maintain. Either way the high profits that flow from a high market share will be gone. Don't give a competitor a free card.

> ➤ Don't let other people play in your game for free.
> ➤ Raise the barriers to entry.

3 Don't fight unless you have to

At the card table: The movies misrepresent poker. The script will call for a final showdown, two players head to head, the final bet called, the cards revealed, the winner sweeping up the mountain of dollar bills, the loser fingering a trigger under the table. In practice getting to the showdown – the final revealing of cards when all bets are completed – is fraught with risk and should be avoided. The showdown is a battle of strength, the final locking of horns in which anything can happen, the underdog can easily get lucky on the last card. Less dramatic for the cameras, but it is far better to win the pot without a fight and therefore avoid the risk of being out-drawn.

How do you avoid a fight? By signalling intention. If you raise and then re-raise an opponent you are signalling an intention that you will back this hand all the way – to a final showdown if necessary. The rational opponent with a moderate hand will read your intention, assess her prospects and avoid the fight by folding. By signalling strength you can win the pot without the need for a final winner-takes-all fight at the showdown. Many people believe that bluffing is the essence of poker. But bluffing is just signalling intention whilst misrepresenting the strength of your hand. A good player will often use the semi-bluff rather than the complete bluff (misrepresenting a losing hand as strong). The semi-bluff is made on a hand, which although not a winning hand now may, with good cards, have an outside chance of becoming a very good hand (e.g. filling a straight). The semi-bluff has two chances of winning. The signalling of a strong hand by raising may win the pot there and then without a fight. Alternatively, if forced to the showdown there is a chance of drawing the cards to win. However, it is worth noting that it can be very hard to bluff beginners or very poor players. If they are not capable of assessing strength or their prospects of winning they will play on to the showdown regardless of your promised (but perhaps exaggerated) strength.

Round the board table: Battles for market share are in neither competitor's interest. If you are market leader you want to avoid a showdown wherever possible. This can be achieved by signalling strength – by leaving the potential competitor or market entrant in no doubt about your willingness to fight if necessary. Like two males preparing to fight in the mating season, a display of force, some effective posturing and a realistic assessment by the weaker party avoids a potentially damaging fight. Market leaders should take trouble to mark their territory and signal the intention to fight at every opportunity. The last thing you want to do is have to engage in battle. But unfortunately, just like poker, there are always fools with money (often from private equity) who will not read the signals and charge into battle regardless of their chances of success. Misrepresenting strength will be useless – the battle will have to be fought. But like a good poker player, companies can exaggerate strength (the semi-bluff) to discourage competitors in the critical stage of a developing market. But the semi-bluff is much more effective if you are seen as a strong and purposeful competitor. It is more effective from Microsoft than a software start-up.

there are always fools with money

> Don't fight unless you have to
> Signal strength and commitment to keep competitors away.
> Misrepresenting strength can be effective at protecting weaker positions.

4 How to fight a strong enemy

At the card table: In poker there are times when you are down to a few loose chips against a player peering over their towering stacks. The situation is serious. The pavement will look very narrow to the drunk – perhaps just one false step away from the gutter. Some promising hands that in other situations could be played with a positive expectation now have to be turned down. Not only is a positive expectation important but every bet has to have a good chance of winning – there is no time left to look at the sum of a portfolio of similar bets, every bet has to be treated in isolation. Now picking the right hand to fight becomes a matter of life or death. Good hands must be passed. Only the best can be backed. You have to pick your fights with great care. Everything is necessarily focused on a couple of opportunities with high probability of winning, but an inevitably low return.

Round the board table: If you are taking on a large well-funded competitor you need to focus. You don't have the resources to compete on several fronts. You must select the one or two places where you can focus resources and have a high chance of making small gains. This strategy

if it does come to a fight you are very unlikely to win

must be repeated until either you can attract more finance or the big competitor is sufficiently annoyed by your attack to buy you out. With limited funds you are not in a position to make high-risk/high-return investments. But it may also be helpful to pick opportunities where the competitor is not at its strongest. Don't pick a fight with a well-funded competitor in the one market that it will defend to the death. Focus on its weaker propositions where it may even fold without a fight – because if it does come to a fight you are very unlikely to win.

It is worth noting that it isn't completely straightforward being on the other side in this situation – competing against a desperate competitor down to his last funds. A desperate competitor will not make the same rational decisions as a better funded player. He will fight to stay alive and will defend his position with great tenacity. The entrepreneurs with everything to lose will fight much harder than the hired hands that the big company will put up against them. They will be forced to take risks – some of those risks may work. Growing confidence, an improving financial situation and the disciplines of having to focus can make them particularly dangerous. The big competitor needs, wherever possible, to raise the stakes to end the threat from a poorly funded and tenacious competitor. Strong signals that you intend to defend your position can be effective here and will deter potential investors from giving them a lifeline.

> ➤ David and Goliath – focus your limited resources on one weak spot.

> ➤ Don't provoke the big competitor in markets where it has signalled (or you can reasonably deduce) their intention to fight.

> ➤ If you are the better funded competitor, raise the stakes and be clear to signal your intention to deter others who may be considering investing.

Rules of thumb

4♣   Signal intention to avoid a fight

3♠   Be honest in your assessments of your own and your competitors' strengths and weaknesses

J♠   Don't make it cheap for firms to compete with you

8♠   Don't fight unless you have to – try to avoid a showdown

Chapter **16**

··

The art of decision making

Management is an art and not a science. There aren't universal laws that can be followed to unfailingly create value. Management is about the exercise of judgement not the application of rules. Judgement that is always subjective and can easily be biased and distorted. The art of management is about understanding where our judgements come from – knowing when to trust and when to doubt our instincts.

On the following pages, I have captured the main themes and included some observations that may help you understand the art of management – the art of decisions.

Managers make decisions...

About the allocation of resources
With other peoples' money which therefore...
...have to be justified to others
That have significance to others
That build on each other
That are misremembered

Managing in the real world

There is the imaginary world of management science where...
We can make well-founded predictions about the future,
Our management theories have the status of scientific laws and
We can reliably identify cause and effect

In this imaginary world we are able to...
Make predictions about the future with the same reliability as (we think)
we are able to explain the past
Eliminate risk by the careful evaluation of situations and the correct
application of theories
Objectively choose the best path every time the path divides
Know that our failures arise because we didn't have all the information
or we misapplied the theory
Identify the lazy and stupid manager by the outcome of their decisions
Assign blame for bad outcomes with confidence
Write management books which give general advice that can be applied
in every situation

But the world we live, manage and trade in is very different...
Actions sometimes have unpredictable and disproportionate effects
No amount of rational analysis can objectively identify the 'right'
answer
The future is always unknowable – we can never eliminate uncertainty
We can't separate cause and effect through observation
Our 'theories' derived from observing best practice are no more than
'rules of thumb' developed in one situation that may or may not be
applicable in another.

Every decision involves a judgement

There isn't an objective method for finding the right decision because...

We can't assess all the alternatives – we have to focus on just a few

We can't predict all of the consequences of an alternative

We never have enough time – we have to decide when enough is enough

We don't have fixed and certain goals

We use our judgement to...

Stop searching for alternatives

Stop assessing consequences

Stop searching for new information

Choose between conflicting goals as they are uncovered

Stop deciding and start acting

Intuitive judgement – the art of knowing

Our intuitions...

Are the sum of all our experiences

...experiences that have been shaped by our environment

Are instantaneous – they just appear in our minds...

Can determine our choices without us ever being aware of them

Are sometimes in conflict with the answers we get from following rule-based logic.

May have to be justified to others (and sometimes ourselves)

Intuitive judgement stops the search by...

Identifying options we like.

Identifying options we recognize

Making do with 'good enough'

Intuitive judgements 'close to home' can be fast and accurate when...

They are decisions that have been made frequently before...

...in familiar contexts...

...with fast feedback...

...for a low proportion of wealth

But intuitive judgement can be led astray when...
Our memories are dominated by one or two past events with high emotional impact
Some of the relevant information is not in minds to influence our judgement
We carry assumptions (prejudices) about cause and effect
We rely on judgements based on very little experience
We ignore the risks that we haven't experienced

Poker and investing

Poker is a metaphor for investing because...
You have to make decisions without all of the information
Each bet is an 'investment' made with the aim of making a profit
The cost, likelihood and return are all unknown and can only be judgements
The best players use intuitive judgements, wrought from experience, to make decisions
The experience of others has been captured in 'rules of thumb'
Poor players (and managers) waste too much money on mediocre opportunities
The best players (and managers) make the most of the best opportunities
Poker isn't about bluffing, it is about communicating, and sometimes miscommunicating, intention

The poker metaphor breaks down because...
Poker is a zero-sum game (what I win, you lose) but...
...business is usually, but not always, about mutual benefit
In poker the only thing we can alter is how we bet (and, indirectly, how others perceive us)...
...in business there are many more variables the manager can control
Poker is played alone...
...business is a team game

Deciding 'far from home'

Intuition distilled from experience is useless when...
You are deciding far from home, making decisions which are...
...rare or unique...

...in unfamiliar contexts...

...where there may be no feedback or it is delayed or ambiguous...

...when all or most of your wealth is at stake

We are overconfident in our judgement because...

We take confidence from other successes in different contexts to...

...back our own judgement

We back previous winners even though...

...separating luck from skill is very difficult when luck can influence outcomes

We copy the success stories of others

When we do have to make decisions far from home we should...

Hire an expert to guide us, although experts are...

...not as good as they think they are...

...likely to diagnose their speciality more often than is justified...

...tell you what they think you want to hear

Learn quickly and make our own map of unfamiliar terrain

Making maps and learning fast

The XP methods deliver value in uncertain environments by...

Accepting uncertainty as a fact; not trying get certainty through over-planning

Accepting that even goals can change

Keeping the business sponsor and the customer as part of the decision-making process

Failing quickly, learning quickly and responding to what you have learnt

Focusing on values and vision to guide the process

What managers tell us about decision making

Because fear is more powerful than greed...

We are risk averse and decline opportunities for gain, but...

We will take a risk to recover a loss, which leads to...

...the sunk cost effect – throwing more money after bad

...that we change our preferences depending on our frame of reference (gain or loss)

If we are above budget we will be risk averse, but...

...below budget we will take risks, although...

...close to extinction we become very risk averse

Managers don't do what the theories say they should do, they...

Don't evaluate all of the options and reduce them to a single measure (net value)...

...they focus on a couple of likely options

...treat likely as 'certain'

...treat unlikely as 'impossible'

Don't see management as a gamble then a wait for the outcome, they...

...manage events, each decision being built on by later decisions

Change their preference depending on the context

Entrepreneurs: big dreams and funding

Entrepreneurs go ahead despite the poor chances of success because...

The availability bias means they misrepresent their chance of success

They build over-optimistic scenarios that only focus on success (inside thinking)

They overestimate their chances of success – most of them think they are better than average

The glamour of success lures people in regardless of the odds (the lottery effect)

Entrepreneurs struggle to find funding because...

The endowment effect makes them overvalue equity so that...

...100% of nothing seems more valuable than 50% of a lot

They misunderstand the 'rules' of courtship with finance providers

They don't see their business proposition as others see it (the outside view)

Rules of thumb

Providing a final '10 rules' for better decisions would be disingenuous. What I have done is brought together the 'rules of thumb' that I have included at the end of each chapter. Rules of thumb aren't 'laws' that have universal application. They depend, like our intuitive judgements, on the environment that gave rise to them. They can be thought of as a distillation of other people's experience. Your own judgement is the only guide to assessing whether and when they should be applied. But remember, your judgement is better than the management scientists would have you believe...

Rules of thumb

On management and competing

A♠ Don't fight unless you have to – try to avoid a showdown

K♠ Changing your mind in the light of new information is a sign of strength not weakness

Q♠ Don't waste time asking people for a rational justification of well-grounded intuitions

J♠ Don't make it easy for firms to compete with you

10♠ Never get so remote from the commercial environment that you stop learning

9♠ Goals are discovered not handed down

8♠ We can't manage uncertainty the same way we have *tried* to manage certainty

7♠ Plan lightly – avoid detailed plans of distant futures

6♠ Use shared values and a clear vision to guide decision making when the path is uncertain

5♠ Build relationships rather than controls

4♠ Practise honesty and openness in communication – courage and determination in action

3♠ Be honest in your assessments of your own and your competitors' strengths and weaknesses

2♠ Be sensitive to the surprising

On investing and entrepreneurship

A♥ Every cost should be seen as an investment for gain

K♥ Overheads are the blind bets we place to be allowed to play the game – keep them low

Q♥ Invest strongly in the rare situations where you have a clear advantage

J♥ Be cautious or decline investments where you only have a small advantage

10♥ Focus on the three numbers that matter: probable cost, chance of success and possible return

9 ♥   See a series of similar investments as a portfolio rather than looking at each opportunity in isolation

8 ♥   Take an outsider's view of your business plan

7 ♥   Pass on a third of the field before choosing the best you have seen

6 ♥   Don't believe your own business plan – it is just one of an infinite number of alternative futures

5 ♥   Know the 'rules' of private equity

4 ♥   You don't lose value selling shares to investors

3 ♥   A good investment will, with reasonable probability, double your money in three years

2 ♥   Ignore sunk costs – each new investment must be evaluated on its own terms

On intuition, judgement, and deciding

A ♦   Intuition gained in one environment can mislead in another

K ♦   Every decision requires a personal judgement

Q ♦   Good management is the art of good judgement – judgement based on experience

J ♦   Good enough is sometimes the best decision

10 ♦   Record your decisions to calibrate your judgement

9 ♦   Expert judgement may be better than yours but it will not be as good as the experts think it is

8 ♦   Test a judgement by changing the frame of reference (making a gain or avoiding a loss)

7 ♦   Success can breed overconfidence

6 ♦   Consider hiring a guide when faced with decisions in unfamiliar terrain

5 ♦   Far from home be prepared to fail fast and learn fast

4 ♦   Trust intuition based on well-grounded experience

3 ♦   Question judgements that are not based on personal experience

2 ♦   You can't make the perfect decision

On chance, luck and gambling

A ♣   Don't judge people by the outcome of chance events

K ♣   A narrow path (limited funds) and big steps (high stakes) just gets you in the gutter more quickly

Q ♣   Close to home you *do* get luckier the more you practise

J ♣   Some winners are fools, some losers are wise

10 ♣   You can't separate skill from luck just by looking at outcomes

9 ♣   Avoid big bets for small advantage

8♣ Avoid long shots

7♣ Raising or folding can be better than calling

6♣ Treat management theories as rules of thumb – not universal laws

5♣ Judge a theory by its predictions not its explanations

4♣ Signal intention to avoid a fight

3♣ Position matters – early movers need bigger advantages

2♣ With limited resources even good bets with positive expectations have to be turned down

Glossary of poker terms used in the book

Ante A bet required by all of the players before a hand begins.

Bad beat Having a hand that is a strong favourite beaten by a lucky draw.

Blind bets Forced bets that the first or second players to the left of the dealer have to place at the start of the first round of betting.

Bluff A bet or raise designed to make an opponent fold even though they may not have a weaker hand.

Call Putting chips into the pot to equal another player's bet or raise.

Community cards In Texas Hold'em and Omaha, the five cards that are dealt face up and shared by all of the players

Chip A token used for betting with a monetary value.

Flop In Texas Hold'em and Omaha the first three community cards that are dealt together.

Flush Five cards all of the same suit but not in sequence.

Fold To pull out of a hand rather than bet or raise.

Full house Three of a kind *and* a pair.

Hand A hand in poker is always five cards.

Hole cards The two cards dealt face down to each player (in Texas Hold'em) which only they can see. (Hence the phrase 'My ace in the hole,' to denote a hidden strength.)

Loose Loose play is betting on more hands than you should.

The Nuts To hold 'The Nuts' means that you have the best possible hand – whatever the other players hole cards they can't beat you. (Hence one of my favourite poker phrases 'Sometimes

even a blind squirrel can hold The Nuts' refers to the fact that even poor players may have the best hand.)

Omaha A game similar to Texas Hold'em but with each player receiving four cards face down (two of which must be used with three of the community cards).

On tilt A player that is betting poorly and is out of control.

Pot The sum of all the bets placed so far in a hand.

Raise To place a bet which increases an earlier bet.

River The fifth and final community card, sometimes called 5th Street.

Semi-bluff A bet or raise with the intention of either getting a player with a better hand to fold or to draw so as to improve your hand.

Showdown Turning over all of the cards once all the bets have been completed.

Straight Five cards, of mixed suits, in sequence.

Texas Hold'em A very popular version of the game in which each player makes the best hand of five cards they can from five community cards and their own two hole cards.

Tight Playing conservatively and only betting on very strong hands.

Turn The 4th community card, also called 4th Street.

Bibliography

Introduction

Ely Devons' allusion to ritual magic can be found in Devons, E. (1961) *Essays in Economics*, Oxford: Greenwood Publishing.

Chapter 1

Rubin's gripping account of his first day in office for President Clinton is taken from his autobiography, Rubin, R. E. (2003) *In An Uncertain World*, New York: Random House.

The quote from Morris Goldstein is reported in Whitehouse, McKay, Davis, Liesman (1998) 'Bear tracks', *The Wall Street Journal*, 18 August.

The puncturing of the 'moral hazard bubble' is referred to in Edwards, F. R. (1999) 'Hedge Funds and the Collapse of Long-Term Capital Management', *Journal of Economic Perspectives*, Vol. 10, No. 2 (spring).

Chapter 2

Des Wilson's compelling account of spending a year on the professional poker circuit is in Wilson, D. (2006) *Swimming with the Devilfish*, London: Macmillan. The extracts are taken from pp.274–275.

The report of the lightning strike on Philips factory is included in Christopher, M., Peck, H. 'The Five Principles of Supply Chain Resilience', *Logistics Europe*, February 2004, p.20. The same incident is discussed in Apgar, D. (2006), *Risk Intelligence*, Boston: Harvard Business School Press.

Mandelbrot's discussion of the volatility of markets is from Mandelbrot, B. (2004) *The (Mis)Behaviour of Markets*, New York: Basic Books.

Ilya Prigogine's description of deterministic chaos is in Prigogine, I. (1997) *The End of Certainty*, New York: The Free Press.

The discussion of the Nissan warranty costs is taken from Bazerman, M. H. (2006) *Judgement in Managerial Decision Making*, 6th edition, New York: John Wiley .

Crozier's study of power in organisations is from Crozier, M. (1964) *The Bureaucratic Phenomenon*, London: Tavistock.

Chapter 3

The text of Darwin's note is from Darwin, C. (1969) *The Autobiography of Charles Darwin, 1809–1882*, edited by N.Barlow. New York: Norton (Original work published 1887).

Undermining the explanatory and predictive claims of management theories is explored in Rosenzweig, P. (2007) *The Halo Effect*, New York: The Free Press.

Apgar's discussion of 'Encyclopaedists' is included in his *Risk Intelligence* (2006) cited above. Etzioni's 'Hypervigilance' is taken from Etzioni, A. (1989) 'Humble Decision Making' in *Harvard Business Review on Decision Making*, Boston: Harvard Business School Press.

The interview with Anna Walker was reported in The *Guardian*, 11 October 2006.

William Ouchi's discussion of the contrasting approaches to goals is from Ouchi, W. (1981) *Theory Z*, Reading, Massachusetts: Addison-Wesley.

The discussion of Darwin's marriage dilemma and the mating habits of the guppy are taken from Gigerenzer, G. and Todd, P. M., and the ABC Research Group (1999) *Simple Heuristics That Make Us Smart*, New York: Oxford University Press.

Chapter 4

The description of the Monty Hall problem is included in Bazerman's *Judgement in Managerial Decision Making* (cited above).

For the discussion on EMAP, see Caroline White 'EMAP slashes digital investment', www.journalism.co.uk, 28/11/02.

Steven Sloman's discussion of the two types of reasoning is covered in Sloman, S. A. (2002) 'Two Systems of Reasoning' in *Heuristics and Bias*, Gilovich, T., Griffin, D., Kahneman, D (eds), New York: Cambridge University Press.

Antonio Damasio's work with brain damaged patients is recounted in his enthralling book Damasio, A. R. (1994) *Descartes' Error*, New York: GP Putnam's Sons.

Damasio's experiments and the experiments detecting sweat gland activity are discussed in Gladwell, M. (2005) *Blink*, New York: Little Brown and Company.

Nassim Taleb's account of his career on Wall Street is included in Taleb, N. N. (2004) *Fooled by Randomness*, New York: Random House.

HMSO 'The Stern Report' (2006).

Chapter 5

Damasio's anecdote and reflections on the limits of rationality are included in *Descartes' Error* (cited above).

There is a thorough discussion of so called 'frugal' stopping strategies in *Simple Heuristics That Make Us Smart* (cited above).

Gary Klein discusses the decision-making strategies of fire-fighters and soldiers in Klein, G. (2003) *The Power of Intuition*, originally published as *Intuition at Work*, New York: Random House. This also includes a discussion of Isenberg's study of how managers think.

Daniel Isenberg's study appeared in Isenberg, D. J. (1984) 'How Senior Managers Think,' *Harvard Business Review*, (6), pp.80–90.

Chapter 6

The history of boo.com is taken from Malmsten, E., Portanger, E., Drazin, D. (2001) *boo hoo*, London: Random House.

I have taken wisdom and rules of thumb from several authors on poker. For beginners I recommend Reuben, S. (2001) *Starting Out in Poker*, London: Everyman.

Other titles that I have used frequently are Skalansky, D. (1990) *The Theory of Poker*, Henderson, Nevada: Two Plus Two Publishing, and Feeney, J. (2000) *Inside The Poker Mind*, Henderson, Nevada: Two Plus Two Publishing.

For the business reader, Apostolico, D. (2005) *Tournament Poker and the Art of War: How the Classic Strategies of Sun Tzu can transform your Game,* Stuart (Lyle) Inc., U.S., has some good insights into tournament play.

The reported conversation with John Duthie is taken from Des Wilson's *Swimming with the Devilfish* (cited above).

The discussion of Monte Carlo engines is from Taleb's *Fooled by Randomness* (cited above).

The survey of managers' attitudes to gambling are taken from the influential article, March, J. G. and Shapira, Z. (1987) 'Managerial Perspectives on Risk and Risk Taking', *Management Science*, Vol. 33, No. 11, pp.1404–1418.

Chapter 8

The story of Long-Term Capital Management is grippingly told in, Lowenstein, R. (2001) *When Genius Failed,* London: Fourth Estate.

Professor Ed Galea's study of North American air accidents is reported in, Galea, E. R., Finney, K. M., Dixon, A. J. P., Siddiqui, A. and Cooney, D. P. (2006) 'Aircraft Accident Statistics and Knowledge Database: Analyzing Passenger Behaviour in Aviation Accidents', *AIAA Journal of Aircraft,* Vol. 43, No. 5, pp.1272–1281.

Chapter 9

Anthony Fisher's story is told in Frost, G. (2002) *Anthony Fisher: Champion of Liberty,* London: Profile Books.

Chapter 10

The original survey of business failure is by Dun and Bradstreet (1967) *Patterns of Success in Managing a Business,* New York: Dun and Bradstreet.

The US census data is reported in Dunne, T., Roberts, M. J. and Samuelson, L. (1988) 'Patterns of Firm Entry and Exit in U.S. Manufacturing Industries', *RAND Journal of Economics,* Vol. 19, pp.495–515.

The Scottish survey was undertaken by Reid and Smith in, Reid, G. C. and Smith, J. A. (2000) 'What Makes a New Business Start-up Successful?', *Small Business Economics,* Vol. 14, No. 3, pp.165-182.

The study of Californian entrepreneurs was reported in Cooper, A., Woo, C. and Dunkelberg, W. (1988) 'Entrepreneurs' Perceived Chances for Success', *Journal of Business Venturing,* Vol. 3, pp.97–108.

The discussion of 'inside' and 'outside' views is in Kahneman, D. and Lovallo, D. (1993) 'Timid Choices and Bold Forecasts: A Cognitive Perspective on Risk Taking', *Management Science,* Vol. 39, No.1, January.

The two studies of the performance of personal investment portfolios were, Barber, B. M. and Odean, T. (2000) ' Trading is Hazardous to Your Wealth: The Common Stock Investment Performance of Individual Investors', *Journal of Finance,* Vol. 55, pp.773–806: and Barber, B. M. and Odean, T. (2001) 'Boys Will be Boys: Gender, Overconfidence, and Common Stock Investment. *Quarterly Journal of Economics*, Vol. 116, No. 1, pp.261–292.

The experiment to replicate the entrepreneurial market entry decision is described in Camerer, C. F. and Lovallo, D. (1999) 'Overconfidence and Excess Entry: An Experimental Analysis', *American Economic Review,* Vol. 89, 306–318.

Chapter 11

The Peter Lynch story and the coins thought experiment are all included in Shefrin, H. (2002) *Beyond Fear and Greed,* New York: Oxford University Press.

The details of the studies of 'hot hands' basketball are in Gilovich, T., Vallone, R. and Tversky, A. (1985) 'The Hot Hand in Basketball: On the Misperception of Random Sequences', *Cognitive Psychology,* Vol. 17, pp.295–314.

The fund managers study can be found in Carhart, M. (1997) 'On Persistence in Mutual Fund Performance', *Journal of Finance*, Vol. 52, No. 1, pp.57–82.

The discussion of overconfidence in experts is in Griffin, D. and Tversky, A. (1992) 'The Weighing of Evidence and the Determinants of Confidence', *Cognitive Psychology,* Vol. 24, pp.411–435.

A discussion of professional conflict of interest is in Bazerman's *Judgement in Managerial Decision Making* (cited above).

Chapter 12

Two introductions to eXtreme programming are, Beck, K., with Andres, C. (2005) *eXtreme Programming Explained*, Boston: Addison-Wesley; and Beck, K. and Fowler, M. (2001) *Planning eXtreme Programming*, Boston, Addison-Wesley.

The XP values are taken from DeCarlo, D. (2004) *eXtreme Project Management*. San Francisco: Jossey-Bass.

The reports of managerial attitudes to risk taking are from March and Shapira, 'Managerial Perspectives on Risk and Risk Taking' (cited above).

Chapter 13

Nick Leeson's own account of the fall of Baring's Bank is in Leeson, N. (1996) *Rogue Trader*, London: Little Brown and Company.

The seminal paper on prospect theory was originally published as Kahneman, D. and Tversky, A. 'An analysis of Decision under Risk', *Econometrica*, Vol. 47, No. 2, pp.263–291, and is included with many other valuable papers in Kahneman, D. and Tversky, A. (eds) (2000) *Choices, Values, and Frames*, New York: Cambridge University Press.

The study of taxi drivers comes from, Camerer, C. F., Babcock, L., Lowenstein, G. and Thaler, R. H. (1999) 'Labor Supply of New York City Cab Drivers One Day at a Time', *The Quarterly Journal of Economics*, Vol. 112, No. 2, pp.407–441.

A discussion of several applications of prospect theory, including the end of the day effect in on-course race track betting is found in, Camerer, C. F. (2000) 'Prospect Theory in the Wild' in *Choices, Values, and Frames*, New York: Cambridge University Press.

Richard Thaler's account of the portfolio of $1 million gambles is described in, Thaler, R., H., (1999) 'Mental Accounting Matters', *Journal of Behavioral Decision Making*, Vol. 12, pp.183–206.

The reports of managerial attitudes to risk taking are from March and Shapira, 'Managerial Perspectives on Risk and Risk Taking' (cited above).

Chapter 14

The experiment with mugs to illustrate the endowment effect is reported in Kahneman, D., Knetsch, J. L. and Thaler, R. (1990) 'Experimental Tests of the Endowment Effect and the Coarse Theorem', *Journal of Political Economy,* Vol. 98, pp.1325–1328.

Index

accidents, misrepresentation of 95–6
88888 account 160–1
alternatives, identifying 24–5
Amazon.com
   Jeff Bezos's early success with 110
   market valuation of $32 billion in
      December 1999 76
   not the first online book store in
      the US 84, 205
American roulette wheel, two zeros
      which provides best odds from
      the house in a casino 72
American sport, dominated by
      statistics 134
ante, bet required of all the players
      before a hand begins 63, 68, **207**
Apgar, D. 13
   Encyclopaedists (collectors of
      information who can't commit)
      29
Aristotle, two ways of reasoning 42
art of management, understanding
      where our judgements come
      from 197
Asia, financial turmoil (1997) 91
assessment of your own and
      competitors' strengths and
      weaknesses, be honest in 195,
      203
association, lucky chair and 97
associative or intuitive reasoning 42,
      49
associative system, useful for
      achieving one's goals 43
auditors
   experiment about sale of company
      142
   prediction and 73

availability bias 95–6, 99, 121–2
   can be misled by and give undue
      weight to emotional factors 102
avoid big bets for small advantage 88
avoid long shots 88

baby-world.co.uk 111
bad beats
   in business 12–13
   in poker 12, 13, 139, **207**
Barber and Odean, study of
      individuals' stock portfolios 126
base rates 122, 124–5, 131, 204
basic probability, rational 'stopping
      rule' 35
basketball, 'hot hand' 135
Bazerman, M. 17, 142
bear traders 71
Beck, Kent 147–8
   Planning eXtreme Programming
      146, 153
Benetton advertising, brand
      recognition and 54–5
best alternative, relies on human
      judgement 21, 37, 59
'best you have seen', sample third of
      the field before committing to
      37, 204
Bezos, Jeff 110–11
blind bets 63, 68, **207**
bluffing 17, 63–4, 85, 193, 200, **207**
Bob
   player of Texas Hold'em for five
      years 91–4
   under Omaha his intuition could be
      liability 92
boiled frog syndrome 98
boo.com 76–8

book publishing
cover price of book needs to be at least five times physical production cost 82
similar investment and risk pattern to poker 73
brain damaged patients, emotional tags and 47
branded outlets, recognition and 55
Britain's National Health Service (NHS), incentivized to achieve targets and performance ratings 33
British roulette wheel, one zero 72
bubbles, hard to spot when you are inside them 78
build relationships rather than controls 157, 203
bull traders 71–2
business
goal of profit may bring conflict with other goals 32
more random than management science has been telling us 144
role of chance in 21
team game usually about mutual benefit 200
business autobiography, decisions that are forgotten 5
business ideas, do seek investment for 186
business plans
don't pretend they are true 187
futility of as predictions of the future 173, 198, 205
opportunity for management to show knowledge of the market and the customer 129
part of entrepreneur's CV not a detailed financial plan for next three years 186, 203–4
planning fallacy and illusions of control 128–9
represent only one of many possible future histories 131, 204
business start, everything to prove 124
business success, more visible than business failure 121
business world, more uncertain than management science has been telling us 16, 198
Buxted Chicken Company 106, 110

Californian entrepreneurs, optimism and overconfidence of 121, 124
call 27, 29, 78–9, 84–6, 88, 204, **207**
Camelot, odds of winning jackpot are about 1 chance in 14 million 53
Camerer, C.F. 165–6
Camerer and Lovallo, experiment 126–7
candidates for a position, making a choice between 54, 56–7
capital flight 3, 7
Carhart, M., study of mutual funds from (1962 to 1993) 136–7
cars, extended warranty to counter uncertainty 17
chance 79, 123–4, 138, 164, 201–2, 204
always involved so can't assume loser is a fool 144, 204
role in business 21
chaos theory, don't need to understand to become better manager 20
China, devaluation (1998) 14
chips 68, 171, **207**
choices, depend on whether we are seeking gain or seeking to recover losses 169
client-auditor relationship, distorted professional judgement 142
Clinton, Bill, loan of $50 billion to Mexico including funds from IMF 2
'close to home'
business models 115
decisions in familiar situations 59, 78, 89, 92–4, 105, 113–14
LTCM and 101–2
power imbalance between investors and entrepreneurs 173
producing a monthly magazine 114
requires you keep learning, record your decisions and look for the surprising 102, 203
we can be quick and effective decision makers 150
we can use intuition from our past experiences 115
you get luckier the more you practise 103, 204
communication, practise honesty and openness in 157, 203

company, looks at two or three
alternative targets before
making an acquisition 25
competing, misinformation and
strategies
know yourself/know your enemy
at the card table 190
round the board table 190–1
competitive advantage, make most of
75, 79, 85, 203
computer, chess playing floored by
number of options 24–5, 27
confidence
may come from experience or
dreams 116, 119
need to be sure it is well grounded
130–1
conflict 31–3, 41, 48, 50, 199
Cooper, A. 121
corporate executives, role as
'guardians' with emphasis on
logistics and organization 33
cost, should be seen as investment
for gain 79, 203
courtship, the entrepreneur and
178–9
Crozier, Michael 18

Damasio, A. 46–9, 52–3, 72
Descartes' Error 47
Darwin, Charles, question of
marriage 22–3, 31, 34–5
DeCarlo, Doug 147, 153
decide, when you think you have
enough information 34, 37, 199
deciding 'far from home'
intuition distilled from experience
is useless when decisions rare
or unique 200–1, 204
when we have to make decisions
far from home we should hire
an expert 201
decision cue, recognition as is the
essence of brand marketing 54
decision maker
limited learning makes for poor 49
will often select route that can be
justified to others 4
decision-making
allocating resources 1

art of is knowing when to stop
searching or when to restart
search 52
can't take chance out of
management 138, 204
crude strategies can be effective
when judgement tuned to the
environment 51
effective way of dealing with
unfamiliar is to learn quickly
150, 156
emotional responses essential for 7
factors that contribute to 173
fast and lean can be very effective
in many environments 55–6
luck is always a part of 61, 201
map making central to in
unfamiliar environments 113,
150, 155
more art than science 89
psychological is quick, clever and
surprisingly effective 30
in rapidly changing and unfamiliar
environments 145
rational acknowledges that
information and time have a
cost 30
reluctance to make decision and
need for more information
recognized by writers 29, 199
theory
is in effect a recipe 23
rational should be thought of as
an ideal 28
we are not always sure what our
goals are 32
decisions
ability to make good in
unpredictable market is
everything 129
art of judging when to stop
searching 59
avoiding by hiding risk aversion
behind claim that more
information needed 29, 200
become self-aware when you make
9
better make us more likely to enjoy
a successful career 5
build on others taken the day or
month before 3–5, 198

decisions (continued)
  chance can unpick the best 19, 204
  consider how they are changing
    deployment of resources 9
  don't judge by outcome of 20, 204
  frequent 93
  getting best possible is beyond us
    34, 37
  intuitive will be most effective when
    we get fast and unambiguous
    feedback 93, 199
  made with someone else's money
    need to be justified 1, 3, 8–9,
    43, 198
  making with imperfect information
    and differing objectives does
    not create a stable system 15
  outcomes of importance to other
    people but are surprisingly
    forgettable 3
  outcomes often not clear cut 7
  record to calibrate your judgement
    9, 99, 204
  require a personal judgemen t 37,
    39, 204
  significant but rare decisions 113,
    200
  some have to be made on the hoof
    28
  time-constrained happen every day
    27–8, 199
  twisting recollection of, we tend to
    misremember what we
    thought at the time 6, 8, 198
  use 'rules of thumb' when we don't
    have or don't trust our own
    experience 81, 203
  we use a host of psychological tools
    to make in the real world 30
deductive logic 23
Deep Blue, made progress by getting
    better at doing what humans
    do 25, 36
'deterministic chaos' 15
Devons, Ely, enduring power of magic
    17–18
Disney, may fund major theme parks
    113
doctors and psychologists,
    overdiagnose rare conditions
    140–1

don't fight unless you have to
  at the card table 192–3
  round the board table 193, 203
don't give opponent free or cheap
    cards
  at card table 191–2
  round the board table 192, 203–5
dot.com dreams, money wasted at
    turn of last century 5, 76, 111,
    129
Dow Jones Industrial Average, fall on
    different days in August (1998)
    14
Dragon's Den
  calculation – 100 per cent of
    nothing 175
  exchange of equity for cash but
    offer sometimes rejected
    174–5
drunken walk, principal law of
    probability 86–7, 102, 171,
    194–5, 204
Dun & Bradstreet, two-thirds of new
    businesses failed within first
    four years 120
Dunne, T. 120
Duthie, John, winner of televised
    Poker Million tournament from
    Isle of Man 70

education, weight on knowing about
    things rather than knowing
    how to find out things 17
Edwards, F.R. 7
Eisner (Disney's former CEO) 92
EMAP 39, 44–5, 203
emerging markets, surge of
    investment in after bail out of
    Mexican bondholders 7
emotion, powerful role in finding
    mate 35
emotional associations, manipulation
    of is one of the dark arts of
    marketing 54
Empirica (Taleb's company), unusual
    business model 167
endowment effect
  global warming and 185
  term for overvaluation of what we
    own 176–8, 202

engineer, can spot warning signs that indicate component is about to fail 140

Enron debacle, auditors pleasing their clients responsible for the crisis 142

entrepreneurial optimism, vs. investor scepticism 124–5

entrepreneurs
  assessing opportunities in cyberspace 62
  best don't waste time and money on the smaller prospects 64–5, 203
  can often exploit new markets better than large corporations 46
  in new territory negotiating investment so get expert on side 186
  over-confidence of 119
  struggle to find funding 202
  ways of convincing themselves that their business can be given high valuation 176, 202
  would-be, chance of achieving goal is about 33 per cent 123–4

entrepreneurship
  67 per cent base rate of failure is reality 122
  glamour of 129, 202

environmental awareness, critical to turtle breeding venture 110

equity, instinctive reluctance to let it go 176

Ericsson
  joint venture with Sony 13
  single-source procurement strategy, Philips plant in Albuquerque 12, 17

estate agent, role of to pick way through conflicting goals and aspirations 32

Etzioni, A., Hyperviligance (collecting more information instead of making a decision) 29

expected utility theory, assumes we make choices that give us biggest perceived benefit 162

experiences
  book learning and case studies valuable but no substitute for personal 50, 204
  gain as many as you can for intuitive decision making 72, 200
  our brains use emotion to give significance to our 51, 198
  priority to those that are tagged with strongest emotional response 48
  some lessons we have to learn from, not from textbooks 49
  take the emotion out of and we can't decide 50
  treat other people's stories with caution 79

expert, anyone with first-hand experience in particular field 139

expert guide, needed to explore unfamiliar domain of trying to raise finance 178, 204

experts
  difficulty of getting most from 145
  first duty is to themselves 142
  overconfidence of 140–1
  overdiagnose rare occurrences in area of their expertise 143, 201
  recognize patterns 140, 143
  tell you what you want to hear 143–4, 201
  tend to over-estimate quality of their judgements 126, 140–1, 143–4, 155, 204
  use when you don't have experience in unfamiliar territory 144
  valuable when they have well-grounded judgement in area new to us 139–40, 143, 204

extinction and success, thin line between 169–71

eXtreme management see XP

Far East, financial crisis 75
'far from home'
  backing a winner for 108, 109–110, 119, 133
  be prepared to fail fast and learn fast 157, 201, 204
  Boo.com managers 78
  business models 115
  copy success of others 109, 110–111

'far from home' (continued)
  deciding to launch a new consumer magazine 114
  decisions rare or unique in unfamiliar contexts with limited feedback 113, 115–16, 200
  decisions in unfamiliar environments 59, 92, 107, 114
  entrepreneurs negotiation an investment agreement making decisions 186
  fast-failing/fast-learning XP tackles decisions 153, 201
  high proportion of wealth put at risk 108
  hire a guide 109, 111–12, 116–17, 119, 133, 201, 204
  how do we make judgements? 122
  learning fast 150, 153
  make a map of the new terrain 109, 112, 113, 116, 119, 201
  power balance between investors and entrepreneurs 173
  rare but significant decisions 105, 108, 113
  slow or no feedback 108, 201
  XP principles provide model for making decisions 156, 201
fear, organizational culture of can be barrier to innovation and change 29
fear of losing, more powerful than our greed for gain so we take risks to cover a loss 171, 201
female guppy, mating strategy 36, 109
Fidelity Magellan Fund, Peter Lynch and 134, 143
fight, signal intention to avoid 195, 205
film production company, may fund one project a year 113–14
Finding an Ideal Mate – The Rational Way 35
fire-fighters and soldiers, single course of action which they carry out 58, 203
Fisher, Anthony
  chickens 105, 106–7, 110
  green sea turtle venture 106–7, 110, 112–13
  rise and fall 139

Fisher, Irving, Great Crash of October (1929) 16–17
flop 27, **207**
flush 27, 86, **207**
focus on three numbers that matter: probable cost, chance of success and possible return 79, 203
fold 27, 63, 78–9, 84–6, 88, 190, 204, **207**
Fowler, Martin
  overhead of data collection can swamp the real work 149
  Planning eXtreme Programming 146, 153
frame dependence, real world examples 165–6
frame of reference, change when thinking about uncertain choice 172, 204
Freeserve, had not yet launched free dial-up ISP in (1998) 74
Freud, Sigmund, conflict between id, ego and super–ego 48
Frost, G. 107
full house 63, 190, **207**

G7 7
GAAP accounting standards, auditors and 142
Galea, Professor Ed, study of accidents 96
gamblers, often misrepresent their own rate of success 72
Germany, internet access 62
Gilovich, T. 135
Gladwell, Malcolm
  experiment with undamaged gamblers 48
  Blink 47
Glossary of poker terms **207**
goal, losing weight conflicting with other goals- eating well and sleeping in 31
goals
  aren't handed down they are uncovered 36–7, 203
  complex, layered and changing 32, 37, 199, 201

different individuals have different 33

help set priorities but don't supersede full set of objectives of organization 34, 37

keep ultimate in sight 153

Goldstein, Morris 7

'good enough' 26, 59, 60
frequent use of 36, 204
use as stop search 34, 57–60, 199

good management, art of good judgement 50, 204

Greenspan, Alan 2, 90

Griffin, D. 140

Grove, Andrew (Intel) 84

gut instinct 43, 50, 130

Hall, Monty (host of *Let's Make a Deal*) 40

hand 68, **207**

hedge funds 9 0

herding, powerful inclination in business and in life 36, 109, 111, 119

hindsight bias 6, 8–9, 93, 112

'history of the future' 122–3
we build on those that dwell on successful scenarios 131

how to fight a strong enemy
at the card table 193–4
round the board table 194

humans
good at spotting patterns, seeking out causes and telling stories 135, 198
sophisticated practical decision makers 8

hunches 4, 43, 47, 116

'idiotic bull, impetuous bear and cautious trader,' alternative histories for 71

'I like it', powerful stopping rule 53, 59, 199

IMF 7, 14

inductive logic 23

information, changing your mind in light of new is sign of strength not weakness 157, 203

information gathering, over-zealous attitude has some unwelcome consequences 28, 199

inside view, entrepreneurs' view focusing on internal variables that can be controlled 125, 127, 131, 174

instinctive judgement, can sometimes be correct 4

international business services company, 'slow and sure' better than 'fast and dumb' 28–9

international company, Monty Hall problem 42

international poker tournaments, money to be won on 63–4

internet companies, setting up in neighbouring towns 15

intuitions
based on emotional impact of past experiences 39, 43, 199, 204
clash between and logic 173, 199
from one environment may mislead you in another environment 92, 95, 103, 153, 199–200, 204
good guide when making decisions close to home but can have predictable errors 102
trust if based on well-grounded experience 60, 204
ways our experience and memories shaped to give us guidelines on how to act in future 58, 199

intuitive judgement
the art of knowing, 'close to home' can be fast and accurate 199
used to stop endless quest for information and start deciding 51, 199

intuitive knowledge, keep watching and learning or it will become stale 99

intuitive reasoning 42–3, 49–50, 92

investment relationships, built on trust which takes time to develop 186

investments
good with reasonable probability will double your money in three years 88, 204

investments (continued)
  never come with exactly
      quantifiable price tags 67
  uncertainty about costs in business
      and poker 81
  understand basic pattern of and be
      aware of the dangers 116
investors
  generalists so need to employ an
      expert 179
  initial decision to back
      management team on intuition
      and then use rule-based logic
      to justify it 186, 199
  understand rules that govern 186
  you don't lose value selling shares
      to 187, 204
Isenberg, Daniel 58
Italy, internet access 62

Japan
  high-risk bonds and LTCM 101
  Kobe earthquake (1995) 161
  recession (1998) 14
Japanese perspective on objectives
      33–4
JP Morgan 62, 76
judgements
  based on imperfect information 138
  every decision involves, no
      objective method for finding
      right decision 199
  everything in poker or in business
      66–7
  good built on experience of one's
      environment 110, 113
  how do we make away from our
      area of experience? 122, 200
  management the exercise of, not
      application of rules 197
  necessary derived from experience
      26
  overconfident in 201
  personal part of decision making
      29, 204
  question of how we distil personal
      experience into 21
  test by changing frame of reference
      172, 204
  wrought from experience are guide
      for making decisions 89

justification
  need to justify decisions to other
      people 173, 199
  public companies and 43–5
  rational, influence on decision
      making 39, 94
just in time (JIT), planning for XP
      projects 148

Kahneman, Daniel 162–3, 177
Kasparov, Gary, versus IBM's Deep
      Blue 24–5
keep learning, stay in touch with the
      commercial environment 103,
      203
Klein, Gary, The Power of Intuition 58

lawyers, overemphasise possibility of
      unlikely outcomes 141
learning, limited makes for poor
      decision maker 49
Leeson, Nick (Baring's Bank) 160–3
legal terms, become powerful when
      company facing litigation 18
long-term capital management see
      LTCM
loss aversion, vs, entrepreneurial
      optimism 120–1
lottery tickets, we rush to buy
      especially when there are roll-
      over jackpots 53
Lowenstein, R. 101
LTCM 89–91
  the downfall 100–2
luck, skill and the business manager
      138–9
Lynch, Peter, managed Fidelity
      Magellan Fund (1977–1990)
      134, 136, 143

maintenance of machinery, key
      uncertainty for workers 18
maintenance workers, guarded
      knowledge of how to repair
      the machines and had great
      power 18
making map and learning fast 201
Malmsten, Ernst 62
management
  art not a science 197
  three options: fold, call or raise 79

management science
  inability to undertake controlled experiments means difficulty identifying cause and effect 19
  theories developed by observing management in top-performing companies 82
management theories
  don't have status of scientific laws 11, 198
  many just stories that give us confidence in ability to control events 135
  rules of thumb not universal laws 20, 83, 205
management writers and researchers, treat assertions with scepticism 20
managerial decision making, key characteristics 1, 153–4
managers
  allocation of resources 1, 3, 8, 198
  alter preferences depending on level of success, did not see risk taking as gambling 154, 202
  approaches to uncertainty and motivation of people 154, 203
  backing a series of high-risk ventures could end in disaster 86–7
  believe they are able to control events and make long-term forecasts in business plan 128
  can walk unaided if learn to live with uncertainty and knowledge of how to make decisions 8
  different reach different decisions about when to stop searching 30
  don't convert all alternatives into single number to make choices 170, 199, 202
  evaluating whether right resources being deployed to achieve desired outcome 64, 205
  focus on couple of likely scenarios 74, 202
  have to accommodate uncertainty 13
  make decision without all the information they have to make a judgement call 29, 198
  more sophisticated decision maker than the theory would suggest 159
  navigating through interlocking decision is mark of good 5
  need new skills for managing in uncertainty 156, 203–4
  not gambling but risk taking 74
  paid to make decisions 3, 11
  play ever-expanding number of roles 3
  poker has much to teach 61
  risking a substantial proportion of company's worth on a single bet is to be avoided 87
  risks faced by 47
  should keep sight of three numbers: likely cost, chance of success and likely return 67, 69, 79
  shrewd can wait for early feedback from the marketplace 84–5, 205
  smart, lean and effective methods to make decisions adapted to environment 59
  spend time working with 'insider's' view and underestimate competition 127
  step-by-step commitment is what they do 153
  task is reduced to selecting one of three options 64–5
  use intuition gained through experience in decision making 81
  watch for patterns that might signal a major loss 83–4
  ways they use intuition 58
managing in the real world, imaginary world of management science 198
Mandelbrot, Benoit 14, 102
'map making'
  shorthand for process of exploring new territory 112, 201
  strategy of 145
March, J.G. 153–4, 170

markets
  more volatile than traditional
    theories allow 14–15, 167
  new have many unknowns and
    higher risks 85
  not closed systems but driven by
    external forces 15
  'sticky' for mugs 177–8
  volatility of has increased 154
MBA programmes and management
    textbooks, describe world
    where rules and markets used
    to explain performance 16, 198
MBA students
  don't have any 'feel' for the
    numbers 69
  opportunities for entrepreneurial
    careers 130
  used as lab rats because they are
    willing and free 169
memory
  can't be trusted with accurate
    assessment of your past
    performance 99–100, 198
  less serious plane crashes and 96
mental models, pictures built up
    through experience of how the
    world works 58
Merton, Robert 90
Mexican default, indirect
    consequences immense but
    less quantifiable 2
Mexican economy, consequences of
    collapse for US 2–3
Mexican government, loan of $35
    billion dollars from American
    taxpayers 2
Mexico, effects of economic
    measures imposed on 6
Monte Carlo simulation 71–2, 82, 86,
    123, 125
'Monty Hall problem' 40–3, 176
'moral hazard bubble' punctured 7
mug's game 177
mutual fund managers, performance
    of 136

NASDAQ index as barometer of
    technology and internet asset
    values 45

NASDAQ, hit high on 10 March 2000 76
'natural' price, buffeted by random
    'noise' 14
'nearly men', few big wins but string
    of losses 72–3
New Mexico, lightening strike 17
Newtonian certainty 73
Newtonian world, predictable causes
    and effects 154
Newton, Isaac, laws of motion and
    gravitation act to create stable
    and predictable system 14
New York taxi drivers, prospect
    theory and 165–6
Nikkei 161–2
Nokia 12–13
nuclear accident, to assess
    probability we focus on issues
    that may cause 122
'nuts, the' 66, **207**

objectives, difference between those
    that are by-product of master
    plan and those that emerge as
    discovery process 33
Omaha (variation of poker) 91, 207
on-course horse race betting 166
online property database, house
    hunting and 31
opponent, competing against, art of
    misinformation and strategies
    for fighting 189
opportunity, don't rush into first
    entrepreneurial 130–31
opportunity cost 5, 75
option traders, survived alternative
    histories 71
organizations
  don't stop learning but strategic
    decision makers do 94
  a few lucky fools in every
    organization 139, 204
Ouchi, William 3 3
outsider view 125, 131, 204
over-confidence
  assumption it can't happen to you
    but one day it will 100
  challenges of expert 112
  component for action 129–30, 203
  curse of 125–7

in entrepreneurs 173
experts and 140–1
leads to illusion of control 131
success can breed 117, 204
overheads, blind bets of business 68, 78–9, 203

pattern recognition, ability to identify different cues that constitute a pattern 140
Pavlov's dogs, associate ringing of bell with being fed 48
people
encouraged to be honest in assessments in XP planning 149
generally risk averse 120, 163
naturally risk averse so organizational culture can be barrier to innovation 29
perfect decision, steps in recipe 23, 204
performance, keep record of 73, 204
performance criteria, never as complex as layered and conflicting goals of the organization 33
performance related pay, setting objectives for 32
pharmaceutical company scenario 164–5
Philadelphia 76ers (1980–81) season, study of data from 135
Philips plant in Albuquerque 12–13
physical sciences, possible to set up experimental situations where everything held same 16
physician, sees pattern in collection of symptoms that seem unrelated to untrained eye 140
plane crash, surviving 95–6
planning, detailed a waste of time, has to be constantly revised 156–7, 203
poker and investing 200
poker player and business manager, three options: fold, call or raise 78
poker players
assessing whether cost of meeting bet is justified since game invented 62–3

at the moment you have to bet nothing is known for certain 66, 200
avoid big bets for a small advantage 87, 204
backing long shots with limited wealth means you end up in the gutter 86, 88, 204
bad beat and 11–12
best have same luck as rest of us 64
best use intuitive judgements wrought from experience 200
can mimic the betting style of hero but needs luck to match success 111
can use either intuitive or rule-based methods for decision making 65
decisions always matters of judgement 29
do two things better than the rest of us 64
experienced understand that a good hand may not be the best hand 127
fold if you are betting first 84
game of skill where players have to make judgements about how to deploy resources 19
good know every bet must be made on its own terms 168
good take bad beats in their stride 139
improve at playing through practising to improve their instincts through feedback 70
inexperienced run out of time 27, 36
internet and new players 70
judgement gained through experience to decide scenarios that need detailed attention 25
lucky chair, four possibilities of 96, 143
never stop watching and thinking at the card table 83
playing eight hands simultaneously is crash course in experience and feedback 70–71
raising or folding can be better than calling 85, 88, 204

poker players (continued)
  rely on instinct most of the time
      68–70
  risks faced by 47
  rule-based assessment of expected
      value and probabilities works
      well for 70
  self-knowledge most important
      aspect of game 190
  should have target rate of return
      per hour 26
  some are more skilful, have better
      understanding of the
      probabilities 138
  three options 63, 76
  top make money by not losing on
      weaker hands 67–8
  warn about making decisions in an
      emotional state ('going on tilt')
      48
  we evaluate risks on current
      standing 170–1
portfolios 126, 169, 204
position matters, early movers need
      bigger advantages 84–5, 88, 205
pot, the 85, 191–3, **207**
preferences, change depending
      whether we see choice as gain
      or as chance to recover a loss
      164, 171, 201
Prigogine, Ilya, 'the end of certainty' 15
private equity, know rules of 187, 204
private equity backed initiative, no
      choice but to carry on even
      when underperforming 46, 50
private equity companies
  investment long-term bet on
      management team and an
      industry 45
  tempted to make a follow-on
      investment rather than accept
      the write-off 168
private equity firm, may make $1
      billion buy-out decision
      113–14
probabilities
  in business and life 122–4, 128–9
  in poker 70, 138, 169
process-driven software project
      failures (1990s), new
      philosophy of software
      development 147

product packaging, covered in
      'affective tags' to create positive
      emotional associations 54
professional investor, aware of base
      rate and individual risk of start
      ups 124
professional private equity investor
  paid to find high-return
      investments 178
  will commission a due diligence
      report from trusted industry
      expert 179, 184, 186
promising options, focus on what
      experience tells you 34
prospect theory
  gains from buyer should be
      separated and treated
      individually 166
  loss to buyer should be bundled
      together into one price 167
  making full use of 172
  not a business model for everyone
      167
  preferences when we evaluate
      gambles for gain and to
      recover loss 171
  pricing and product options 172
  way we make choices when faced
      with uncertain outcomes 163
psychological tools, no help in
      unfamiliar situation 30
psychology, poker and 64
psychology of buying, understood by
      sellers before prospect theory
      166
psychology of choice 162
psychology of value curve and
      endowment effect, behind
      abhorrence to paying tax 176
public companies
  difficulties in making major long-
      term strategic changes 43
  management structure 46
  prone to constant justification of
      large investment decisions to
      shareholders 49–50

raising 27, 63, 86, 193, **207**
rare events, dangerous and can wipe
      out a decade's gains in a single
      day 100

'rational' decision makers, best alternative unswayed by subjective judgement 21

rational 'marginal value' theorem, foraging animals and 25–6

rational reasoning 42

necessary to justify well-grounded intuitive decisions 50, 203

reality, 67 percent base rate of entrepreneurial failure is 122, 198

reasoning, emotional responses play a vital role in 48

recognition

name recognition as proxy for other cues 56–7

stop searching and 54, 57, 59–60, 199

recollections, biased towards recent and most memorable events 121

'reference group neglect' 127

Reid and Smith, study of 150 new businesses in Scotland 120

restaurant industry, failure rates of independent restaurants 80 per cent in first two years 120

'right', myth of 29

'right' decision, just as far out of reach 30, 199

risk

business models and 98–9, 113–14

can be managed 154

can change perception of depending on how much money we have 169, 198

portfolio of in hands of players who understands probabilities can have high return 169

view dependent on how we are performing 170

risk averse, when a gamble may give us a gain 163–4, 171, 201–2

risk aversion, can make us turn down one-off gambles even when they have positive expectation 171–2, 205

risk blindness 97–8

risk and reward, two distinct patterns of 114

risk seeking, when we are facing a loss 163–4

river cards 12, 27, 170, **207**

Rogue Trader (film about Nick Leeson) 160

Rosenzweig, Phil, Halo Effect, The 23

Roth, Joe (chairman of Walt Disney) 127

roulette, alternative histories 71

Rubin, Robert E. (Secretary to Treasury for President Clinton) 2–3

$23 billion bail out for Russi a 7, 14

decision on what to do with $35 billion of US taxpayers' money 4

traits of good decision maker 6

In an Uncertain World 2

rule-based logic, doesn't have a chance against our intuitions 176

rule-based system of reasoning 42, 49

adept at ensuring one's conclusions are sanctioned 49, 53, 70, 94

system that poker players can use 65

rules of courtship and marriage for private equity 179–80

business plan can't be part of your vows 181

courtship will take a long time 180

investors' idea

investor will want to leave relationship with as much of their fortune intact as possible 183, 203

reserve right to bring their mother if they don't like the way you run the house 183–4

reserve right to evict you and move in their lover 184

they will want to charge you rent on the family home 184

you will be paying for the wedding and covering the costs of all their guests 184–5

keep playing the field 180–8

misunderstood by entrepreneurs 202

rules of courtship and marriage for private equity (continued)
there is no marriage until the ceremony is over 181–2
will always be a fight negotiating the pre-nuptial agreement 182–3
'rules of thumb' 202–3
avoid big bets for small advantage
at the card table 87
round the board table 87–8
avoid long shots
at the card table 8 6
round the board table 86–7
keep watching, keep thinking
at the card table 83
round the board table 83–4
on chance, luck and gambling 204–5
on intuition, judgement and deciding 204
on investing and entrepreneurship 203–4
on management and competing 203
position matters 205
at the card table 84
round the board table 84–5
quick short-hands to help you find a 'good enough' option 82, 204
raising or folding can be better than calling
at the card table 85
round the board table 85–6
specific to particular variations of poker 82
your judgement is guide to when they should be applied 202–3
Russia, cash crisis (1998) 14, 101

S&P500 index 134
S&P500 options 90
sales teams, have power to remove uncertainty and become influential 18
Salty, Samer, on the internet 62
Samuelson, Paul, coin toss wager 66, 154, 162, 168–9
San Francisco, blind to risk in 97
scenario building, process that would-be entrepreneur has to go through 123
Scholes, Byron 90

science of management
Newtonian outlook 16
planning fallacy 128–9
sick patient that stands up with help of two crutches 8
searching, quest for alternatives and information 51
semi-bluff 193, **207**
senior management, power with role as planners and forecasters 18
Shapira, Z. 154, 170
sheep and businesses
decision of when to move vital for survival 26–7, 35
floored by too little information 27, 36
Shefrin, Hersh, *Beyond Greed and Fear* 137–8, 143
showdown
in poker 63, 191–3, **207**
try to avoid in business 195, 203
sins of omission, more serious than sins of commission 29
Sloman, Steven 43
'slow but sure' mantra 29
Smith, Adam, *Wealth of Nations* 14
social sciences, experiments rarely if ever possible 16
somatic markers (emotional tags), associated with aspects of our experience 47, 72
South Korea 7
Spain, internet access 62
sporting performance, random sequence 135–6
sports, do players have streaks? 134–5
spreadsheets, sophisticated analysis of 69
Stack, Charles 84
Star Trek's Mr Spock, unable to experience emotion 47–8
step-by-step commitment, not what management textbooks recommend 153
Stern Report 185
stock market, backing winners on 136–7
'stop search' 30, 34–6, 51–3, 57–60, 199

strategy consultants, good at providing rational justifications for important decisions 95, 103

'streak shooting' in basketball 135

strong positive associations, powerful subconscious effect 53

students, given detailed information about sale of a company 142

subconscious intuitive reasoning, effect of stopping search before it has even begun 52

Summers, Larry 2

sunk costs 171
  calculate in evaluation of further investments 172
  do not include in your evaluation of further investments 172, 204
  effect 187, 201
  high-risk investment with hope project can be turned from loss to profit 168
  impact of 173
  tempt us to keep gambling to recover what we have already spent 171

surprising, the, being sensitive to what is going on in your peripheral vision 88, 100, 103, 203

Taleb, N.N.
  experiments with a Monte Carlo engine led him to become an option dealer 167
  luck with stained tie 96
  In an Uncertain World 2

technology bubble in (2000), collapse inevitable with aid of hindsight 16

Texas Hold'em (variation of poker) 12
  knowledge of probabilities and information gained from opponents' playing styles 27

Thailand 7

Thaler, Richard, combining of bets 169

theories, be wary of that seem to explain past but can't predict future 20

theorists, ideas on decision making 7

throwing dice 120

'tilt', refers to fact that your sense of balance for making sound judgements has gone 48, **207**

tobacco-related deaths 122

track record 134

traditional management, responds to change by tightening controls and redoubling planning 150

transaction costs, women and fewer in portfolio 126

transactions, hard to achieve between investors and entrepreneurs 178

turn in poker 12, 27, **207**

Tversky, A. 140, 162–3

UK National Lottery, pays out only 50 per cent of ticket sales as prize money 53

UK's Dragon's Den TV programme, Excel and 69

uncertainty
  ability to reduce can give individual or department a lot of power 17–18
  can't manage in same way we tried to manage certainty 20, 203
  no amount of research and analysis can remove 16
  we have to learn to manage with 11, 18
  we pay money to remove it 17

underlying rate, look at what statisticians call the base rate 122

US
  Congress opposed to 'bail out' of Mexico 2
  dot.com boom 74
  illegal immigration to if Mexican economy collapses 2
  rise in websites from 2, 000 to 400,000 in three years 62
  wide price spreads (1999) 101

US-Mexico saga, $35 billion gamble 6

valuation and the equity that has to be given up, owners' expectations and reality 175

value judgements, were wrong in boo.com 77

values, guide in XP when goals and solutions are negotiated in the process 150
values and vision, needed to guide decision making when path is uncertain 149, 157, 201, 203
venture capitalists, wary of start ups 124

Walker, Anna, interview with Health Trust CEO 33
wasp, foraging strategy 26
weather forecasters and bridge players, immediate feedback on their decisions 93, 140
what managers tell us about decision making 201–2
managers don't do what the theories say they should do, they 202
Wilson, Des
bad beat 13, 19
conversation with John Duthie 70
Swimming with the Devilfish 12
winners
one good outcome and we label people 110
problems of backing 145, 201
wins and losses, asymmetry of 72
wise loser and lucky fools, behavioural clues that help us separate 139

would-be entrepreneurs 121, 125
www.babyworld.com 74–5

XP management
approach that allows us to learn quickly and keep focused on core values 156, 201
built around people and processes 149
characterizes best practice in organizational decision making 151
difference between and traditional project management 149–50
goes back to the guiding values and principles when project goes off course 150
planning trap and 146
XP project
complex high-speed, self-correcting venture 147
developed to create business value in fast moving environment 150
is process of discovery, both goal and route are going to evolve 149
planning essential focused on foreseeable horizon not the distant future 148
scenario of gem stones 151–2

zero sum game, between management and investors 185
poker is 200